11-30-76

MURDER IN SPACE CITY

HENRY P. LUNDSGAARDE

Murder in Space City

A Cultural Analysis of Houston Homicide Patterns

New York

Oxford University Press

1977

Library of Congress Catalogue Card Number: 76-9229
Printed in the United States of America

For permission to reprint passages from the works indicated grateful acknowledgment is made to the following:

City University of New York for Morton Bard and Joseph Zacker, "Assaultiveness and Alcohol Use in Family Disputes," in *Criminology,* Vol. 12, 1974.

Princeton University Press for Paul Bohannan (ed.), *African Homicide and Suicide,* copyright © 1960 by Princeton University Press. Reprinted by permission of Princeton University Press.

Southwestern Methodist University School of Law for Charles P. Bubany, "The Texas Penal Code of 1974," in *Southwestern Law Journal,* Vol. 28, 1974.

Northwestern University School of Law for Henry Allen Bullock, "Urban Homicide in Theory and Fact," in *Journal of Criminal Law, Criminology and Police Science.* Reprinted by special permission of the Journal of Criminal Law, Criminology and Police Science, Copyright © 1955 by Northwestern University School of Law, Vol. 45, No. 5.

University of Houston School of Law for Robert A. Carp, "The Harris County Grand Jury–A Case Study," in *Houston Law Review,* Vol. 12, 1974.

Macmillan Publishing Co., Inc., for Arnold L. Epstein, "Sanctions," in *International Encyclopedia of the Social Sciences,* copyright © 1968 by Macmillan Co.

Munksgaard for Verner Goldschmidt, "Primary Sanction Behavior," in *Acta Sociologica,* Vol. 10, 1966.

University of California Press for David G. Mandelbaum (ed.), *Selected Writings of Edward Sapir in Language, Culture and Personality,* copyright © 1949 by The Regents of the University of California; reprinted by permission of the University of California Press.

West Publishing Co. for William L. Prosser, *Handbook of the Law of Torts,* 3rd ed., 1964.

Macmillan Publishing Co., Inc., for Alfred R. Radcliffe-Brown, "Social Sanction," in *Encyclopaedia of the Social Sciences,* copyright © 1934 by Macmillan Co.

American Anthropological Association for David M. Schneider, "Political Organization, Supernatural Sanctions, and the Punishment of Incest on Yap," in *American Anthropologist,* Vol. 59, 1957.

Houghton Mifflin Company for Norbert Weiner, *The Human Use of Human Beings,* 1967.

University of Pennsylvania Press for Marvin E. Wolfgang, *Patterns in Criminal Homicide,* 1958.

To Anette, Peter, and Thorsten

Acknowledgments

It is fitting to first acknowledge the patience, assistance, and love over the past four years of my wife and two perspicacious sons. They, more than anyone else, have lent encouragement and understanding from the inception of the study to its completion. My former colleagues, Professors James L. Watson and William A. Stini, have contributed many constructive criticisms and suggestions. I also wish to thank Dr. Paul Lin for his active role in the codification and computer processing of the homicide case data. Kenneth G. Norman worked diligently to document the judicial outcome of many individual cases decided after my departure from Houston. The study itself would not have been possible without the generous hospitality and cooperation of Deputy Chief H. D. Caldwell and Captain L. D. Morrison of the Houston Police Department. Many individual homicide detectives and police clerks have rendered different kinds of assistance. I want to acknowledge specifically the help of Lieutenant F. C. Crittenden and homicide detectives T. E. Baker, D. L. Collier, G. Sharp, K. D. Porter, J. L. Reed, and H. R. Trimble. Ms. Donna Friedman worked for nearly an entire year transcribing the homicide cases and Mrs. Barbara Pirtle typed countless drafts of the text and tables. The University of Kansas provided partial support for clerical assistance, computational time, and travel expenses connected with two return visits to Houston. I wish to thank the Houston Chamber of Commerce for providing the excellent photograph of Space City. The authors and publishers who have permitted me to include brief excerpts from their scholarly articles and books also have my gratitude. It has been my good fortune to work with Robert J. Tilley, editor, and Carol Miller, assistant editor, and their colleagues of the Oxford University Press.

CONTENTS

PHOTOGRAPHS

MAPS

1
Introduction

Homicide is, no matter what else it may be, a social relationship. It might even be called the most definitive of social relationships. Like all other human social relationships, it must take place in terms of culture. It can, therefore, be studied with the ordinary tools of social anthropology, no matter what other tools may also profitably be brought to bear on it. African Homicide and Suicide, *Paul Bohannan (ed.)*.

Murder as a product of culture is what this book is all about. The study specifically looks at how and why in 1969 nearly 300 Houstonians died as a result of homicide and why more than one-half of their killers escaped official sanctioning and judicial punishment. The focus is on those homicide episodes that involve "normal" killers and those incidents that illustrate different kinds of interpersonal and social relationships between killers and victims. One may ask, for example, what difference it makes, and to whom, whether the person killed is the spouse or the friend of or a complete stranger to the killer. How do official legal sanctions and public sanctioning agents differentiate between lawful and unlawful killing? And how do we explain why a large number of persons resort to lethal violence in response to seemingly minor trespasses upon their property or to outside censure of their feelings about personal freedom? Although the book focuses on the detailed analysis of homicidal episodes in one American city in one particular year, the study is intended to provide an empirical basis for the explanation and understanding of interpersonal violence in the country as a whole.

The characterization of the majority of Houston killers as "normal" implies only that such persons were not evaluated psychiatrically as part of the official homicide investigation. A killer, generally speaking, seems not to be labeled and treated as a psychopathic personality type unless the act of killing is directly associated with some form of sexual deviance, overt sadism, or behavior defined as insane. The recognition on our part of the fact that some of the cruelest death experiments in human history were conducted by some of Germany's most distinguished physicians, who in their time were regarded as perfectly sane, calls attention to the very difficult problem of categorizing killers per se as insane or as abnormal or psychopathic personality types. The problem has been extensively treated in psychological studies of homicide and, of course, occupies a central role in the continuing debate over the insanity defense in criminal law.[1]

I have used the term *murder* in the title although only a small percentage of the killings in 1969 resulted in the killer being convicted of legal murder. But the term itself, which under Texas state law legally denotes proof of both malice aforethought and intent to kill, calls attention to the legal differences between homicide and murder. The use of this definition, however, would reduce the problem of killing in Houston and elsewhere to insignificant proportions, legally. On the other hand, the term *homicide* broadly applies to the killing of any human by another. We must therefore distinguish between an act of killing as lawful homicide and an unlawful act of killing as a species of murder, manslaughter, or negligent homicide. It is all too easy to kill someone by an act of omission, such as failing to render aid to a person in peril of his life, or one can kill unintentionally and without malice by, for example, backing one's car into a child playing in a driveway. Criminal law nominally distinguishes among these different forms of killing in accordance with intent, motive, and the circumstances surrounding each act. The application of formal legal criteria of unlawful behavior under most circumstances is made difficult by the lack of precision in the criteria used to differentiate lawful from unlawful homicide. Legal definitions and interpretations applied to any given set of facts also may at times be very much at odds with general community feelings of morality and justice. Different legal interpretations of unlawful homicide by state courts, state legislatures, and federal courts amply illustrate how time, place, and historical or political circumstances similarly affect the interpretation of homicidal behavior as a criminal act.[2]

I have also deliberately used *Space City,* and not *Houston,* to call attention to another important point. Houston, since the establishment of N.A.S.A.'s Manned Space Craft Center in the 1960s, has attracted several hundred of the nation's finest scientists and engineers to the city. Since its establishment early in the nineteenth century, Houston has grown from a small inland seaport and commercial town to one of the world's leading industrial centers. The city in one decade has earned a world-wide reputation as a center for technology, science, and medicine, and as a center of national and international commerce. The fact that such a concentration of human talent, technological knowledge, and capital in one city co-exists with one of the nation's highest per capita rates of serious crimes against the person is evidence that the most "civilized," "modern," or "enlightened" society may fail to apply its resources to the correction of conditions that breed violence and allow human failure.

And, finally, I should add that it would be a mistake for me, or any anthropologist, to conclude that a purely cultural explanation can account for the frequency of homicide in Houston or elsewhere in the nation. A number of anthropologists, biologists, ethologists, criminologists, sociologists, and psychologists have devoted their careers to the search for solutions to human aggressiveness and interpersonal violence. I recognize the legitimacy of these efforts to link human violence to biochemical factors, environmental stress and crowding, or the well-recognized criminogenic conditions of the depersonalized environment of inner city areas. Yet, it is unlikely that simple practical and theoretical solutions will be found to complex social and cultural problems. Anything short of a cultural explanation, however, will not only fail to explain the present data, but it will impede comparative research in this and other societies through the vain search for simple causes of complex forms of human behavior.

The scientific and popular literature on the subject of human violence is indeed very extensive and, generally, inconclusive. Statements by the eminent ethologist Konrad Lorenz in his book, *On Aggression* (1966), and the readable playwright-cum-science writer Robert Ardrey's works, *The Territorial Imperative* (1966) and *The Social Contract* (1970), to the effect that mankind is saddled with an instinct of violence, have met with sharp criticism by scientists of varying backgrounds (and scientific competencies) in the study of human violence.[3] Volumes 12 and 13 of the Staff Reports to the National Commission on the Causes and Prevention of Violence catalog and summarize many, but not all, views on violence from the disciplines of anthropology, biology, sociology, psychology, and psychiatry.[4] The observation by Michael Couzens at the Brookings Institution that "with all its legal and scholarly buttressing, the final report remains a political instrument with political objectives" should neither deter nor discourage the serious student of violence from using the Staff Reports as a base line from which to formulate fresh hypotheses and perhaps even generate new insights and explanations.[5] In fact, a principal reason for choosing 1969 as a target year for this study was to permit ready comparisons of national data with homicide data from Houston.

Interpersonal violence has only recently become the subject of interdisciplinary study and research. The need for such study is best illustrated by Wolfgang and Ferracuti who have proposed the development of an "integrated theory" that combines the empirical data from different scientific disciplines with an "analytical synthesis" that permits a general theory of criminality. Although their own study falls short of the goal, the publication of their book, *The Subculture of Violence* (1967), introduced a perspective that holds considerable promise for what might become a new "paradigm" for behavioral research and theoretical understanding of human violence.[6]

Is it possible, for example, to explain the rise in the rate of homicide and aggravated assault over a given period of time as an increase in the number of persons who, for some reason or another, have become "extremely violent"? It would, of course, only be empirically sound to evaluate such data in terms of their relative statistical significance, i.e., to discern if there is a rise in violence relative to the size of the population before deriving some sort of violence index. The statistical and analytical problems that arise from such questioning of the data are at the least difficult. Yet it is precisely in this area that most criminologists have attempted to generate hypotheses about violent behavior. Wolfgang's (1958) study of homicide patterns in Philadelphia, verified by the replication of his findings in Pokorny's (1965) comparative study of homicide patterns in Houston, does not lead to any general theory of homicide behavior. Bensing and Schroeder (1960), both legal scholars, similarly provide a relatively recent example of the correlational approach to homicide. Their study of homicide in Cleveland, along with that of Bullock (1955) in Houston, accounts for the numerical distribution of homicides without explaining, on a general comparative level, how their findings either support or disprove previous theories. The problem here relates to what is meant by explanation and how, in both methodology and theory, it is possible to separate the concept of explanation from that of understanding.[7]

The explanatory power of the correlational methodology, as it is used by most sociologists and criminologists, is well exemplified by Wolfgang's development of the subcultural hypothesis. In this book I explore Wolfgang's admitted inability to account for different rates of homicide in America and England. I hypothesize that the explanation for observable differences in the homicide rate of any two communities, such as, for example, Philadelphia and London, will involve significant differences in the cultural traditions of those communities. American and English cultural traditions, similar as they may appear to be, do differ significantly in the most basic cultural sanctions that prescribe and proscribe acceptable expressions of individual violence.[8] To validate this general hypothesis is not an easy task and it seems almost trivial to say that cultural differences determine the kind and degree of violent behavior exhibited by peoples in different cultures. Yet one must then ask by what other theory and methodology it will be possible to describe the difference in the level of interpersonal violence found in such similarly sized urban aggregates as, for example, Tokyo and New York City? The limitations on statistical explanation at this level of abstraction are all too well known to most social scientists.

The historical explanation of American violence provides a convenient contrast to analyses that are basically functional and sociological. The summary chapters in Volumes 1 and 2 of the Staff Reports generally attribute violent behavior in the United States to a historical continuity of the "frontier tradition" and "the vigilante tradition," as well as to racial segregation, economic expansion, and political assassination.[9] Shirley's *Law West of Fort Smith* (1968) vividly illustrates what life and death under the "frontier tradition" was like.

Although it would indeed be a mistake to deny the continuation of frontier-like attitudes into the twentieth century, it would also be prescient to accept any explanation of violence based *solely* on historical factors. It is therefore admitted that historical factors, especially as they account for the limitations of judicial and police control of individual violence, may only partly explain why the members of a certain culture employ violence to resolve conflict.

Although–as Aubert's study, "Some Social Functions of Legislation" (1966), has demonstrated empirically–there may be wide discrepancies between legislative intent and actual compliance with a given statutory law, it is not unreasonable to suspect that homicide is more likely to occur where criminal statutes, court decisions, and police procedures allow citizens great latitude and discretion in the use of personal violence. Similarly, there is little doubt that the belief of many Americans that citizens have a constitutional right to freely carry and use firearms in some ways contributes to the seriousness of the injuries of victims of aggravated assault.

Brief consideration may now be given to the place of psychological explanations of violence in the formulation of the present study. Psychological explanations, generally speaking, primarily rely on what Brown in his *Explanation in Social Science* (1963) calls "intentions," "dispositions," and "reasons." A hypothetical example of a psychological explanation of homicide might thus include a discussion of the murderer's purpose or "intentions" to reduce psychological tension or it might provide a psychiatric evaluation of the murderer's life history and personality profile. Such data describe the killer's behavioral repertoire and explore his reasons for killing his victim, e.g., by learning what reasons provide the best explanation of the killer's behavior. These modes of explanation of violent behavior, framed in a somewhat different language, are exemplified in Toch's *Violent Men* (1969), an innovative study. Toch's analysis, from a study of persons incarcerated for crimes of violence, is founded directly on the broad assumption that Americans are "a violent people." He further assumes that some citizens are more violence prone than others. A relative propensity for violence is reinforced by an interaction in specific social contexts that may involve either positive status reinforcement among peers or expose individual feelings of low self-esteem or inadequacy. In brief, Toch concludes that "Violent Men have propensities for violence that are built into their personalities and modes of functioning . . ."[10]

The Volume of Killing

Homicide is one of the ten principal causes of death in Texas (see Appendix E, Table I). In the whole of the United States in 1969, there were 7.2 reported homicides per 100,000 inhabitants. Texas, along with Florida, ranked fourth among the states with 11.3 homicides per 100,000 persons (Table II). The greater metropolitan area of Houston has a population of about 1,878,327 persons, which makes it the nation's sixth largest city. Over the years, Houston has had one of the highest per capita homicide rates in the nation. For the year 1969, the basis for this study, the reported homicide rate in Houston rose to an all-time high of 23.3 known homicides per 100,000 city residents. A more complete picture of the frequency of interpersonal violence in Houston is obtained by adding some 8,944 cases of assault and battery also reported to the police that year (Table III).

It cannot be disputed that the relative frequency of interpersonal violence in Houston is high. (The measure of frequency, which is adjusted to the international base for measuring demographic rates, is obtained by dividing the number of homicide and assault victims by the number of persons in the city population.) Extreme care, however, must be exercised in interpreting the significance of the frequent occurrence of serious offenses against the person. Houston is not a typical American city and Texas is not a typical American state. The high frequency of homicide is not in itself indicative of either lawlessness or social disorganization. The Reverend Billy Graham's characterization of Houston as "the murder capital of the United States" is as misleading and inaccurate as the Houston Chamber of Commerce's proclamations that their city is the Shangri-La of capitalism and Western civilization. These views are vividly expressed in Bainbridge's *The Super-Americans* (1961). His eminently readable account of life "in the land of millionaires" contrasts sharply with the more narrow and brash self-glorification of the Houston business community in the aptly entitled multi-authored book, *Big Town, Big Money* (1973). Blair Justice's *Violence in the City* (1969) balances the picture by illustrating how many Houstonians, representing different interest groups, learned to work together and thus avoid the destructive racial riots that brutalized social and racial relations in other large American cities during the turbulent 1960s.

In Houston and elsewhere there is wide disagreement about the significance of the frequency of homicide and interpersonal violence. On the one hand, there are both public officials and private citizens who do not view homicide as cause for alarm. This lack of concern stems in part from the observation that most killings and fighting occur among racial minorities and others at the bottom of the social hierarchy. On the other hand, there are those, even among behavioral scientists and criminologists, who take general exception to the significance of criminal statistics. According to their view, misguided law-and-order fanatics and police bureaucrats use ever increasing annual crime rates to justify their requests for additional manpower and institutional funding.

It is not very difficult to challenge the accuracy of official statistics. For instance, the Houston Police Department can only record those crimes that are known or reported to the police. The District Attorney's office only counts those offenders who actually enter the judicial process. And the City Health Department simply records mortality statistics reported by physicians and public medical officials.[11]

Fortunately, homicide statistics are less subject to many of the inaccuracies found in other kinds of criminal statistics. Homicide victims can be identified and counted, even when badly decomposed, and every suspected homicide victim in the Houston area is autopsied by a forensic pathologist to establish the exact cause of death. Police department and coroner reports simply count and tabulate the number of known homicide victims discovered every year. This of course leaves room for uneven record keeping and, as we shall observe later, homicide cases vary in the amount of official attention they receive.

Houston's official annual homicide rate is computed by counting the number of victims (per 100,000 city residents) actually *known* to the police during the calendar year. All homicide victims, therefore, are included for statistical purposes in the year in which their bodies or remains have been recovered by the police. It follows then that the official annual homicide rate may vary from the actual rate. If, for example, the 27 homosexual torture victims, who were killed in 1969 but whose remains were discovered by the police in 1973, had been retroactively counted as part of the official 1969 homicide rate, the rate for that year would have increased by 10 percent. The reader should keep in mind that, in view of the relative frequency of homicide and other forms of assault and battery, the number of officially reported homicides in any given year provides a conservative index of the total volume of interpersonal violence (Table IV).

If, on the other hand, one looks at conviction statistics for known killers, it can be learned that the murder rate is significantly lower than the reported homicide rate. By counting only those cases resulting in a murder conviction against a killer or killers, the city, comparatively speaking, has an extremely low murder rate. The problem here, which should indeed amount to a methodological fallacy, would be to treat as significant only those cases that result in a severe penalty for killers.

Even if, in order to place the Houston data in national and cross-cultural perspective, it were to be argued that the homicide rate per se can be used as a rough index of community violence, it can be argued logically (but not culturally) that Houston has a very low homicide rate. A comparison of the Houston homicide data with those from other countries, using demographic yearbooks compiled by the United Nations, shows that Colombia, Mexico, Nicaragua, and South Africa have much higher death rates attributed to homicide than those of Houston, Texas, or the entire United States. The Demographic Yearbooks of the United Nations, however, list 50 different kinds of causes of mortality and include in one category (category "BE 50") deaths attributed to "all other external causes" including homicide. The determination of an accurate homicide rate, cross-nationally, would require much stricter standards of medical reporting than now prevail. Only a complete autopsy of every unnatural death by a trained forensic pathologist would yield information accurate enough for comparative statistical analysis.

By way of another quite exotic example, one can readily illustrate the inherent dangers of any comparative statistical analysis that fails to include qualifications derived from an appreciation of cultural variables. In a small Mexican village of approximately 1,900 Mayan Indians, the homicide rate in 1964 rose to a phenomenal 251.2 killings per 100,000 population![12] The problem here, of course, is to compare comparable community situations and to balance quantifiable and nonquantifiable cultural facts, and to put the matter simply, to try to learn how people in different cultures and communities themselves perceive interpersonal violence and homicide as a critical problem of social order and control. Statistical frequency tabulations, and the relative significance attributed to numerical data, must always be interpreted as reflecting any number of observer and contextual biases.

Official recognition of violence as a problem of American culture was most forcefully made on June 10, 1968, when the late President Lyndon B. Johnson, by executive order, instructed the National Commission on the Causes and Prevention of Violence "to undertake a penetrating search for the causes and prevention of violence–a search into our national life, our past as well as our present, our traditions as well as our institutions, our culture, our customs and our laws."[13]

In an earlier but similar recognition of this nation's growing crime problem, President Johnson established the Commission on Law Enforcement and Administration of Justice on July 23, 1965. One finding of the Committee was a rough estimate of the economic impact on the nation as a whole of crimes against the person. *Measured in terms of earnings lost by homicide and assault victims and their families, the cost to the people of the United States probably exceeds $850 million.* The findings of these two commissions established beyond any doubt that the level of interpersonal violence in American culture has passed the point where the statement that violence "is as American as apple pie" is a debatable one.[14] The recognition of the violent traditions in American culture differs materially from the use of criminal statistics as a sort of public scare tactic as is, for example, illustrated by the crime clock displayed by the Federal Bureau of Investigation in Washington, D.C. This clock, which records the frequency of serious crimes in the United States, shows that a "murder" occurs every 39 minutes, a forcible rape every 17 minutes, and a robbery every two minutes. There is merit in the criticism of such display tactics voiced by former Attorney General Ramsey Clark, who said, "the clock presents a two-dimensional world that is unreal–minutes measuring occurrences–but there are many dimensions to this world and we must measure more than two if we are to know anything about crime."[15]

Although statistical analyses of important and quantifiable variables in the Houston homicide data are included in the book, the study deliberately emphasizes a descriptive case-by-case analysis of actual homicides. Statistics are given when it is necessary to establish frequency, volume, and correlational occurrences of quantifiable variables. But we need to know considerably more about homicide and interpersonal violence than these statistics reveal if we are to understand the cultural nature of such complex forms of social behavior.

The Research

My curiosity was first aroused in 1970 when I went to live and teach in Houston. As a stranger to the community, I noticed almost constant but exceptionally brief accounts of slayings in and around the city in the news media. These accounts indicated that homicides occurred almost daily somewhere in the city. I was continuously struck by two facts: (1) Except for truly sensational slayings, homicides were not treated as front page news. (2) Despite the cursory nature of most such reports, it could be seen that the killings resulted from seemingly trivial victim provocations. For example, one man killed another because the latter stole the parking space desired by the killer to be. Another man shot a bartender after an argument over a five-cent increase in the price of beer during the hours of entertainment. An off-duty police officer working as a security guard was shot when he asked a man to lower the volume of his piano playing after midnight. The officer, in turn, killed the piano player and the incident was classified as a justifiable homicide. The frequency of homicides arising from such slight provocation called my attention to homicide as a subject worthy of anthropological inquiry.

Some of the principal assumptions that have guided the study include: (1) Homicide differs from other forms of violent behavior primarily in the mode of expression and seriousness of outcome; (2) homicide, as exemplified in the 1969 data, requires the broadest possible analytical perspective if explanation is to be attempted; (3) homicide, as a cultural phenomenon, requires a separate analytical treatment because it represents the extreme point on a hypothetical continuum of interpersonal violence. In the City of Houston, the ratio of homicides to other offenses against the person is approximately one to 32. Homicide, therefore, is much like the tip of the proverbial iceberg because it is the most readily evident form of violent human behavior.

During 1972, I received permission from the chief of police to review all 268 official homicide cases on file for the year 1969 in the Homicide Division of the Houston Police Department. This particular year was chosen for several reasons. First, three sociological studies of homicide in Houston, Bullock (1965), Caldwell (1963), and Pokorny (1965), as well as the publication in 1969 of the voluminous study of the National Commission on the Causes and Prevention of Violence, permit comparison of the 1969 Houston data with both a local and a national sample. Second, it was not possible to include cases still under police investigation or cases still in the process of adjudication before the criminal courts. As it turned out, I was able to discover the final outcome for all but 29 cases. Some of these had not yet been solved by the police or prosecuted by the district attorney.

The individual case data, because of their confidential nature, could not be reproduced or removed from the premises of the Homicide Division. I was, however, permitted free access to the 1969 case files provided that I would work on the premises of the Homicide Division, where a small interrogation room was made available to me. This arrangement proved advantageous since it made it possible to seek supplementation and clarification of the file data from homicide detectives. Each case was read in its entirety and the significant facts were directly taped on a tape recorder. To ensure anonymity of all the principals in a case, including the detectives responsible for the case reports, all names have been fictionalized. A case numbering code was adopted to allow any investigator with access to the police files to check or expand on the information summarized in the case descriptions.

The individual case data were also supplemented by interviews with homicide detectives, forensic pathologists, and lawyers familiar with the peculiarities of the Texas system of criminal justice. Official court records were examined to obtain information on sentencing and court disposition. During brief periods in 1972, 1974, and finally after January 1, 1976, I also observed the investigation procedure itself to learn, at firsthand, how different detectives working together on one case collated information and decided what information was to be treated as relevant or irrelevant for their purposes. After I had taped all the known cases for 1969, I accompanied different homicide detectives, working both day and night shifts, on their investigations of current cases. Observation of homicide scenes around the city, and my presence during police interrogation of killers and eyewitnesses to homicides, made me increasingly aware of both the limitations and potentialities of information contained in the previously recorded data. Homicide officers, in addition, significantly enlarged my appreciation of the homicide investigation by accompanying me to such novel but to them familiar scenes as the emergency ward and morgue at the Ben Taub Hospital, the dispatcher's office at Police Headquarters, and the city jail. Finally, I was given "the guided tour" through high crime localities and neighborhoods.

Police files are not organized for scientific research, but the record of the entire police investigation includes much valuable information. Although the information collated in one case report had been gathered by different individuals, who by training and experience look only for certain things and disregard others, there is enough similarity between cases to justify a comparative analysis. Each case report contains information on the following: location of the killing; description of the complainant; type of premises in which the homicide occurred; time of the incident; sex, race, and age of the principal parties present at the scene; detailed reconstruction of the offense; suspects and persons arrested at the scene or shortly after the killing; description of the scene of the killing; physical evidence collected at the initial investigation; coroner's report; hospital report; and witness statements. Witness depositions are usually taken by detectives as soon after the incident as possible. Much of this information is sorted into discrete and comparable variables, which can be analyzed quantitatively. Moreover, the descriptive first-hand information in written confessions, witness affidavits, and detective reports yields valuable information, which is statistically significant and thus can be analyzed to ultimately explain homicide and related forms of violent behavior. Although witness affidavits may be later challenged as inadmissible or hearsay evidence if a case comes to trial, they are notarized and signed. Photographs and crime laboratory reports are added to each case file as they become available. Of particular anthropological interest is the data concerning relationships between killers and their victims. In the 268 cases for 1969 may be found examples of almost any dyadic combination of killer and victim relationship.

Case-by-case analysis and comparison of the homicide cases in 1969 indicate that killers and their victims tend to be more alike than different socially; that homicidal behavior occurs in a limited number of settings and social circumstances; and that similar cases generally evoke similar responses in official sanctioning. An official response refers to the actions of the police in apprehending and processing a homicide suspect together with the subsequent acts of city attorneys, grand jury members, jurors, judges, and all other persons called upon to finally dispose of a homicide case. The way a particular killer is treated is governed by very complex cultural rules. These brief introductory comments shall be limited to the statement that sanctions against homicidal acts are consonant with cultural attitudes concerning the degree to which such acts are private or public matters. Lawlessness appears to be most often ascribed as taking place in the "public" realm or as to acts that involve killers and victims who are strangers.

In some instances it was impossible to categorize the relationships between the principals in a homicide case. For the purposes of analysis, categories of killer and victim relationships were distributed as follows: (1) 77 cases involve relatives, (2) 68 cases involve friends and associates, (3) 55 cases involve strangers. Some 28 cases filed separately under justifiable homicide were reviewed but were treated separately from the analysis of killer-victim relationships resulting in a different judicial outcome (see Chapter 6). On the basis of this 200-case sample, it is evident that the severity of the penalty for killers correlates inversely with the degree of intimacy between killer and victim. Thus, 61 percent of killers of relatives escaped any form of legal penalty; 53 percent of killers of friends or associates similarly escaped any form of legal penalty, and 36 percent of killers of strangers escaped legal punishment. Conversely, not one person who killed a relative received the death penalty, only one received a life sentence (for killing both his parents), and 16 (21 percent) received prison terms of varying duration.

None of the killers of friends or associates received a death penalty, and only two of them were sentenced to life. Of the others, 25 (37 percent) received some kind of prison sentence. Of those who killed strangers, five (10 percent) received a life sentence; and 23 (42 percent) were sentenced to serve a prison term. The average prison sentence, in years, for killers in the three categories was eight years (relatives), ten years (friends and associates), and 28 years (strangers). Of those actually sentenced, killers of relatives received sentences ranging from three years to a maximum of 19 years; killers of friends and associates, sentences from a minimum of one year to a maximum of 75 years; and for killers of strangers, sentences, other than the death penalty, of three years to 99 years.

These facts, culled from police files and public records in the Criminal Court Archives, were subsequently tabulated and processed by computer. The tabulations generally show that if a person kills a relative he is more likely to escape any form of criminal sanction than if he kills a complete stranger. The most notable exception to this general finding occurs when the killer-victim relationship specifically involves two persons who are status reciprocals in the parent-child relationship. In such cases, the parents receive a disproportionately lighter sentence for killing their children than do children for killing their parents. The number of relatives, and persons listed as friends and associates, who escape any form of legal sanctioning is four times greater than that of persons who killed strangers. It also appears that there is a direct causal relationship between a killer's social status, the situational context in which he kills his victim, and the severity of the official penalty applied to his act. To sustain a murder charge under Texas criminal law the prosecuting attorney's indictment must demonstrate, to the satisfaction of a jury, that the killer not only intended to kill his victim but that his act was motivated by malice aforethought. It is quite easy to perceive a vague psychological element of "malice" if the killing directly threatens public safety and if the act is combined with a property offense. It appears that Texas grand juries, aware of judicial permissiveness in cases in which a person defends himself after provocation, do not negatively sanction persons who kill their relatives within the private domains of domestic groups.

It is principally because most homicides involve "last straw" encounters between so-called intimates that I have chosen to view homicide as a very special kind of dyadic social relationship. Also, the emphasis on the social context in which violence occurs is an essential and much ignored element in the explanation of specific forms of violence. Bohannan et al. (1960) found, for several different African societies, that personal violence is contextually defined and differentially institutionalized by different social groups. The concept of subculture, as often used by sociologists and criminologists, has proven useful only to a limited extent. The limitation derives from the difficulty of applying the subculture concept for a given population. The boundaries of the population defined as sharing the same subculture cannot be precisely defined. Although the subculture hypothesis, in combination with Sutherland's classic differential association theory, has indeed shown itself to be useful in explaining juvenile delinquency or the formation of criminal gangs in specific studies, it confuses social group membership with a juxtaposition of individuals with similar experiences into analytical categories.[16] It is my view that the patterns of homicidal behavior for which excellent descriptive data are available involve at least two kinds of sanctions: (1) the organized negative sanctions of criminal law and public sentiment prohibiting and forbidding the taking of human life; (2) the diffuse positive sanctions that approve of individual aggression and violence, including killing, given specific situations and acceptable motivational circumstances.

One of the more difficult problems with the Houston data concerns the continuity in time of violent behavior patterns in the face of rather dramatic sociocultural change. The American frontier is gone, but somehow we see pale reflections of elements of the past recurring in an urban context.

Sanctions are clearly more than reactions to breaches of conduct or expressions of approval for conformity. Sanctions must be part of the cultural ideology and values so that human action is integrated and social activities coordinated. Social integration, and in turn cultural stability, must to a large extent result from a compromise between the allocation of authority and social privilege and the preservation of individual choice and freedom of action. Societies change, and individuals constantly adjust motives and decision-making choices, in response to internal as well as external demands for change. A clear understanding of sanctioning processes can undoubtedly help us understand how and perhaps why total cultural systems both sustain and replace traditions in response to the changing demands of human existence. An excerpt from Sapir's brilliant essay, "The Unconscious Patterning in Society," may help clarify how the concept of culture pattern, which includes sanctioning mechanisms, can be applied to the study of homicide:

> All cultural behavior is patterned. This is merely a way of saying that many things that an individual does and thinks and feels may be looked upon not merely from the standpoint of the forms of behavior that are proper to himself as a biological organism but from the standpoint of a generalized mode of conduct that is imputed to society rather than to the individual, though the personal genesis of conduct is of precisely the same nature, whether we choose to call the conduct individual or social. . . . The patterns of social behavior are not necessarily discovered by simple observation, though they may be adhered to with tyrannical consistency in the actual conduct of life. If we can show that normal human beings . . . are reacting in accordance with deep-seated cultural patterns, and if, further, we can show that these patterns are not so much known as felt, not so much capable of conscious description as of naïve practice, then we have the right to speak of the "unconscious patterning of behavior in society."[17]

It is a principal aim of this study to describe, discover, and analyze those cultural patterns that ultimately manifest themselves in the high rate of homicide and related forms of interpersonal violence in the urban Houston community.[18]

Another very basic question to be addressed relates to a basic theoretical issue in anthropology. It concerns the ability of an outsider to a culture to describe accurately and without ethnocentric bias how participants or members of that culture conceptualize some part of experience. This problem may be exemplified by briefly considering the two recent ethnographic descriptions of violent cultures. In one of these general studies, Langness describes incidents of cannibalism, sexual aggression, and homicide for different societies in New Guinea. Any Western reader would agree that the ethnographic data from this area support Langness and others in the conclusion that extreme forms of personal violence were at one time accepted as entirely normal.[19] Similarly, Chagnon's study of the Yanomamö tribes of Brazil depicts a culture and a people embroiled in a continued state of chronic intertribal and intracommunity fighting. Such fighting is not only viewed as normal but is considered desirable.[20] In both studies, the anthropologist made a judgment similar to the one I have made above. On the basis of actual behavior, it is possible to characterize and evaluate the significance of violent behavior relative to other aspects of the culture. Native conceptions of peace, amicability, or friendly interaction, although important for a basic understanding of motivation, do not alter the outsider's interpretation and classification of observable behavior. The data on Houston homicide permit us to explore unconscious cultural patterns of violence, which, through a multitude of sanctions and sanctioning processes, sustain and perhaps even promote a high level of interpersonal violence. It could also be said that the frequency of violence, especially in urban communities in Texas and elsewhere in the nation, has reached such a level that the efficient operation of entire communities as socially cooperative entities is threatened by behavior that is poorly understood by the members of those communities. As a people concerned with furthering civilized life, we face tenacious cultural problems for which existing remedies are inadequate.

Publication of psychological and sociological studies of violent behavior has succeeded in calling attention to the magnitude and seriousness of violence as a social problem. But there have been very few attempts to conceptualize the problem of aggression and violence in American society as part of implicit cultural patterns that are sustained and nourished by slowly changing social values and social institutions. The anthropological approach provides an empirical basis, founded on a detailed comparison of actual case materials, for both theoretical and applied discussion of urban violence as a cultural phenomenon. I am firmly convinced that as the anthropologist shifts his attention from small, isolated, non-Western communities to urban centers he will find that the traditional research tools developed in studies of these communities are entirely appropriate to the analysis of specific social problems within the urban setting. The implications for kinship and family studies, social organization, and legal and political behavior are clear. The anthropologist who turns his attention to the study of complex societies should not abandon his traditional toolkit for the ready-made methodological and theoretical perspectives of his colleagues in the social sciences. The anthropologist must seek, rather, to add the very special perspective derived from participant observation arising from a long tradition of field work in non-Western and preindustrial cultures. Anthropologists have been trained to pay attention to all facts and all aspects of social life, no matter how small, that ultimately combine to make a cultural description possible.

Police and law enforcement agencies in general, and our belabored criminal justice and social welfare systems in particular, have proven entirely inadequate in dealing with the cultural problems generated by increasing levels of violent behavior and homicide. There is a need for more imaginative solutions than have so far been attempted.

Plan of the Book

The book moves from an overview of the principal events in a typical homicide case, through three chapters that describe and analyze different killer-victim relationships, to a discussion of the distinctions between lawful, unlawful, and lay conceptions of homicide. Additional data in the charts, tables, figures, maps, and appendices are cited in each chapter. Chapter notes, which are not extensive, are used primarily to refer the reader to comparable findings of other studies of homicide and to general works on the subject of violence.

In many ways I consider this book a voyage of discovery for both the writer and the reader. I have sought to present as many descriptive data as possible and to allow the reader enough room to think of interpretations and conclusions that may differ from my own. I have tried to make sense out of something which, happily, to most Americans is strange and senseless behavior. The reader will undoubtedly find the case material brutal and unpleasant. Indeed, if the reader felt differently, there would be little hope of ever correcting the social, economic, and cultural conditions that needlessly prevent a large number of Americans from achieving their full potential as productive members of society and as civilized human beings.

Chapter 2, on the homicide investigation, summarizes how each and every homicide case is processed by the police, the district attorney's office, the courts, and the coroner's office. I feel that it is absolutely essential for the reader to "walk through the homicide investigation" to realize how the focus, once a person has been killed, and emphasis on the part of governmental officials at different levels and at different capacities quickly shift from a concern with the victim and his survivors to apprehension of the killer. An autopsy is performed on the victim so that we may know the official cause of death. In Houston, the victim's survivors and relatives receive no compensation or indemnity whatever for the loss of their family member. The killer is protected by a whole series of legal rights, he is never tortured or seldom even reprobated for his act; he is simply processed by a judicial system that, as elaborated in Chapter 6, is closely allied with general cultural values concerning the rights of individuals to defend themselves and others, the rights of persons to bear arms, and the rights of accused to draw upon lawyers, psychiatrists, character witnesses, and others who can in any way justify or ameliorate his behavior.

Chapters 3, 4, and 5 provide the bulk of the substantive data of homicide cases from 1969. These cases have been divided into three general categories of killer-victim relationships (domestic relations or relatives, friends or associates, and strangers). Only a fraction of the cases for 1969 have been described, and I have chosen them on the basis of how well each case represents the relationships within a particular category and how well, alas, each case has been officially documented. Each of the three basic killer-victim relationships is compared to the judicial outcome for killers in each category. The study clearly shows how the killer-victim relationship determines the seriousness of the outcome for the killer. Some unique "frontier-like" aspects of the Texas penal code, which result in very few convictions against killers, are reviewed in detail in Chapter 6. The interrelationships between cultural values and the judicial processing of homicide offenders are explored to illustrate the interconnections of the different parts of the cultural system.

Chapter 7 concludes with a brief overview of general sanctioning theory. It is finally argued, on the basis of the descriptive case-by-case analysis presented in Chapters 3 through 5, and the analysis of quantifiable variables, that the study of sanctions and sanctioning behavior can help us to see how human violence is subject to the laws of culture and therefore open to change.

2
The Homicide Investigation

Introduction

American culture symbolically assigns each act of homicide to a place on a continuum. At one end of the continuum, killings are classified as honorable, excusable, justifiable, and permissible; at the other end, they are tragic, negligent, and criminal. The act of homicide, by definition, always embraces two or more persons. The actual slaying may either represent a surprise attack by the killer or evolve from the mutual interaction and communication of the killer and his victim. Assassination and contract murder exemplify homicidal acts that require neither interaction nor any form of communication between the principals. At the opposite pole, the act of killing serves to terminate a social relationship between two persons involved in mutual and frequent communication and interaction. The characterization of any particular act of homicide as excusable or criminal is an extremely complex affair.[1] In this chapter, I will explore and emphasize the bureaucratic response as exemplified by one police case. This case may also serve to exemplify the systematic and official step-by-step investigative and judicial response to a homicide. Initially, the official determination of culpability or innocence and the attainment of justice depend directly upon the official police evaluation of the facts and circumstances that lead somebody to kill a fellow human being.

The victim, who is formally and officially labeled "the complainant," becomes the fictitious party to any future official and legal actions against the killer. The victim also becomes an official entity in quite a different way. His brain, spinal cord, and all vital organs are removed together with laboratory samples of his spinal fluid, blood, and urine. The body is dissected in a postmortem medical examination to determine the official cause of death. The results of the medical examination, the facts believed to have motivated the killer to act, and the subsequent legal assessment of all the evidence in the case determines the final disposition of the case and its outcome.

Homicide Case No. 170 illustrates how the basic facts of a case are assembled and officially processed. The information contained in an official police homicide report, which determines whether or not the police or the city attorney will initiate a criminal action, is tailored in such a way that only some of the facts, the motivational circumstances, and information on the killer-victim relationship are recorded and included in the official police report.

The official evidence is selective because only certain information is sought. A case report, therefore, includes and excludes descriptive information that may be of interest to laymen, scientists, or other non-official persons. But the information collected by police officers and other public officials involved in a homicide or criminal case, which obviously is biased by bureaucratic and judicial conventions, does not of course preclude scientific use of the same facts as data. The data that can be culled from police files must simply be put to the same critical tests for accuracy that other data collected by observation or formal elicitation of verbal statements are put to. The following discussion of Case No. 170 is aimed principally toward the clarification and illustration of the kind of police report that, for scientific and comparative purposes, serves as a reliable source of raw culturological data.

Homicide Case No. 170

Shortly after noon on January 9, 1969, an 18-year-old Black male flagged down a patrol car. The young man informed the officers that his older brother had been shot. As the uniformed officers drove the youth to his home they radioed the dispatcher who in turn immediately notified both the Homicide Division and the Office of the Medical Examiner. Two homicide detectives working the day shift were assigned to "make the scene" by the on-duty lieutenant of detectives. The two detectives assigned to the investigation thereafter assumed principal responsibility for investigating the killing. A county ambulance, with two attendants and a deputy coroner from the office of the county medical examiner, were simultaneously directed to the scene from Ben Taub Hospital. The deputy coroner viewed the victim at the scene and issued a preliminary finding: The complainant, Donald McGrew, was dead. The body was removed by ambulance to the county morgue at Ben Taub Hospital where all shooting victims from the general Houston area are brought. The detectives were now ready to collect and record the necessary facts from the scene and the witnesses. These facts, which later in the day would be summarized in a typewritten report prepared by the two homicide detectives, were to form the basis for the legal action, which, as a matter of required routine, would at once initiate and end the role of the police in the shooting. Since there were several witnesses who could testify about the possible motives for the killing, and because the killer called the police sometime later to give himself up, the police investigation was concluded in a matter of days.

The killing was assigned an official case number (170) and the victim's name was filed in alphabetical order in the 1969 homicide case record and officially "cleared" by the Homicide Division. Excerpts from the case file, which have been edited for clarity, read as follows. The names, home addresses, and other identifying features of all principals, however, have been fictionalized to preserve the confidentiality of the police reports.

The details of the offense were learned from witnesses Mary McGrew, a Black female, age 17; Beverly McGrew, a Black female, age 15; and Herman McGrew, a Black male, age 18. All the principal witnesses are siblings to the complainant and the defendant. They all stated that the complainant and the defendant got into an argument about the manner in which the defendant had been treating their sisters and other people. The defendant's sister, Mary McGrew, and his father had attempted to file official charges against the defendant the night before the commission of the crime because, as Mary McGrew said, the defendant had told her that he wanted to have sexual relations with her. According to the witnesses, the complainant and the defendant had a loud argument about the defendant's sexual overtures toward their sister. The two youths were arguing in one of the family bedrooms when the witnesses heard a shot. The defendant ran out of the house. The complainant walked 18 feet from the bedroom into the hallway. He fell and died in that hallway.

The three affidavits that follow are quoted in full to illustrate how the homicide detective manages to uncover those facts that are crucial to the official investigation and disposition of the case. It must be remembered that the legal process starts with the homicide detective's evaluation and recording of the facts he has been trained to regard as significant and meaningful.[2] The brief affidavits, which may be contested by the defendant's attorney if the case is ever brought to trial, form part of the basic or raw data incorporated in the official record of any killing. The three oral statements, simultaneously elicited from witnesses by three different detectives, overlap to such an extent that one might conclude that the statements had been elicited by the same person. This is an important point to keep in mind.

> My name is Beverly McGrew. I am 15 years old. I live at 715 Vermont Street. I go to school at E.O. Smith Junior High School and I am in the 8th grade. On Thursday, January 9, 1969, I was kept home from school by my father because I was up late last night from being at the police station. I had gone to the police station with my father and two sisters, Mary and Kathy, to file charges against my older brother, Don. Don had gone under my sister's dress and we came down to report him. Today at about 11:30 A.M., Don came into Mary's and my bedroom and he started cursing Mary because she had told our father what he had done. He also started to curse me. Don threatened to kill me and Mary if we told our Dad what he had done to us. I told Don that I wouldn't say nothing but I told my Dad anyway. In a few minutes Don came back into the room and he spat in my face and started cursing me again. He had found out that we had come to the police station to

report him. When he spat in my face I didn't say anything back to him. When he spat in my face one of my brothers, Ray, walked in the door and then Don started cursing and hitting Ray. Don then said to Ray, "Nigger, I ought to kill you." Ray then told Don, "Why don't you leave me alone." Don kept cursing and hitting on Ray and teasing him, "Why don't you pull that little gun you have got?" Ray said, "I don't want to shoot you so why don't you leave me alone?" Ray said that he did not want to shoot him because Don was his brother. Don said, "Don't ever let me hear you call me your brother again or I will kill you." Ray then went out on the front and in a couple of minutes he came rushing into the house with a pistol in his hand. Ray then ran into the living room with the gun still in his hand and shot Don. He didn't say anything to Don before he shot him. He shot Don one time. When he shot Don, Mary, my older brother Herman, and I jumped up and ran outside the house. We ran around the block to my sister-in-law's house and Herman stopped a policeman driving down the street and told him what had happened. I don't know where Ray went after he shot Don. I was brought to the police station a little while later to make this statement.

My name is Mary McGrew. I am 17 years old and live at 715 Vermont Street with my father, my brothers, and my sisters. I go to Junior High School and I am in the 9th grade. I also work part-time in the kitchen at Ben Taub Hospital from 4:00 P.M. to 7:15 P.M. About three months ago, my brother Don got out of jail. He had been there for about four years. Since coming home, he has been acting crazy. Yesterday, Wednesday, January 8, 1969, Don came in where I was taking a nap and tried to get me to let him sleep with me. I wouldn't let him do that but I could not get him to leave me alone. Don made me take my drawers off and lay across the bed, cock my legs up so he could see if I was a virgin or not. Then he stuck his fingers inside of me and kept telling me how he was going to have me. Finally he quit. Later that night I told my father what happened and he took Don into the bathroom and tried to talk to him but he could not talk any sense into him. Later my father, two sisters, and I went to the juvenile division and talked to the police about Don. They gave us an address where we could file on Don and send him to the crazyhall. I talked with my sisters and they told me that Don had been looking up under their dresses also. Before we came to the police station I met my brother Ray down the street and I told him about it. Ray had told me to tell him if Don tried anything. Ray told Dad to get something done about it. Today Don came into my room and told me and my sisters that he was going to break my leg and kick my ass. He spat in my sister's face and he tried to spit in mine but I got out of the way. My brother Herman called from work around noon and asked me what had happened. Don was on the other phone listening. I told Herman what had happened but not everything. Herman and Don got to arguing and Don told Herman that he would kill him when he saw him. My brother Ray came in about this time. Ray was hurt on the job and is not working. I told Ray not to leave because Don was going to jump on me. Ray said he was tired of him messing with us and he was going to put a stop to it. "If Daddy will not do anything to the boy, I will have to do something." Ray went into the room where Don was and they started to argue. They kept arguing . . . I heard a shot. Beverly, Herman, and I ran outside and down the tracks. We decided to come back. We found Don dead in the front doorway. Ray was gone. I have read the above statement and find it to be true and correct.

My name is Herman. . . . I am 18 years old. I live at 715 Vermont Street. I am unemployed and not attending school at this time because I am sick. On January 9th, somewhere around noon, I was in the kitchen of my house fixing to iron some pants. My brother Don was in the kitchen with me. He left the kitchen and went into his room. In a few minutes I heard Don and Ray arguing at the front door. It was quiet for a few minutes and Don came back into the kitchen. To get to the kitchen he walked through the room where I was ironing and said, "Herman, you don't know how to iron." I told him that I didn't care and he then said that the pants I were ironing looked like his. I told him they weren't his and that I had bought them. He then left the kitchen and walked through the bedroom and into the living room. I heard the shot while I was getting some water in the kitchen. Don came into the kitchen holding his stomach. He came from his room. He then went back toward the living room and I got scared and ran over to my brother's house around the corner to tell my father. My father wasn't there. I then saw a police car in the street and I stopped it and told the officer that my brother had just been shot. I showed the policeman where my brother was. After I brought the policeman back to the house I learned from my sisters that Ray had shot Don.

In addition to the three affidavits, the homicide report includes a brief summary by the two detectives placed in charge of the case. Their summary reads as follows:

Kathy McGrew, a Black female, age 15, was not at home at the time of the offense. She says that Don often tried to play with her and her sisters. Nathaniel Miller, a Black male, age 22, who lives close to the family residence, also was not home at the time of the offense. He says that Ray McGrew had bought a gun recently. He says that the gun is a small revolver; possibly a .22 caliber pistol. He adds that Don McGrew often made rash statements and that he, Nat, has heard that Don has tried to play with his sisters' sexual organs. He has not seen him do this, however. . . . The person wanted, Ray McGrew, is unemployed at this time. He was previously employed at a restaurant on Main Street about four months ago. He was born in Houston in June, 1948. He has a previous police record. He was last seen running north down the railroad tracks shortly after the offense. The subject took the weapon used in the offense with him. The suspect, Ray McGrew, is also listed as a suspect in a residence-burglary case, a misdemeanor theft case, and assault to murder case W-06198. The complainants for those cases have been listed. . . .

As the police were initiating a routine search for the suspect, Raymond McGrew, they received a call from Raymond who said that he wanted to give himself up. He gave the police an address and a patrol car was dispatched to apprehend and arrest the suspect. Ray stated to police officers that he was wrestling with his brother and that the gun had discharged into the complainant's body. Ray was brought to the Homicide Division where detectives officially charged him with murder in Judge Richard Miller's Court.

The results of the autopsy were now inserted into the complainant's official case file. There were no signs of alcohol or drugs in the body of the deceased. "It is our opinion [the official medical opinion] that Donald McGrew, the decedent, came to his death as the result of a gunshot wound in the chest."

Shortly after these facts on the case had been compiled, and while the defendant was awaiting further official action in the city jail, the District Attorney's office obtained permission of the Justice Court to dismiss charges against the defendant. Ray was released from custody. He was a free man. But Raymond McGrew can reenter the legal process at a later date if the police are able to change his status from "suspect" to "defendant" in his previous acts involving burglary, misdemeanor theft, and assault to murder. The likelihood of future arrest for any of these offenses is unknown. One thing is certain, however, Raymond McGrew can never again be charged with his brother's murder and the fratricide is no longer the subject of official interest or concern. The questions the disposition of the case raises are many: One might first ask how Raymond McGrew escaped punishment of any sort; what kinds of official procedural and statutory rules were invoked to clear Ray of the slaying of his brother; how many persons with similar backgrounds are today free citizens; and by what official reasoning does someone like Raymond go unpunished?

These are difficult questions to answer; some of them have no clear answer. What can be done, however, is to look further into the data and seek plausible answers. There are complex cultural reasons as to why killings within domestic groups in Texas, and perhaps elsewhere as well, are officially treated as nonthreatening to the viability of the society in general. On the other hand, the robber, the thief, and the "morally corrupt" are perceived as dangerous to the society.

It is my purpose to link the specific examples of values, attitudes, and beliefs about homicide to a cultural and symbolic system, including a judicial subsystem, that socializes its members to distinguish between acceptable and unacceptable patterns of human behavior and interaction.

The Medical Investigation

Even the most objective among us cannot remain entirely unmoved by the sight or description of an autopsy. The reader who may lack any familiarity with human anatomy or who finds the thought of dissection repugnant can follow the arguments by skipping along to the next section. But the official postmortem examination represents such a fundamental part of any homicide investigation that its description cannot be omitted.

Section 1, Article 49.25 of *Code of Criminal Procedure of the State of Texas* (hereafter cited as Tex. Code Crim. Proc.) enjoins all Texas county governments with a constituency of 500,000 or more persons to maintain an office of medical examiner. The office in Houston, with principal laboratory facilities at the Ben Taub Hospital, employs two full-time forensic pathologists together with a supportive staff of dieners (laboratory helpers), deputy coroners, ambulance drivers, and others. Houston is one of the few cities in Texas to employ full-time forensic pathologists. The principal duty of the medical examiner's office is to investigate and determine the cause of death of persons who have died under any one of the following circumstances:

1. When a person shall die within twenty-four hours after admission to a hospital or institution or in prison or in jail;
2. When any person is killed; or from any cause dies an unnatural death, except under sentence of the law; or dies in the absence of one or more good witnesses;
3. When the body of a human being is found, and the circumstances of his death are unknown;
4. When the circumstances of the death of any person are such as to lead to suspicion that he came to his death by unlawful means;
5. When any person commits suicide, or the circumstances of his death are such as to lead to suspicion that he committed suicide;
6. When a person dies without having been attended by a duly licensed and practicing physician . . . [or] . . . When the local health officer or registrar of vital statistics whose duty it is to certify the cause of death does not know the cause of death . . . (Tex. Code Crim. Proc. Sec. 6, p. 545).

In all deaths resulting from homicide or suicide, whether the cause is proven or only probable, the medical examiner routinely performs an autopsy of the victim. On May 4, 1972, I accompanied two homicide detectives to the county morgue at the Ben Taub Hospital to observe an autopsy and to interview informally one of the forensic pathologists who was on duty in the morgue. The presence at the autopsy of an anthropologist, or any outsider for that matter, did not seem to bother the medical staff nor, according to the homicide detectives, did it appear to affect their daily routine. Observers, such as physicians, medical students, or nursing students, are frequently present at an autopsy. Detectives from the Homicide Division are routinely assigned to attend autopsies of suicide and homicide victims.

The ambulance that brings the body of a victim to the morgue parks at a special, quite inconspicuous, loading platform at the rear end of the hospital. An elevator, said to "provide the slowest ride in town" takes the body down to the morgue. Two attendants thereafter transfer the body from the stretcher to a table-high steel tray. The body is rolled over a large weight scale and its weight, minus the known weight of the tray, is recorded. The morgue attendants now proceed to remove the clothing from the body. Scissors are used for expediency and convenience. All personal items, and especially those that help establish the identity of the dead person, are removed. The body may be sponged off if there is any visible blood or dirt. A paper sheet is then draped over the now naked body and, finally, a cardboard identification tag, showing the relevant information about the deceased, is tied to one of the big toes.

If anyone must further identify the body at the morgue, the body will be placed on a sliding tray in a large refrigerator. If the body already has been officially identified, and if nobody is to view the body prior to autopsy, it is rolled into a large refrigerated room housing as many as twenty bodies at one time. This room, or "the cooler," has two doors. One door leads directly to that part of the morgue where private citizens may come to identify a body. Another door, at the opposite side, opens into the autopsy laboratory.

The autopsy room, which is in a part of the morgue complex, resembles a large and quite ordinary human anatomy teaching laboratory. Two large steel platforms, equipped with sinks and running water, delimit the principal working area for two independent teams of autopsy personnel. Each steel table is equipped with an elevated table-like platform. This platform is used by the pathologist for the dissection of individual body organs as these are detached and removed from the body by two dieners working together. The body itself is usually dissected in a steel tray that can be rolled into place next to the examination table. A foot pedal under the examination table allows the pathologist to operate a dictaphone while using both hands for the dissection and examination of the organs. As the autopsy gets under way, the pathologist records his observations; they are, in turn, transcribed and filed as part of the permanent official record. Although the exact method of dissection varies with circumstance and place, the general autopsy procedure cited below synoptically describes the medical details of a typical autopsy.

Before any incisions are made on the body, the two dieners report their initial overall observations to the pathologist who, in turn, records the information. The information tag tied to the body when it arrived at the morgue is removed and that information is recorded. Additional information on the dead persons's sex, age, race, height, and general state of nutrition follows. The limbs, the lower jaw, and the musculature are inspected for signs of rigor mortis. Body discoloration, together with other early signs of putrefaction, is noted. The exact time, the principal or primary cause, and manner of death are the three most important facts to be established by the autopsy.[3]

The body is opened with a Y-shaped incision that connects the distal ends of the two collar bones and extends, from a point over the xyphoid or breast bone, downward to the pubic symphysis. The ribs are cut with shears and the thoracic and abdominal areas are completely exposed and thus made readily accessible. The two dieners now proceed to dissect and remove individual organs. Samples of urine, spinal fluid, and blood are collected (a 0.10 percent, by weight, of alcohol in the blood is regarded as evidence of being intoxicated). Careful attention is paid to the position and condition of each organ before it is removed. The heart, lungs, and viscera are removed and transferred to the dissection table where each organ is weighed and inspccted by the pathologist. Organ tissue samples are selected and stored separately. When the body cavity has been emptied of all organs, the spinal cord can be removed. The tongue, pharynx, larynx, and the entire neck area is removed en masse without disturbing the external features of the lower face region.

At this point in the procedure, the two dieners will usually concentrate on the removal and preparation of different organs and anatomical structures. Each eye is removed, without disturbing the lids, and examined. One diener moves to the end of the autopsy tray and opens the head. An incision is made from ear to ear at the back of the neck. The skin flap, with hair left intact, can then be pulled forward to cover the face. The skull is now completely exposed. An electric saw is used to cut the bone so as to permit removal of the top of the skull or the calvarium. Final removal of the calvarium may require the use of hammer and chisel. The brain and portions of the spinal cord are now removed. The brain is weighed and then dissected carefully. The near-empty skull cavity is closely inspected for fractures.

The autopsy concludes with a general repair of the body. The method of dissection permits ready concealment of the fact that what is left is essentially an empty hull. The dissected organs are discarded in the laboratory after study and the remains can be released to a mortician for funeral service and burial.

A few additional minor points need to be made. First, the medico-legal autopsy differs from a regular medical autopsy in several important ways: It is not undertaken to increase scientific understanding of disease processes but used, in an applied sense, to determine an official cause of death and gain expert forensic evidence for adjudication. Second, the expenditure of time, money, and medical expertise in the investigation of violent or undetermined death seems, on a broad and cultural scale, to stress that society seems prepared to go to great lengths to find the exact cause of a murderous act, whereas socially it often fails to direct its available resources at the prevention of similar crimes. The young pauper, who in life seldom benefits from the blessings of modern medicine, will in death be dismembered and disemboweled by some of the foremost medical practitioners in the country.

The Police Investigation

The Homicide Division of the Houston Police Department is responsible for the investigation of all actual and alleged offenses against the person and the apprehension of criminal offenders. The principal offenses investigated by the Homicide Division, ranked in order of relative workload frequency, include homicide, assault, threats, rape, suicide, and other offenses involving acts of personal violence.

The Homicide Division is staffed by one captain, five lieutenants, 40 detectives, and five clerks. The division is regarded as one of the most prestigious and selective units within the police department. Homicide detectives frequently express their feelings of pride and elitism. They are assigned to this division on the basis of such factors as emotional maturity and stability, personal and social adjustment, and a high sense of public duty. The homicide detective, perhaps more so than other police officers, is confronted with human tragedy daily and he is under constant pressure to exercise self-control when faced with danger.[4]

The detective who arrives at the scene of a homicide is, generally speaking, a person who has broad previous experience in various kinds of police work. He has spent considerable time as a uniformed patrol officer and he has passed civil service and police department examinations to earn the rank of detective. The officer must be a high school graduate with some college experience. Most detectives have spent at least two years in one of the armed services and some have worked for other police departments before they joined the Houston Police Department.

An official investigation in the Homicide Division is initiated either by a citizen's complaint or by direct police action. Since the division is responsible for all offenses against the person, there is a continuous demand for some kind of police response.[5] Such action may seem as trivial as the bureaucratic handling of a private altercation between a wife and husband, or it may be as complicated and time-consuming as the brutal sex and torture murders publicly revealed by Elmer Henley's confession to the police in 1973.[6]

The following paragraphs trace the general outlines of a routine homicide investigation. Perhaps it would be better to say "typical" rather than "routine" to characterize an investigation that begins with a call to investigate a shooting and ends with the culprit's peaceful surrender to the police. This is how most investigations occur, rather cut and dried and without publicity or mystery.

Homicide detectives usually first enter the scene of a crime if a death has occurred or if there is the likelihood of a fight or assault victim dying. The shortwave police radio in the division office is tuned to the general police patrol frequency but homicide detectives on patrol do not respond to shooting or disturbance calls unless the police dispatcher requests their presence. Because of the specialized nature of the homicide investigation, the division communicates on its own radio frequency. Detectives, who often cruise around the city, keep the car radio tuned to the special division frequency while awaiting a call. Once a call comes in, the lieutenant on duty in the Homicide Division will assign a team of detectives to investigate the killing. The two detectives who "make the scene" hereafter assume principal responsibility for clearing the case. The puzzle-solving attributes of fictional whodunit murder mystery stories are entirely missing from the majority of cases investigated by the Homicide Division. The official clearance rate, which in the past was 90 percent or better, attests to the open and shut nature of most homicide cases. Yet there is a vast difference between guessing a suspect's identity, or apprehending the most probable offender, and legally convicting a killer on the basis of evidence that will convince a judge and jury about the guilt of a person charged with criminal homicide. It is principally for legal reasons, therefore, that even the routine homicide investigation must devote as much manpower and technical expertise to each case independent of such factors as complexity or simplicity of circumstances leading to a killing.

The proliferation of mystery movies and television series depicting violent behavior and crime, together with a steady output of fictionalized accounts of police work, has served to emphasize rather than dispel much of the mystery and puzzle-solving mystique of the detective-killer relationship. The theme is repeated *ad nauseum* in the context of the courtroom battle of wits between the district attorney and defense attorneys armed with clever procedural insights and factual surprises uncovered by private detectives who supposedly surpass the police in fact-finding and basic intelligence.

The normal homicide investigation, and the legal disposition of a particular case, is as routine and about as melodramatic as the detection and prosecution of a federal taxation case. It is not deemed newsworthy by the press and media and it is usually not sensational enough to invoke public interest.

The call for a homicide investigation initiates a series of official bureaucratic procedures. The aim of the investigation is twofold: (1) to determine the cause of death of a victim and (2) to apprehend, arrest, and charge the person or persons legally responsible for the act. Unlike other kinds of police work, *a homicide investigation by definition cannot include any form of prevention.* The determination of the cause of death is largely a medical problem. Therefore, the homicide detective works closely with the medical examiner. It is common practice for the detective to view the dead victim at the morgue and to measure and describe visible wounds on the body. The officer fingerprints the victim and he may collect external tissue and hair samples for laboratory analysis together with the victim's clothing. These items and the victim's personal effects in possession at the time of death are collected and brought to the Homicide Division. The victim is also photographed so as to show all wounds and to illustrate the type of injury that resulted in his death. The officer may return to the morgue at a later date to witness the autopsy of the victim. Knowledge of the cause of death, and the recovery of expended bullets or other evidence about the exact means of killing, form an important link in the investigation, which at this point usually involves piecing together disparate kinds of evidence.

The officer who investigates the scene of a homicide is, as noted earlier, usually not the first official to enter the case. Uniformed patrol officers, ambulance drivers, and any number of eyewitnesses may have "disturbed" the scene at which the killing occurred. Because the homicide detective only rarely enters a pristine, undisturbed scene his observation and description must encompass every conceivable detail. Most case reports include a meticulous cataloging of such seemingly trivial facts as the dress of the victim, the position of the victim, the locality of the killing, the weather and lighting conditions, and a host of small details that may be relevant to the subsequent investigation and possible prosecution (see Appendix A). Some detectives include detailed measurements of the scene and they frequently augment such measurements with schematic drawings. Of equal importance is the description of any "real evidence" found at the scene. The recovery of weapons, articles lost or left behind by a fugitive killer, poison containers, bullet holes in a wall, or broken pieces of equipment or furniture may acquire special significance in the subsequent investigation. Such standard crime laboratory tasks as the collection of fingerprints, blood or hair samples or the identification of tool marks are performed by special police officers from the Bureau of Technical Services.

The interrogation of witnesses, associates of the victim, and the apprehension of the killer call for the homicide detective to exercise his professional skills directly. Although written and signed affidavits by eyewitnesses may be challenged by a defense attorney in open court, statements by eyewitnesses and the defendant can be crucial to the outcome of the case. It must be emphasized that the homicide officer, after consultation with his superiors in the Homicide Division, can recommend that no legal action be taken against a killer. The reverse situation may also prevail. That is, the district attorney may recommend dropping a case for lack of sufficient legal evidence and a detective may, on his own volition, attempt to collect further evidence so as to arrest and charge a suspect. The decision whether to arrest and charge a possible suspect may be a very difficult one to make. If a suspect is apprehended before the police have collected all revelant facts and in effect "made a strong case" against a suspect, the suspect may shield himself behind any number of legal rights and procedural safeguards that essentially remove him as a source of valuable information from the investigation itself.

The final police job may be that of testifying at the defendant's trial. The high acquittal rate for murder suspects by some well-known and colorful Houston attorneys attest to the difficulty of obtaining convictions in homicide cases. The grand jury system, and the many idiosyncratic features of Texas criminal law, combine to make the conviction of killers a 50-50 proposition. In the end, therefore, the most conscientious homicide investigation may terminate in the freeing from legal prosecution of the suspect. The point is worth emphasizing: Texas criminal law and general beliefs concerning rightful and wrongful behavior, although interrelated, can be viewed as separate facets of the cultural system. Under law, the police must investigate and prepare cases for prosecution by the district attorney. (See Appendix D, Chart I, for an overview of this process.) In the cultural subsystem of "justice" or mores concerning permissible behavior, a known killer may not be charged at all. His act of slaying may be viewed and judged, socially and legally, as reasonable, honorable, and socially acceptable.

Legal Disposition of Case No. 170

Case No. 170 was officially cleared by the Homicide Division of the Houston Police Department the moment the principal suspect was apprehended, arrested, and officially charged with a specific offense. On the basis of the evidence provided by the Homicide Division, the special nature of the case, and other factors not made public, the district attorney entered a motion of *nolle prosequi*. The Justice Court granted the motion and the suspect, Raymond McGrew, was discharged from police custody.

The district attorney could have pursued a quite different method of procedure. He could have asked for an indictment leading to a jury trial or he could have bound over the defendant for the grand jury. The grand jury, after being instructed on the different legal or statutory interpretations applicable to the evidence in Case No. 170, could have issued a "true bill of indictment" with the result that the defendant would be formally indicted for the offense of murder and therefore be legally required to stand public trial. The grand jury might also have returned a "no bill" and the defendant would be absolved of any further legal responsibility for the slaying of his brother in this case.

One of the most engrossing problems raised by the 1969 homicide data concerns the relationship between an act of killing and the final legal outcome for the killer. At this point, it must suffice to mention that as many as 69 homicide suspects were neither charged nor indicted for any offense and that in certain kinds of familistic killings the odds are better than chance (50 percent or better) that the killer will avoid any form of legal punishment. In later chapters, I will discuss fully how the data from 1969 suggest that the majority of persons charged and arrested by the police for felonious homicide are freed in a matter of hours or days following the homicide. A homicide may be legally justifiable, excusable, or highly approved as a form of social conduct. The labels felonious homicide or murder only apply to killings that result in an official, legal, and negative organized sanction against the probable killer. The passing of time between the commission of the act and final legal disposition may, as hinted at above, be a matter of a few days or several years. Unlike many other criminal and civil offenses there is no statutory time limit on prosecuting a homicide suspect. Finally, the common assumption that most criminal offenses lead to adjudication in courts is false.

The majority of homicide cases are dismissed by the police, the district attorney, or a grand jury. If a murder case goes to trial the odds are slightly against the defendant unless, of course, he has secured the services of experienced criminal attorneys who long ago adopted the view that one wins a case by removing the spotlight from the defendant and by pointing the finger at the victim and the society, and away from the suspect. The saying attributed to one such attorney that "no property needs stealing but a lot of people need killing" says more about the effect of attitude and social mores than law as the decisive factors in winning an acquittal for a client.

If the defendant in Case No. 170 had been formally indicted, it would have been easy to apply this typical defense strategy: the defense attorney could emphasize the bad moral character of the victim, buffer his assertions by calling attention to the victim's past criminal record, and, finally, tell how the victim's family had taken him back and tried to help him after he had served his prison sentence. The defendant, it may be recalled, was defending his sisters and acting as *patria potestas* in place of his father.

The defense attorney could alternatively have chosen a more formal approach by, for example, building his case on a theory of accidental or negligent homicide or on a citizen's rights of self-defense and the right to kill. Article 1221 of the Texas Penal Code gives great latitude for a person to kill another in the necessary defense of either person or property, in response to threats or fear of danger from the victim, or any other "reasonable" provocations that may have caused the killer to fear for his life. Article 1225 explicitly states that "the party whose person or property is so unlawfully attacked is not bound to retreat in order to avoid the necessity of killing his assailant" (Vernon's Penal Code, 1961, p. 547). With specific reference to the situation described in Case No. 170, the statute would not require that the defendant run from the house, call the police, or refuse his brother's challenge to fight him with a deadly weapon.

Perhaps the most interesting observation that can be made with respect to the entire homicide investigation is the overwhelming concern with the discovery of motivational factors at the expense of a concern over consequences. The investigative system is designed to reveal and evaluate the motivations for killing. The larger question: The consequences of homicide to a victim's survivors, and ultimately society at large, although not altogether ignored, is viewed as outside the scope of official responsibility.

3
Homicide within Domestic Groups

Introduction

This chapter examines homicides among members of domestic groups. These homicides involve persons, as assailants and victims, who are related to each other, live together in the same household, or who occupy complementary familistic status positions within definable social units. Such units can be variously characterized as households, families, kinship groups, or even homes. No less than 41 percent of the killings reported for 1969 involve assailants who in one way or another could claim membership in the same domestic group as their victims. Assailants and victims within domestic groups most commonly are related to each other as husband and wife, in-law and daughter- or son-in-law, or co-resident and co-resident. Homicide within these groups also takes the form of patricide and matricide, filicide, and—as in Case No. 170 described in Chapter 2—fraticide. The members of domestic groups will hereafter be referred to as *intimates* or persons who interact with each other socially and economically on a regular face-to-face basis and who usually are status reciprocals in a familistic relationship.[1]

A domestic group may be defined as a social unit composed of two persons or more who share the same domicile and cooperate minimally to form a singular economic entity; it lacks both the temporal perpetuity of consanguineal kinship groups and the legal status of corporations. A typical domestic group may in some instances display the attributes of a nuclear or an extended family, a household, or a home. But membership in a domestic group is neither limited to kinspeople nor is it restricted to consensually cohabiting adults and their legitimate or illegitimate children. A domestic group may be composed of adults cohabiting as "common-law" marrieds together with children from previous unions or their relatives and close friends. Group composition, both in terms of the kinds of relationships and physical size, varies within as well as between different domestic groups. Members of a domestic group may hold property in common or one or more of the principal members may hold exclusive rights to properties enjoyed by the membership at large. Members may leave to form separate domestic groups and new members may be added. The stability of domestic groups derives from the predominance of husband-wife and parent-child relationships. The greatest source of intragroup friction, together with a noticeable lack of temporal continuity of group membership composition, probably originates in a loosely structured and poorly defined form of group authority. Husband-wife killings typically evolve from basic conflicts over the allocation and exercise of authority.

Homicidal incidents might ordinarily be expected to be evenly distributed more or less randomly among the affluent and the poor, small and large domestic groups, or among different racial and ethnic isolates within the city population. In the 1969 data, homicide occurs most frequently among the poor, within relatively large and crowded domestic groups, and among Blacks. Yet it must be emphasized that the data do not permit us to say that poverty, residential crowding, race, ethnicity, or personal income can be treated, individually or collectively, as principal causes of either homicide in particular or crime in general. It may be reasonably inferred from the data, however, that a large and disproportionate number of Black homicide assailants and victims share a life-style and a common cultural milieu that, among other things, dehumanizes by its abject poverty, impoverishes by low educational achievement and high unemployment, stigmatizes by racial discrimination, and generally perpetuates values that contribute to highly concentrated homicidal incidents only loosely tied to specific neighborhoods and city areas.[2]

Houston is one of the few American cities of its size without uniform and strict city-wide zoning laws. The absence of zoning, which over time has produced a checkered distribution of commercial, industrial, and residential properties, is said by Houstonians to give the city its undeniable flavor of urban vitality or élan. The phenomenon of urban growth and change is particularly evident in the central city area now completely encircled by "the loop" or Highway 610 (Map I).

It is within this central area that one can observe spectacular billion-dollar shopping and commercial centers connected by some of the most affluent single-family residential areas in America. But a sharp contrast in residential density, relative wealth, and general physical appearance of neighborhoods can also be observed by walking through any area of the city. Even the motorist cannot fail to notice the nuances in affluence and poverty as he tries to beat the traffic. Urban growth and decay is readily evident everywhere in Houston. Yet, compared to other similarly sized American cities, Houston cannot be said to have a clearly demarcated ghetto area or an inner core.[3] The characterization of different city areas in terms of official U.S. census tract data must therefore be undertaken with great caution.

We are, of course, interested in learning more about the relation-

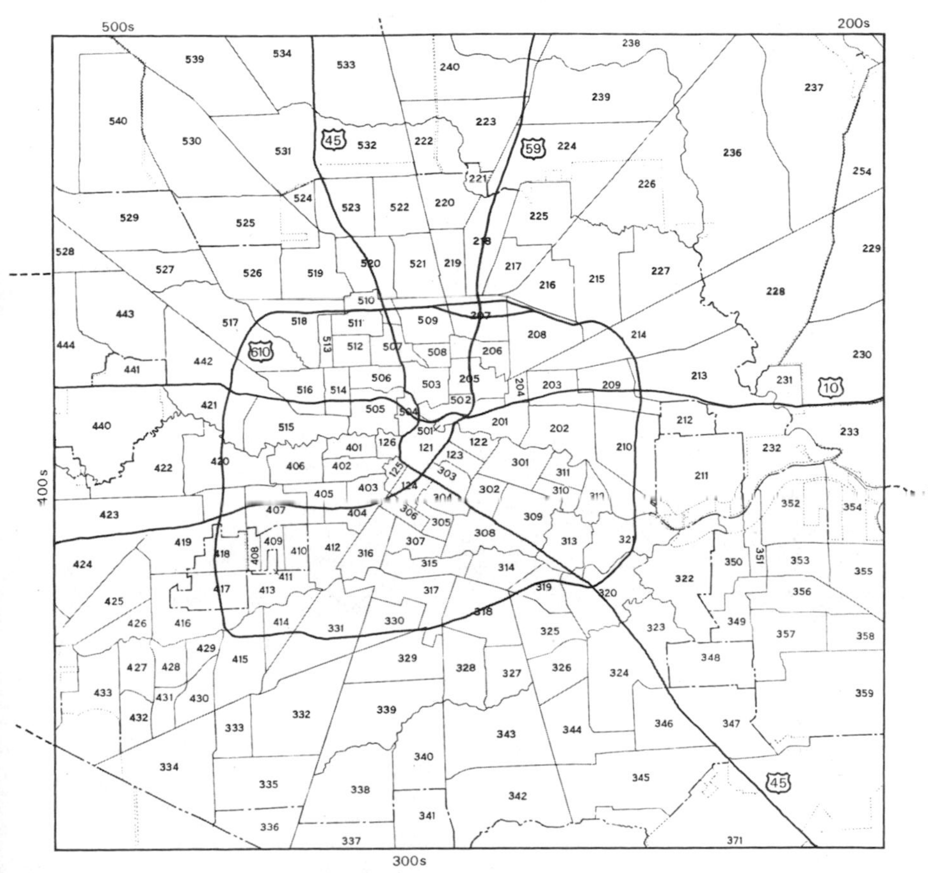

Census tracts of Houston

ships between the population characteristics of high crime neighborhoods and the general economic, educational, and housing conditions that contribute partly to the milieu in which interpersonal violence regularly occurs with such high frequency (Maps I, II, and III).

No less than 78 Houston census tract localities were official homicide scenes in 1969. The precise distribution is depicted on Maps II and III and in Appendices B and C. In the following paragraphs we shall consider eight census tracts in particular to learn as much as possible about the demographic and socioeconomic patterns that characterize areas in which there is a high concentration of homicidal incidents. It is

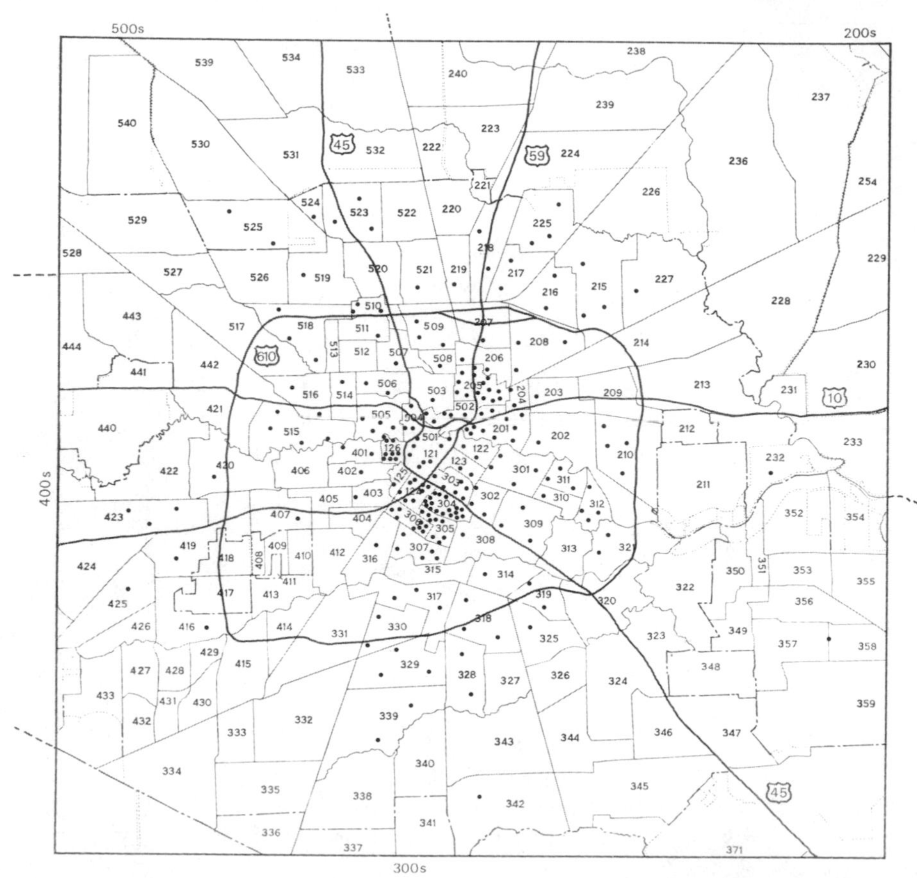

Census tract distribution of homicide incidents

essential, of course, to keep in mind that, given the available data, one can only and then cautiously attempt to characterize in general terms the environment that is shared by homicidal assailants and victims (see Chapter 7). Economic, demographic, and residential attributes permit only a tenuous inference about the effect of the environment on the behavior of assailants and victims. Firsthand field data on kinship, social organization, and personality formation within the environment is sorely needed before we can develop sound hypotheses about the relationships between total environmental factors and individual acts of violence. Here it must suffice to discuss the available statistical data and to interpret the

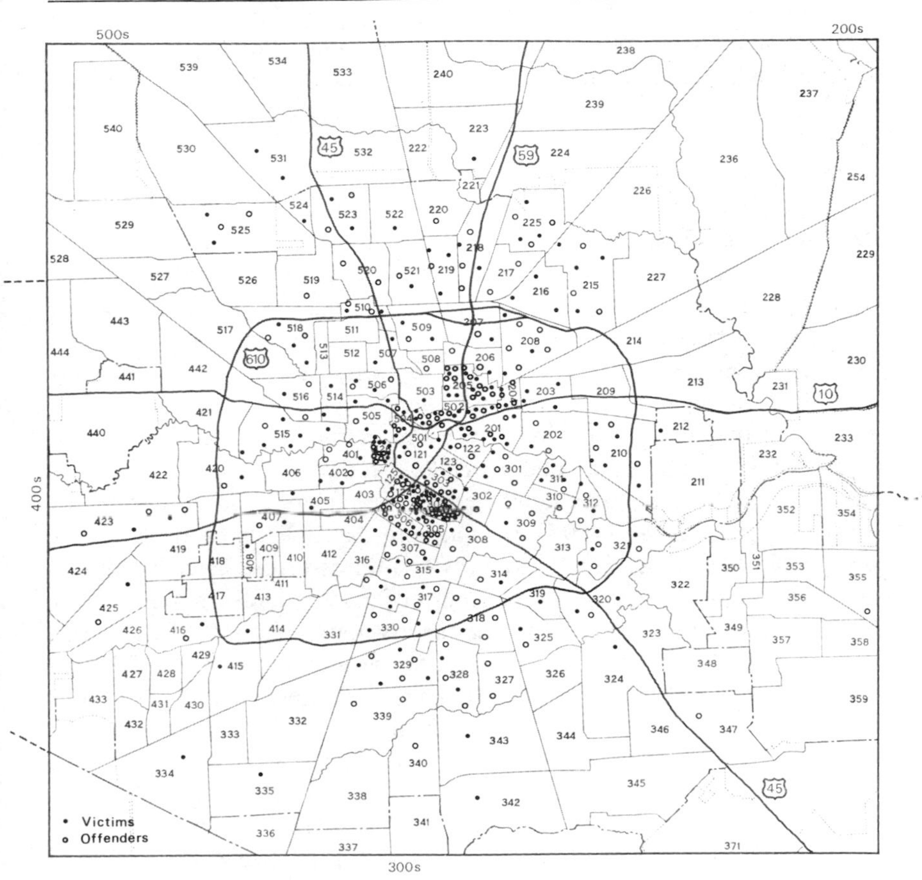

Residential location of homicide offenders and victims

meaning of these data as best we can in terms of the descriptive information found in individual homicide reports. The homicide case data from 1969 have been compared with the population and housing characteristics of the general Houston population as compiled in the official U.S. census of the population.

Eight tracts (124, 126, 201, 205, 303, 304, 305, and 502) have been chosen as a sample. The principal criterion for selecting these rather than others is that the homicide frequency count in all of them is five or more. The choice of five or more homicides as the cut-off point is arbitrary. When a census tract locality had a frequency of five or more homicides, and when other tracts did not, it is assumed that the environment exhibits some elements or characteristics that either facilitate or precipitate violent behavior. The eight tracts selected for closer study are taken to be representative of those tracts in which the incidence of homicide, and by implication other forms of interpersonal violence, was very likely more than a chance occurrence. In an attempt to keep the description as simple as possible, averages are only computed from the census data on the eight census tracts. It must be emphasized that statistical variables are quite arbitrary and, at best, only suggestive of the relationships between population housing characteristics and interpersonal violence. *It is therefore not suggested that there exists any causal relationship between particular housing characteristics and homicide.* The etiology of homicide clearly involves more than demographic and housing factors. With all this in mind, let us look at the data.

Table V (Appendix E) illustrates the racial and marital statistics for the sample population. It is clear at once that Black persons and married couples are predominate. Roughly two-thirds of the 78 census tracts in which one or more homicides occurred in 1969 had a population of 400 Blacks or more. Table VI further shows how tracts with the heaviest concentration of Blacks also experienced the greatest number of homicides. All in all, the sample data indicate that those tracts having the highest incidence of homicide were more than 90 percent Black in composition. There is one exception to this pattern: Census tract 224, in northeast Houston, comprises 247 Whites and 3,525 Blacks (93 percent). No homicides were reported for that census tract in 1969. This exception illustrates and emphasizes the absolute necessity of cautious generalization. On the strength of the evidence provided by the 1969 data it must be concluded that there is no *causal* relationship between race and the propensity toward violence. What we do see in the data is concomitance; that is, poor persons living in crowded housing and existing in a dehumanized environment happen to be mostly Black. Consequently, most homicide assailants and victims are Black. The census tracts with the highest concentrations of Black residents, except for census tract 224, manifest all the social and economic characteristics found in blighted inner-city areas throughout the nation. Individuals are poorly educated and underemployed (Table VII).

Table VIII shows that less than 25 percent of the residents here are high school graduates. Low educational achievement, in terms of the completion of a very minimum education in basic social skills, need not necessarily correspond to a high rate of unemployment. But it limits choice, opportunity, and ultimately, income potential in the employment market. The unexpectedly low unemployment rate in the eight-tract sample (5 percent) is not synonymous with prosperity, however. The average number of families in the sample was 1,974, with 723, or 36.60 percent, of these families having an income below the established poverty level. The mean income in 1969 for these families was $5,277. Although the U.S. Census tabulates separately the general and social characteristics of the Black population, the greatest significant difference between the general population and the Black population is seen in the mean income of the two populations. The general population showed a mean income of $5,277 per family, whereas the Black population had a mean income of $4,486 per family. Interestingly enough, however, the percentage of families below the poverty level did not vary significantly between the general population (37 percent) and the Black population (37 percent) (Table VIII).

The average number of Black families in each census tract, based on the eight-tract sample, was 1,881. Of these families, 702 or 37 percent, had a family income below the poverty level. The mean family income of those at the poverty level was $1,935. And 451 families in the sample, or 24 percent, received public assistance in the form of welfare payments.

Table IX compares the tenancy characteristics of the general population with the eight-tract sample. The difference between the general population and the sample populations is not particularly large. But the differences are not small enough to be ignored because the Black population comprised 94 percent of the sample. The remaining 6 percent is what accounts for the difference (Table IX).

Differences between the general population and the sample population increase for certain characteristics as the White population increased in proportion in the racial composition. The characteristics that yield pronounced increases as the racial composition changed include income and education. The mean income, for example, of census tract No. 125 (5 percent Black) was $13,701. The percentage of high school graduates was 43 percent. One case of homicide was reported for census tract No. 125 in 1969. Neither the assailant nor the victim, however, was a resident of that tract. Clearly, then, such characteristics as family income and educational level are interrelated. A higher income level is related to a higher level of education. Both income and educational level relate to better housing and standard of living. The relevant characteristics, therefore, should be treated in clusters (i.e., variables such as income, education, and occupation can be grouped together and treated as units for purposes of comparison). Exactly how these characteristics cluster remains to be analyzed in multivariate contexts.

What has been documented so far tells us very little that every American already does not know from casual reading of the daily papers: Violent crime is concentrated among the poor, the uneducated, and the unskilled labor force. What the papers usually fail to tell us is that the majority of victims of crime also are poor, uneducated, and only marginally benefit from the affluent society. If a person happens to be Black, poor, and uneducated, the forces that conspire against his social success may be insurmountable. None of these factors alone may motivate persons to perpetrate violence against others. But it is not difficult to understand how interpersonal aggression and violence can become adaptive strategies for survival when so many other avenues to social participation in the world's most affluent society remain closed. The family, the household, or the domestic group quite naturally becomes a principal stage for personal interaction. It is on that stage that persons learn that violence does help resolve interpersonal problems. The individual's inabilities to cope with the outside world narrow the focus of aggression and violence inward toward his primary group of social relations and peers.

Assailant-Victim Relationships

Wolfgang in his excellent book, *Patterns in Criminal Homicide* (1958), which is a sociological study of homicide in Philadelphia, discusses at length the phenomenon of *victim-precipitated* homicide. According to Wolfgang

> The term *victim-precipitated* is applied to those criminal homicides in which the victim is a direct, positive precipitator in the crime. The role of the victim is characterized by his having been the first in the homicide drama to use physical force directed against his subsequent slayer. The victim-precipitated cases are those in which the victim was the first to show and use a deadly weapon, to strike a blow in an altercation—in short, the first to commence the interplay of resort to physical violence (ibid. p. 252).

This definition, as Wolfgang acknowledges, is too legalistic and too narrow to be of much use in work with police case reports.[4] One could also define victim-precipitated crime as any act that invites a criminal response such as leaving your doors unlocked or displaying large amounts of cash in an "unsafe" neighborhood. What is important here is not whether the victim of a homicide delivered the first blow but rather that the assailant and the victim were reciprocals in some kind of a status and role relationship. Husband and wife, parent(s) and child, sibling and sibling, or friend and friend occupy reciprocal social statuses and may, depending upon the context and type of social interaction, interpret and play different roles *vis-à-vis* each other. A misunderstanding, or an outright disagreement, between two persons can result from conflicting views of the acceptable enactment of a role. A wife who expects her husband to be courteous and loving sees the husband role differently from her husband who may see himself as provider and family autocrat. A marriage license does not specify what roles go with the conferral of married status. Marriage, in other words, only establishes a formal and reciprocal status relationship in which the principals are more or less left to determine the kinds of roles that may prove satisfactory to them as a couple.

A social status is a position within a social structure that confers various rights and duties on individuals of a particular status. The concept of status personality is frequently used to denote the total number of status positions that any given individual may hold at any one time (e.g., husband, father, employee, friend). The ambiguity, and indeed conflict, inherent in playing any particular social role derives from the reciprocal nature of social relationships. Any two individuals who occupy reciprocal or complementary status positions *vis-à-vis* each other must rely on a continuity of mutual understandings concerning goals and interests. If there is an opposition or a conflict of these interests, or if they literally cease to be mutual or shared, the nature of the reciprocal status relationship is changed. Divorce, for example, terminates status relationship created by marriage and the individuals are released from the performance of duties and the exercise of rights conferred by the status of husband and wife. Legally and logically this is so true that we often fail to appreciate the difference between the structural and the psychological dimensions of human behavior. A relationship between two persons can be changed structurally by altering the status of each person. A psychological bond between two persons may never really allow a relationship to be terminated although the status of the principals has been formally changed. This phenomenon is particularly evident in killings that involve former spouses or even ex-boyfriends and ex-girl friends. The divorced man who kills his ex-wife's new husband is implicitly acknowledging a psychological relationship that has only been legally and structurally dissolved. We should now discuss victim-precipitated homicide in a broader perspective. Victim-precipitated homicide occurs when one of the status reciprocals in a social relationship fails to meet (1) the expectations that are either culturally defined as part of such a status or (2) those expectations created by mutual understandings between the two reciprocals. This perspective can clarify the motivational factors of some killings that otherwise may appear to be utterly senseless.

The 1969 data indicate that nine husbands killed their wives, 15 wives killed their husbands, four "common-law husbands" killed their "wives," and nine "common-law wives" killed their "common-law husbands." All these killings occurred within the context of a shared domestic environment. Perhaps most surprisingly we learn how the legal penalty for this offense pendulously swings from a 90-year jail sentence to no charge and self-execution of the killer by suicide. The cases, which will be briefly summarized below, confirm the two-dimensional and reciprocal nature of the status relationship: (1) the formal, public, official, and legal conceptualization of marriage as a contractual arrangement and (2) the informal, private, consensual, and customary conceptualizations concerning appropriate and inappropriate role behavior associated with spouse status. Each case, if the information warrants, will be treated in relationship to the kind of case dispositions noted in Tables X, XI, and XII.

Husband-Wife Killings

Case No. 125 was resolved by the killer's suicide. The police report notes that the deceased couple, a woman, age 46, and her husband, age unknown, was discovered by their daughter. The woman had been shot through the back of the head with a .25 caliber pistol and her husband had shot himself through the temple. The husband, according to his daughter, had recently been released from a Texas hospital following a lengthy treatment for alcoholism. Both parents were reported to be alcoholics. The police noted a large garbage can filled with empty beer cans in the apartment and the best explanation for the act seems to be that the homicide-suicide was committed in an alcoholic stupor. The autopsy report attached to the case indicated that no alcohol was found in the blood of the wife. No autopsy report on the husband was filed with the police.

The next case, No. 167, bears a striking resemblance to the above. An elderly White couple was found dead by their daughter. The woman's age was given as 69 but the man's age was not given. The wife was dressed in her nightgown and she was shot with a .38 caliber revolver in the back of the head. She was seated before the television set, which was still running when the bodies were found. The daughter told the police that her father had a violent temper and that her deceased mother took special pleasure in needling him. What finally precipitated the man to act and kill his wife is unknown. The fact that the husband killed himself may say something about his way of solving problems. The ready availability of a firearm also must have made his fatal decision somewhat easier to execute. One can only guess that in both cases, which presumably involved persons who had been married for a long time, the homicide-suicide solution seemed easier than separation, divorce, or the continuation of an unsatisfactory and mutually frustrating relationship.

The Homicide Division telephone answering service is kept continually busy with complaints of marital fighting and brutality. The official response is bureaucratic: The police can only respond to formal complaints or those executed in writing at the police station. There is some indication from the case data and conversations with homicide detectives that many incidents that begin with a complaint to the police eventually terminate in a killing. Spouses who formally "file" against each other have a distinctive advantage, legally, if the relationship sometime in the future results in the killing of an abusive spouse. The record of violence has been established by the recognition of the threat and it can help the assailant in a self-defense plea. In the following case a husband kills his wife with a shotgun. The police in this case found sufficient grounds for bringing the facts of the case before a grand jury. That jury, in turn, issued a no bill for the husband. His killing was well inside the boundaries of a legally excusable act.

A Black male, age 70, killed his 55-year-old wife by shooting her in the chest and throat with his 16-gauge shotgun. According to witnesses, neighbors in the apartment complex where the couple resided, the couple had a loud and continuous argument the night before the killing. Their verbal arguments had erupted into a fight during which the woman took a knife and cut her husband's finger. The finger was stitched at the hospital, but later in the day the fight continued and this time the woman shattered a mirror in her husband's face. Witnesses report that the husband was heard yelling at his wife indicating in no uncertain terms that he would kill her. The wife left the house and returned shouting that she was going to kill her husband. The man didn't take any chances. He shot her through the screen door and according to one eyewitness the man came outside to look at her and said, "There she is, I told her I was going to do it." Another neighbor who called an ambulance said that the man came out in the yard and said, to the people in the crowd, "Call somebody to come and get her or I will shoot her again." Other witnesses and neighbors interviewed by the police reported that the elderly couple drank heavily and had quarreled since the day they moved into the apartment complex. This was not the first time that others had heard one of the two threaten the life of the other. After the husband had been cleared by the grand jury he wrote a formal letter to the authorities: "I, ________, hereby give my permission to Arthur Brown to pick up and keep my shotgun out of the property room at the city of Houston, Harris County, Texas, in connection to the charge of murder filed against me." The shotgun was released to the legally exculpated killer.

In Case No. 92 the police made a thorough investigation because there was considerable doubt whether the victim, a 46-year-old Black female, was killed with a .32 caliber pistol by her husband or if she committed suicide in her husband's presence. The circumstances of the case were sufficiently complicated by circumstantial evidence and by the fact that the principal witness was the woman's young son by a previous marriage. The assailant, a Black male, age 46, was indicted by a grand jury but found "not guilty" after the trial of his case. The ten-year-old boy's verbatim statement encapsulates the sad facts of the marital relationship.

> My name is Daniel Drury. I am 10 years old. I live at . . . with my mother and stepfather. I am in the 5th grade and go to Houston Gardens Elementary School. Yesterday evening, about 6:30 P.M. or 7:00 P.M., my mother wanted to go see my brother who is in Ben Taub Hospital but my stepfather did not [want to go]. My parents left home and dropped my stepfather at Phillip's Place on the way home and stayed for about 30 minutes. I don't think my mother or stepfather had any trouble while at the beer joint (Phillips). We went on home and I went on to bed which was about 9:00 P.M. She told me to go to sleep and not eat anything. She was going somewhere. I then went to sleep. My daddy came home about 10:00 P.M. and I woke up when he came in the door. He asked me where my mother was. He had been drinking. He told me over and over that I lied. He then went and got the pistol. He said that she could not outsmart me [him] and that he was smarter than she was. They argue a lot about my daddy not working and going out and spending his money getting drunk. He then left. He called back and asked me on the phone where my mother was and I told him that I did not know. I then went back to sleep. I woke up again by my mother and daddy arguing. They were in my room. My daddy slapped my mother in the face and then went out of my room. I heard them argue more and heard mother tell him that she had seen him kiss another lady. The next thing I heard a shot and heard my mother say "O, Henry, you shot me." I heard daddy go call an ambulance and say that a lady had been shot while he and her had been wrestling over a gun. He called back again for an ambulance. He went into the bathroom and got a wet towel and went back where mother was and I don't know what he did then. He then went next door and got Mr. G. to come over. The ambulance and the police came and I told them what happened. I went and stayed until about 3 A.M. with Mrs. G. My uncle came and got me. Later I was brought to the police station and told Detective A what happened. . . .

The follow-up investigation, among other things, revealed that the victim's husband had been seen by eyewitnesses to physically assault his wife on at least ten previous occasions and that the husband was a heavy drinker. The autopsy did not reveal any alcohol in the wife's blood or spinal fluid. The husband's police record indicated that he had been arrested for carrying a pistol and that he had been listed as a material witness in a cutting. In 1962, before he was married to his now deceased wife, he was wanted for aggravated assault. The wife's circumstances at the time of her death were not too encouraging: Her other son was hospitalized at the Ben Taub psychiatric ward, she had a daughter who was serving a prison sentence in an Austin city jail, and her stepson—who was married to her daughter imprisoned in Austin—was serving a jail sentence elsewhere. Perhaps the Houston jury found enough loose ends in this case not to render a guilty verdict against the husband or perhaps they were persuaded by defense lawyers that the deceased was crazy enough to have precipitated her own death. One cannot know the details of this and similar cases but we can begin to see the very subtle interplay between the public sanctions that define marriage as an institution and the private sanctions exerted by individuals who, by choice, live within the broad guidelines outlined by their culture.

The victim in Case No. 67, a young married Black female, age 21, met her death by strangulation. Her 30-year-old husband was apprehended by the police and remains, at the time of this writing, either a prime suspect or a defendant now represented by an attorney. In many cases, as we shall see, a case is incomplete or disjointed as is this case. Many factors are at work: the police work necessary to uncover legal grounds for an arrest, the time schedules of crowded courts and busy prosecutors and defense attorneys, and last but not least, the medieval recording system that frequently makes it impossible to discover the final outcome of certain cases. As mentioned in Chapter 2, the police are not routinely notified of the outcome of a case once it has left the homicide division and is turned over to the district attorney. Obfuscation by a slow moving bureaucracy is the fate of many police cases once they have been processed by the judicial machinery.[5]

Case No. 168 seems particularly tragic in that it is a homicide that involves two 18-year-old Mexican-Americans, recently married, with a five-month-old baby. The young wife furthermore was found to be four months' pregnant with a second child and the shooting was a tragic mistake. The young husband was charged with negligent homicide and sentenced to serve three months in jail. What had happened, briefly, was this. He was in the kitchen of the couple's small apartment together with three of his friends. The atmosphere was friendly and the wife was preparing a meal of pancakes. The husband casually took a .22 rifle from behind the refrigerator and began to toy with it. He pointed it around the room and the rifle went off. The bullet entered the right eye of his wife and the young woman died on the kitchen floor. The husband's friends called the police.

The details of Case No. 102 were quickly pieced together on the scene of the killing. A 32-year-old Black man shot his wife with a .32 caliber revolver as they were struggling over possession of the "family pistol." The killing was witnessed by the couple's 15-year-old daughter who submitted a written affidavit to the police. According to the young girl, her parents were arguing over the family budget. The girl's statement reads as follows:

> I live with my mother and stepfather together with my two brothers and two sisters. I attend Baldwin Junior High School where I am in the eighth grade. . . . This morning my mother told my stepfather that she was going to cash a check. He told her that he was going to cash the check to pay the car note. Mother told him that he could not pay the car note this week because he had other bills to pay. Mother was sitting on the footstool in the living room reading the paper. My stepfather was sitting in another chair in the same room. He got up and went into the bedroom and got the gun off the bookcase at the headboard of the bed. He told mother that he was tired of this goddamn shit and he said that when he had the gun in his hand. He put the gun in his pocket. Mother told him, "That is what I wanted you to do. Now that you have got the gun, use it!" She told me to go gather up the clothes for the laundry. I left the room and went to get the clothes. I heard three shots. I ran back into the room to see what had happened. My stepfather told me that he had killed my mother and for me to go and call the police . . . mother was lying on the floor in front of the dresser and her eyes were closed. I called her but she did not answer. . . .

The defendant was tried in the court without a jury, found guilty, and sentenced to serve a seven-year sentence in the Texas Department of Corrections. Can we conclude that the homicide was "victim-precipitated" or perhaps "situation-precipitated"? The technology for an expedient killing was readily available, the argument over money focused other strains and tensions between the couple, and the wife's "I dare you" was more than a kind verbal dig. Why did it happen?

Case No. 191 begins as a domestic quarrel. A 37-year-old White woman and her 42-year-old husband were drinking and quarreling. The woman first ran next door to her sister's apartment but only found her 11-year-old nephew awake. She left her sister's house to seek assistance from a neighbor. Her husband intercepted her as she crossed their driveway, a further argument ensued, and the woman shouted for help as she walked away from her husband. The neighbors found the woman lying bleeding on the sidewalk and called an ambulance. The husband told police that the whole thing had started because his wife didn't love him anymore. The husband's interpretation of their relationship, together with the ensuing quarrel fueled by the mutual consumption of alcohol, finally led him to pull out a pocketknife and stab his wife in the chest. The husband was indicted, tried, found guilty of murder, and sentenced to serve a ten-year term in the Texas Department of Corrections. Expressions like "I don't love you anymore" clearly have the potential for initiating an argument. They challenge the *raison d'être* of the relationship and must therefore be retrieved, rationalized, or simply erased if the relationship is to continue. It is also possible, as was evident in Case No. 191, that the two principals, rather than negotiating back and forth to achieve a status quo or facilitate a detente, will readily escalate from emotional threat to physical action. In the following case, the husband responded to a similar but more serious emotional injury by killing his wife without further argument or negotiation.

The spouses in Case No. 233, a Black male, age 25, and a Black female, age 22, were engaged in sexual intercourse when the wife continually called out the name of another man who was known by the husband to be a former boyfriend. The husband, according to his statement to police officers, completed the act then got up and put on his clothes. He took out his .22 automatic pistol and shot his wife in the chest. The couple's two three-year-old twin daughters were at the scene when the killing took place. The man, at first, told police officers that a neighbor had killed his wife. Sufficient doubt was raised by the husband's conflicting statements, and the absence of an eyewitness or other direct evidence supporting his story, that the first jury trial was declared a mistrial. A second trial was held and the husband was found guilty of murder in the first degree. He was sentenced to serve a life sentence in the Texas Department of Corrections.

We cannot second-guess the two juries or the two judges charged with evaluating the circumstances of the killings in this and the previous case. One element, however, seems bothersome; that is, the different judicial weight assigned to the initial provocation. Does the provocation of words like "I don't love you anymore" and calling somebody else's name during the height of intercourse mean a difference between spending ten years and a lifetime in jail? But this must raise the question of possible judicial capriciousness and arbitrariness in assessing the degree of victim-provocation, assailant response, and final punishment.

Wife-Husband Killings

Nearly twice as many more wives than husbands killed their spouses in 1969. Since men, as both assailants and homicide victims, outnumber women by a ratio of approximately 4 : 1, the wife-husband type of killing is the most typical form of homicide involving women as assailants. The most interesting statistic concerns the disposition of homicides in which the wife became the principal assailant. Nine of 15 wives were brought before the Houston Grand Jury and no billed, the police did not file a charge in one case and dismissed another, one case was brought to an inconclusive trial (the outcome, at the time of this writing, is still undetermined), one wife received a three-year probationary sentence, and the outcome or legal disposition of yet another two cases remains unknown. Insofar as the available data permit, we shall look at each case and search for any motivational and situational factors that led these wives to terminate the marital relationship by homicide.

Case No. 2 adds a touch of chivalry to the marital tragedy. On Oct. 17, 1969 at 9:15 A.M. a 29-year-old Black woman shot her husband in the stomach with a .22 caliber revolver. After the shooting, which evolved during the course of an argument over money, the woman drove her husband to the Veterans' Administration Hospital where he was interviewed by the detectives from the Houston Homicide Division. The husband, prior to his death on January 9, 1970, executed a handwritten affidavit that, in part, reads as follows: "On Friday, October 17, 1969 at 9:30 A.M. my wife and I had an argument over money matters and in this argument we had a gun. In the scuffling over the gun it accidentally was discharged, the bullet striking me in the stomach. Being her husband, I do not want to file any charge against her, and if I do not get well I still do not want the law to file any charge against her." The husband's statement by itself could not exonerate his wife and did not preclude official police action. The police arrested the wife on January 12, 1970, and referred the case to the grand jury. The grand jury in turn issued a no bill and thus closed the case.

Case No. 159 closely approximates Wolfgang's definition of victim-precipitated homicide. The husband was intoxicated (0.27 percent alcohol level in his blood), he verbally provoked his wife by threatening to kill her with a knife, and he physically assaulted her by trying to choke her. It appears that the husband, a 50-year-old Black male, had arrived home around 1:30 A.M. His 45-year-old wife offered to prepare some food for him but he began to use abusive language, calling her a "smart bitch" among other things, and he began to beat her. She fled into the bathroom but he followed her and continued to beat her. She escaped once more but her husband ran to the kitchen and picked up a steak knife, which he said he would use to kill her. The woman managed to retrieve their .22 caliber pistol from the closet and she fired six shots at her husband. The bullets hit his chest, back, and left arm. Although it appears that the first bullet stopped her husband's attack it is evident, from the bullet entry in his back, that she continued to fire the pistol after he had turned away. The grand jury did not make an issue of the obvious "overkill" factor and dismissed the case with a no bill.

It is impossible to reconstruct the mutual understandings and misunderstandings about a workable marital relationship from the acts of the principals in Case No. 15. A man is prepared to choke and beat his bride of six weeks and yet emotionally unprepared to grant her a divorce. The husband, a 37-year-old Black male, was killed with a .22 caliber pistol by his 27-year-old wife at 11:05 A.M. in the family residence. The wife had five young children from a previous marriage. The wife's mother lived in the house next door and it is evident that the victim had failed to get along with either his wife's children or his mother-in-law since the marriage. During the short duration of the marriage the husband had managed to threaten the children, alienate his mother-in-law, and physically maltreat his wife on several occasions. The husband had threatened his wife and added that he would kill her if she ever dared file charges (of assault) against him with the police. One Sunday, after he had once again beaten and choked his wife, the woman moved next door to her mother. The husband unsuccessfully tried to talk his wife into coming back to him, but she resisted and finally went to see an attorney for the purpose of obtaining a divorce. After visiting her attorney she called her husband, who at the time was working as a gas station attendant, to advise him of her actions. His reply was brief: "I will fix you when I get home." In response, the woman and her mother together with the children locked themselves in the house fearing what would happen next. The husband showed up and he asked to be let in. His mother-in-law refused. He got angry and said that he would kill his wife. The mother-in-law went away from the door to call the police. As she left, the man pulled off the screen door and broke down the front door. The wife, in the meantime, had armed herself and she met her husband in the hallway. The man began once again to curse her and he repeated his threat that he would "fix" her. She emptied the magazine of the automatic weapon and her husband fell dead on the floor. It turned out that the pistol was on file with the police department as a stolen weapon. The wife was arrested and booked on suspicion of murder. The grand jury reviewed the facts of the case and issued a no bill on February 19, 1970.

The facts in Case No. 38 were related to the police by the assailant and her 17-year-old daughter who had witnessed the killing in their home. The husband, a 48-year-old Black male, was killed by his wife, age 45, at 2:50 A.M. following a fight. The couple had two children. The argument that led to the killing apparently got under way early in the evening. Finally, after the couple had retired together, the husband kicked his wife out of bed and told her to sleep in their daughter's bedroom. On the way to the bedroom the wife secured the family revolver which, she said, she placed under the mattress of her daughter's bed. Shortly thereafter she went to get a drink of water in the kitchen. She brought the revolver with her–just in case! Her husband left his bed and came after her. The wife fired two shots hitting him once in the head and once in the back. She explained to the police that her husband had come straight at her and that she fired in self-defense. The instant widow first called the Deacon of their church and he, in turn, informed the police. The Houston Grand Jury did not find any grounds for indicting the woman so the case was no billed.

Such familistic killing sometimes occurs outside the home, as in Case No. 49. Here a woman, a 35-year-old Black female, had gone to a local cafe to get her husband to come home. Her husband, age 53, left the cafe and was heard arguing with his wife outside the cafe. She apparently yelled that she was tired of seeing her husband fooling with "them whores" in the cafe and he was overheard to shout that she should remove her eyeglasses. They fought on the sidewalk and during the fight the woman took a .22 caliber pistol from her purse and fired. A witness said that the man tried to raise himself after the first shot had been fired and that the woman then shot him once more. The woman threw the weapon into a nearby car and then waited for the ambulance that took them both to Ben Taub Hospital. Homicide detectives were able to interview the husband before he died and he stated that he was willing to prosecute the person who had shot him but that he didn't know who had done it! One of the eyewitnesses swore to the police that he had shouted to the woman not to shoot the man when he saw she had a gun. The grand jury's finding of insufficient cause, a no bill, must have viewed the woman's armed defense as well within the law or, could it possibly be that the jury is responding stereotypically to killings among intimates as an affair between private persons and not within the purview of the public interest?

The principal eyewitness to Case No. 64 was a 12-year-old girl. She had the misfortune to become, on the one hand, a part of the argument that led to the killing and, on the other hand, to witness firsthand the ugly scene of a homicide. The girl's mother, a 28-year-old Black female, and her stepfather, age 28, were arguing. The argument escalated and suddenly intensified when the man began to hit his stepdaughter. The woman contested his authority and got a small pocketknife from the kitchen drawer. As the couple argued further, blows were exchanged, and the wife used the small knife to make two penetrating stab wounds. One in the neck and one in the right side killed her husband. The woman was arrested, advised of her legal rights, and put in the city jail. She did not feel that she needed an attorney and she volunteered a written confession which the police presented to the district attorney who, in turn, used the confession and the two eyewitness reports to present the case to the grand jury. Both eyewitness reports, one by the defendant's 12-year-old daughter and another by a friend of the couple, were deemed sufficient grounds for issuing a no bill. It is of further interest to note that the second witness's account indirectly tells us something about the neutral or non-interventionist pose frequently adopted by persons who become the perhaps unwilling witnesses to an act of violence. The witness, a male, was visiting this family together with his wife and three small children. He and the family stayed long enough to witness the couple's fighting and they saw the complainant hit the defendant's little girl. The case report contains no further comment about the role of the outside visitors.

The reader should now recall the warning that it is much too simple to use single variables, such as race or sex, to explain violence and homicide. Case No. 93 exhibits many of the characteristics of the previous cases except that the couple here is a White male, age 45, and his 41-year-old wife. The couple had two teenage daughters who stated to the police that they had become so accustomed to their parents' frequent fights that they had learned to sleep through the noise. On this fatal morning, at 2:15 A.M., the two girls were awakened by a shot. The police were called and they found the girls' father lying, still conscious, on the bedroom floor. As the police officers entered they could not help notice that the couple was still arguing! The woman told the police that she had shot her husband because he had been abusive and tried to beat her.

Her husband told the police that they had been arguing because she had been drinking and had called him a son of a bitch. The man then told the police officers that he felt sure that he was going to die but that he did not want to file charges against his wife. The woman was taken to the Homicide Division while her husband was rushed to the hospital. When the husband died on the following day the police filed murder charges against the widow who had already secured the services of an attorney and been released on bond. On December 18th, the grand jury dismissed the case with a no bill *and* the grand jury wrote an official note to the police ordering the release of her .22 caliber pistol.

In reading and studying these homicide cases one gets the feeling that the actors in these strange social scenarios are indistinguishable from ordinary people yet they seem to walk around as sticks of dynamite that may go off at the slightest disturbance or provocation. In Case No. 140 the triggering device is a $42.00 loan. The actors are husband, a Black, age 44, and wife, age 52. It all started quite innocently. The couple, who had their home in Belville outside of Houston, were dining at the home of the defendant's cousin. According to this cousin, who became a principal eyewitness to the killing, the couple arrived on time as expected. The husband bent down for something and a piece of paper fell out of his pocket onto the floor. His wife saw the paper and announced that it was a receipt from a loan company in Houston for the amount of $42.00. The husband and his wife started to argue over the note, she complained that he had been borrowing money without her knowledge, and the husband picked up a knife from the kitchen counter. The wife's cousin took the knife away from him. The man's wife then grabbed her husband by the wrist and held him. The husband started to kick and bite. He bit his wife on the nose, causing a small cut. The wife was frightened although her husband stopped biting her after she had pleaded with him to let her go. She went into another room where she removed a knife from her purse. She explained to the police that she knew that her husband carried a knife on him and that he, on previous occasions, had pulled his knife on her. The husband approached and he apparently tried to get his own knife out of his pocket. His wife held his wrist and they struggled over control of the wife's knife. In the scuffle the knife lodged in the husband's chest. He exclaimed, "I've been stabbed. I'm feeling weak" as he dropped to the floor. The woman's knife had entered the heart necessitating open heart surgery at the Ben Taub Hospital. The operation was a success but a member of the medical staff called the Homicide Division and announced that the man had died in his hospital bed at 3:30 A.M. The subsequent autopsy showed no trace of either alcohol or barbiturates in the husband's body. The wife was no billed by the grand jury.

Case No. 198 was also no billed by the Houston grand jury. In reading the case we get the distinct impression that the victim was a dangerous person who, in the end, compelled his wife to use extreme force in self-defense. The complainant was wanted by the Houston police on an aggravated assault warrant initiated by his wife on March 4, 1969. It is not known why the police had not found the violent husband before he placidly turned up as a corpse at the city morgue.

Excerpts from the wife's affidavit relate the precipitating circumstances of the homicide as follows:

> I am 22 years of age . . . and live with my five children. My mother . . . lives (on the same street). My husband . . . and I have been married for six years. We have been separated several times during this length of time. He drank quite a bit and when he would get drunk he would come home and jump on me and beat me up. I would go and file charges on him and then would go and drop charges on him. He and I have this time been separated for about nine months. However, he has come to my house and broken in several times. When he would come to the house I would leave and go to my mother's or sister's house. After he would get up the next day, he would leave and I would go back home. On Saturday afternoon, about 5:30 P.M., I went to my sister's house on Chase Lane and I stayed there for about 30 minutes. I left there and came back to my mother's house and I stayed there until about dark. I then left my mother's house and went home. I got to my house about 8 P.M. When I got home I saw that there was a light on in my bedroom and I knew that I did not leave the lights on. I went on in and my husband was laying across the bed with his clothes on. I asked him what he was doing and he stated "I'm going to kill you." When I told him that he had stolen my gun he stated again that he was going to kill me and that he was going to do it tonight. The pistol is a .22 caliber. I know that he stole this gun because this was the gun that he had tonight. At this time he started cursing me and calling me all kinds of names and I told him to go ahead on home before he disturbed all of the neighbors and I would not have a place to stay. He then went to the front door and slammed it shut. This door locks when it is shut and he could not get back in. When the door shut I turned around and ran toward the bedroom and at this time

he stuck the pistol through the hole in the door and he shot at me. He actually shot two times through the door. After the shooting he stayed about 15 minutes more out in the yard. I knew he was out there for I could hear him. Everything then got quiet. Before the things got quiet outside I tried to send my children to my mother's house so they could call the law. They did not go because he had stopped them. He told them that they were not going anywhere. I . . . could not hear him. [Apparently a young boy was dispatched and managed to escape notice from the husband as the boy ran to his grandmother's house to call the police.] About the time when he [my son] left the house I went . . . and got my .22 caliber rifle. I did not call the police for I was scared to go outside and I do not have a phone. When my husband came back to the house he knocked on the back door and he then went to the windows and tried to get in and he took the screen off the back window. After he took the screen off the window he came back to the door. . . . I put a latch on the back door. . . . He told me again to let him in and I would not do this. He told me that "I have mine and you have yours" [weapon] and that he was coming in. This time he knocked the back door open and he was standing in the doorway. . . . I shot at him about three times. I don't know whether I hit him or not. He backed off the steps and staggered on. I took off running down to my mother's house. I told my mother what had happened and my little sister then called the police.

The circumstances leading up to the killing qualify as the perfect legal defense for excusable homicide, i.e., the individual was threatened, the assailant had a motive and the means to execute his threat, and the potential victim was in her place of last retreat. The no bill issued by the grand jury was, to say the very least, legally wholesome.

Intent or motive is always a crucial factor in determining criminal culpability. In Case No. 82 the killing resulted from a scuffle in which killing was not contemplated. The police investigated the circumstances of this case and decided that the killing had resulted from the accidental discharge of a firearm and that no charge should be filed against the person who fired the pistol. But the ready availability of the means to kill, in this case a .38 caliber pistol, can be as decisive as the motive to kill.

The Black couple, the husband, age 34, and the wife, age 37, had been married 14 years. They had four children, ages 14, 8, 7, and 6, plus one teenage daughter from the wife's previous marriage. The quarrel, which escalated into a fight involving some of the children, began in the evening when the wife criticized her husband for having relations with another woman. One daughter testified that she had overheard her mother state that she had discovered her husband in the other woman's bedroom. The following day, at about noon, the husband wanted the car keys, which the wife had taken to prevent him from leaving the house again. The man pushed his wife down into a chair and refused to let her up. The teenage stepdaughter came into the room and she began to pull at her father so as to help her mother up from the chair. The man slapped the daughter and she fell back across the coffee table. The wife retrieved a pistol from under a chair in the living room and she pointed it toward the floor warning her husband that he should stop beating the girl. The intent here, allegedly, was to scare the husband into compliance. At the same moment the eight-year-old daughter came running into the room and grabbed her mother. The pistol discharged and the man fell to the floor. When asked by the police why she had pulled out the gun, the wife replied that she was afraid that her husband would seriously hurt the daughter who was five months' pregnant. The yet unborn child would now enter a world without a father or grandfather, and the other children would have experienced firsthand how some domestic problems may be resolved by direct recourse to physical violence.

Domestic quarrels do not always occur within the privacy of the home. In Case No. 69 a Black couple, a woman, age 43, and her husband, also 43, settled their differences in a public bar. The bartender, who nearly got shot himself when the woman began firing a small .22 caliber pistol at her husband, told the police that he was talking to the man when his wife came into the barroom and told him, the bartender, to move over. The loud background music muffled the conversation between the two but it was clear to witnesses that the woman's purpose was to talk her husband into leaving the bar. She left the bar and returned minutes later with a pistol. She walked over to her husband and said something to the effect that he was a S.O.B. and that even if he had come home with her, she would shoot him. After shooting her husband she turned around and took a shot at the bartender, grazing his shoulder with the bullet. She then left the bar. The husband raised himself up from the barstool, walked slowly toward the pool table, and fell dying to the floor as he attempted to hold onto the pool table. The official outcome of the case, I conclude, must reinforce the behavior and form of dispute settlement witnessed in this case. The woman was charged with her husband's murder as well as unlawful possession of a firearm. The bartender apparently did not file a complaint with the police although he was nearly killed himself. The case went to trial, without a jury, and the presiding judge found the defendant not guilty after he heard the testimony. Charges are still pending against the woman for carrying a pistol. The reader may wonder why this woman, unlike all the assailants in the previous cases, was charged for illegally carrying a pistol. Texas law is vague on this point. If you merely possess and use a gun in your own territory it is within the law. In some cases, or if the police want to make an issue out of it, a person will face several different charges relating to the commission of a crime. Unfortunately, this practice opens the way to expedient plea bargaining procedures, which, in the end, speeds official and bureaucratic processing of criminals but, alas, makes mockery of justice.

In the following case (No. 76), we learn, for a change of pace, about the circumstances of a homicide as summarized by newspaper reporters. The newspaper account fails to mention, among other things, such interesting facts that the deceased was found shot in his bed without any signs of a struggle, that the assailant Mrs. G. pleaded self-defense, and that the police were met at the scene by Mrs. G. and no less than two attorneys who had instructed their client to say nothing to the police. The case received a great deal of publicity in Houston–it is not every defendant in a murder case who can bring in a district judge to act as a character witness–and it is, to my knowledge, not concluded as of this date (1974).

On Friday, June 1, 1973 (p. 12, Sect. 1), there appeared the following report of the case. The headline "Judge Says He Noticed G. Difficulties" is an open invitation to the curious. Let's read on:

> U.S. Dist. Judge S. has testified he twice noticed indications of marital difficulty between his federal court reporter, Mrs. G., and her psychologist husband.
>
> S. testified Thursday during Mrs. G.s trial for the pistol slaying of her husband Aug. 4, 1969. Mrs. G., 39, pleaded self-defense, saying Mr. G., 35, threatened her with a gun.
>
> A few weeks preceding the shooting, S. said, Mrs. G. called him saying she could not come to work because her husband had locked her in their bedroom.

S. said Mrs. G. came to work on a later occasion wearing sunglasses and planned to wear them into court. He said she told him her eyes were discolored because Mr. G. had hit her.

S. said he did not see her eyes but accepted her word.

Attorney W. testified that Mrs. G. told him March 27, 1969, she had suffered threats and "physical abuse at the hands of her husband," and wanted a divorce.

W. did not file divorce papers, he said, because he felt it would be safer for Mrs. G. and her three children if they moved away from the house and he obtained a restraining order against G.

On April 4, 1969, W. said, G. learned of his wife's intentions of divorce and called him. He said G. made no threat but left the impression that he (W.) should "be cautious." W. said he received a similar call from G. a month later.

Ms. P., court reporter and friend of Mrs. G., testified she had seen bruises and marks on Mrs. G. on different occasions and knew of her marital problems.

Ms. P. said she became concerned about Mrs. G. two days prior to the shooting and called her at home. Mrs. G. acted like "a puppet on a string" in answering questions about her safety, Ms. P. said, and she believed that Mr. G. was eavesdropping.

Rev. T. of Annunciation Greek Orthodox Cathedral said Mr. G. helped direct programs for children at his church but appeared "very unstable" during his last few years and T. suggested he seek psychiatric help.

Mr. G. refused to seek help Rev. T. said, and blamed his wife for his condition for his previous psychiatric care [sic].

Some of the elements of the above case are repeated in Case No. 86. The principals here, a Black male, age 31, and his wife, age 28, were both unemployed and on welfare. They shared a small apartment with their six children. The killing here also evolved as part of an unsatisfactory marital relationship and the victim's body was found in his bed. In this case, the wife stated to the police on their arrival that she had waited until her husband was asleep before she shot him with a shotgun. The events, as related in the wife's affidavit, were roughly that the husband had come home intoxicated around 10:30 the previous evening. He accused his wife of seeing another man during the day and, as a gesture, he picked up his shotgun and held it against his wife's head while he allegedly said, "I ought to shoot you right now." He then put the gun on the bedroom dresser, crawled into bed, and then said that he would get her before the night was over. One of the six children tried to interfere with the parents with the result that the man got out of bed and spanked her using his belt. Sometime later, with yet another scene with the children, the wife's brother came to the house. He left at 11:30 P.M. The husband finally went to sleep. His wife waited about 15 minutes then she entered the bedroom, removed the shotgun from the dresser, held it about 15 inches away from her husband's chest, and fired one fatal shot. She then left the house but was talked into going back by a neighbor. The neighbor called the police who arrived at 1:10 A.M. The wife, who explained further to the police that her husband had hit her with a tire iron during their earlier fight, was arrested and booked for murder. The case went to trial and the wife was found guilty. *She received a three-year probationary sentence.*

The outcome in the two remaining cases within the wife-husband category has not been determined. But each case is quite explicit about the relationships between the principals who, as it may be recalled, are seeking to enforce their conceptions of the relationship upon the situation and the reciprocal person in the status relationship.

Case No. 117 involves a triadic or three-way relationship between a White woman, her divorced daughter, and the woman's present husband (the daughter's stepfather). The divorced daughter, age 21, had recently obtained her divorce and subsequently moved into the apartment occupied by her mother, age 43, and her stepfather, age 48. The threesome began to drink together around four o'clock in the afternoon and eventually left the apartment to continue their drinking at the Stampede Club on Alabama Street. The older woman got quite intoxicated; she began to quarrel with both her daughter and her husband, accusing them among other things of sleeping together, and, in the daughter's own words: "Mother tried to get me to dance with Bob and I finally did dance [with him] one time. After this, Mother got real mad and accused me of trying to make out with Bob. She stayed mad until we left about 11:00 P.M. Just before we got into my car, I grabbed her and shook her and told her that this was the last time she was going to accuse me of trying to fuck any man of hers. . . ." The quarrel continued and the mother threatened to take her own life. She also said that she would blow her husband's brains out. Bob was sitting on a lawn chair when the .22 caliber bullet ended his life. The autopsy revealed a 0.09 percent alcohol content in the victim's blood. The wife was arrested but apparently not searched thoroughly. The next morning she was found comatose in her jail cell. She was rushed to Ben Taub Hospital and treated for a suspected overdose of sleeping pills. She recovered in the emergency ward while her husband's body was being dissected in the morgue one floor below.

The last case of a wife-husband killing involves a Black woman, age 21, and her 21-year-old husband. The killing occurred at 10:00 P.M. with one eyewitness. According to the eyewitness, who was the next-door neighbor, the couple did not get along because the husband was very jealous of his wife and they had many fights. On the fatal evening, the wife asked her husband for his permission to attend a "Jewelry Party." At first he gave his permission and the woman took their nine-month-old child next door to the babysitter. While she was there the husband came over and suddenly grabbed her by the throat. They left the apartment physically fighting. The wife had armed herself with a steak knife and while they were fighting outside by the driveway she stabbed her husband in the chest. The wound was fatal. Several bystanders could have stopped the fight but nobody interfered. In fact, in reflecting on all the cases in which third parties have been present, it only seems that young children have tried to physically intervene in a fight.

Common-Law Marital Killings

The designations *my common-law husband* and *my common-law wife* signify a relationship or union that is entered into solely on the basis of mutual consent. The relationship, unlike an officially sanctioned marriage, is created by cohabitation and dissolved by either unilateral or bilateral withdrawal from the relationship. The distinction between the status of "spouse" and "common-law spouse" is not made in homicide cases and it will not be used here unless it appears to be significant. The patterns of killing and adjudication vividly illustrate this fact. The 14 additional "common-law" marital killings in 1969 show the following distribution of variables: four men killed their wives and ten women killed their husbands. One man was not indicted, one case has been reset for trial, and the two other men received five- and 19-year jail sentences, respectively. Except for one case, for which the final outcome has not been determined, all female slayers escaped legal punishment. Other things being equal, one should theoretically expect about as many husbands as wives to become homicide assailants and a parallel distribution between the two sexes in legal sanctioning. The data indicate some quite obvious differences, both behavioral and legal, between the act of killing your husband and the act of killing your wife. If the source of these differences can be discovered we may have come one step closer to demonstrating the usefulness of the culture concept in explaining interpersonal aggression and violence. In the following cases, therefore, we shall look very closely for both situational and interactional variables that characterize these special killer-victim relationships.

Although the assailant in Case No. 132, a White female, age 28, did not characterize her relationship to the victim, a 39-year-old male, as a "common-law marriage," the couple had been living together for some time prior to the killing. Both were habitual drug users. At the time of the killing, however, neither appeared to be under the influence of drugs or liquor. The police report does not reveal many details about the relationship, but the final events were reconstructed on the basis of statements by the woman to the police at the scene. According to her, the couple were drinking around town and got into an argument. The man hit the woman in her face. When they arrived home they continued to quarrel and she locked herself in the bathroom. As the man kicked down the door he was met by a single shot from a .45 caliber pistol bearing the woman's initial on the handle. He turned and ran toward the bedroom. The woman followed him and squeezed off five more shots. She then loaded a shotgun but did not shoot the victim again. The grand jury, apparently, did not consider carefully the question of the necessity of shooting the fleeing victim more than once. To resist by force, to kill, and to overkill may have merged as equivalents in the minds of those who issued a no bill in favor of the woman who, incidentally, told the police that she did not know how to handle a firearm! The woman was not charged, since she legally could not be, for the possession of a firearm. The male assailant in the following case escaped a murder charge, however, but he was charged with the felonious possession of a dangerous weapon, since he killed his wife outside the protective privacy of their home.

Case No. 200 comes close to fitting the definition of a victim-precipitated homicide. A Black couple, a male, age 39, and his wife, age 36, had been living together for eight months before the shooting. The woman had, according to her sister, thrown her husband out of their apartment two weeks before the fatal incident occurred. Neither the parting, nor the relationship itself, had been a happy and pleasant one. The woman had on at least two previous occasions shot at her husband without, however, inflicting any serious injuries. Around 11 P.M. one night the woman began to look for her husband in and around the taverns in the downtown district of the city. She was seen carrying two knives and, playfully, held one knife against the chest of a mutual acquaintance to press him for information about her husband's present whereabouts. She was overheard by several witnesses to say in so many words that she would find and kill her husband. When the two finally met the woman advanced, knives in hand, toward her husband and he fired four .22 caliber bullets that hit their mark. The woman died on the sidewalk before several eyewitnesses. The police arrived, the man handed over his pistol, and the relationship was definitively broken. The case illustrates how a couple, who apparently fights regularly to resolve differences between self and other definitions of the terms of the relationship, cannot dissolve the relationship merely by moving apart or, in the case of a legally married couple, by divorce. A gnawing grudge, on the part of either or both, may, as in this case, call for a more final solution of differences than can be provided by their physical separation.

The grudge factor, which essentially means that one or both members of a reciprocal relationship ideationally continue the unsatisfactory relationship past the point of structural dissolution of formal ties, appears to be a consistent motivational factor in common-law marital killings. The exact marital status of the principals in Case No. 71 is not known. There is reason to believe that the case could have been included in either the previous section on marital homicides or in the following section on homicides among ex-spouses. The concern here, of course, is to emphasize that some cases by their very complexity may be fitted into different analytical categories.

The sister of the defendant, a Mexican-American male, age 38, informed police investigators that her brother had gone to the hospital on the day preceding this double killing. He had complained of a backache. The doctor, however, had told the sister that there was nothing wrong with her brother's back and that he had a mental problem. On the following day, rather late in the evening, the man went to visit with his wife who was staying with her sister. The couple's five children were staying with their mother. Everybody present expressed surprise at his visit because they had been told he had been hospitalized for further observation. He apparently did not care about staying in the hospital and stated to his sister that he wished to go away with the children on a vacation. He loaded his five children, together with two of his sister's children, into his pickup truck. As the children were waiting for their father/uncle, they heard several shots from the house. The defendant had shot both his wife and his sister-in-law with a .22 caliber pistol. He yelled at his sister, who lived across the street, to give him some money. She complied and the man left with all the children. What followed then was a movie-type chase scene in which the sheriff shot out the rear tire of the pickup truck as the man tried to escape through the fields in Sugarland outside Houston. The defendant used his own children for cover to prevent the police from firing. Finally, he surrendered–with a reloaded .22 pistol–still holding his three-year-old son.

Despite the incomplete data on this case, it is possible to envision that the factors leading to the act, a double-killing at that, involved several unknown dimensions of the killer's form of mental illness together with some complicated family relationships: the wife and her sister, the sister's husband and their children, and the killer's own children. One thing appears to be clear, the defendant must have perceived his wife and his sister-in-law as standing between him and his children. He chose a desperate and shortsighted solution to a complex problem.

The words, "Harold, you have done shot me" were the last words spoken by a young 24-year-old Black female as she died in front of her home at 11:00 P.M. on April 9, 1969. The assailant, a Black male, age 22, put his .22 caliber automatic pistol on the hood of his Thunderbird and waited for the police. The killing had occurred before several eyewitnesses who, it should be noted, had attempted to separate the couple during their fight. There is no indication as to the nature of the problem between this man and his common-law wife of more than a year. They had fought in the car and the woman was heard to refuse her husband's command to leave the car and to come into their house. She shouted that she did not want to go into the house just to be beat up some more. The man was tried for murder, found guilty, and sentenced to five years in jail.

Case No. 182 unfolded before the eyes of the victim's 87-year-old grandmother. Her granddaughter, a Black female, age 22, was approached by her husband, age 41, after the couple had been separated for about three weeks. The assailant had come to the house to see his children, age 2 and age 3, and the couple got into an argument. The argument ended when the husband pulled a .25 caliber automatic pistol and shot his wife in the head. He ran away from the house but shouted that he would give himself up. The woman was dead on the spot. The husband surrendered to the police. He is now serving a 19-year term for murder in the Texas Department of Corrections. The 19-year prison term, as appropriate as it might seem, contrasts sharply with the 5-year sentence handed down in the previous case. The circumstances in the two cases, which admittedly must have been more complicated than indicated by the police reports, do not appear all that different. This point will be taken up later. It must suffice here to note that similar offenses do not necessarily result in roughly equivalent judicial outcome. In the remaining nine cases in this category, in which the assailant is the common-law wife of the victim, in not one case was a prison sentence imposed. A gun may appropriately be called "the great equalizer" insofar as it refers to the power of offense and defense conferred upon any user whether strong or weak or old or young. Yet the very noticeable difference in judicial outcome between male and female homicide assailants strongly suggest that we must look toward broader cultural patterns, such as values and attitudes toward masculinity and femininity, to fully understand the phenomenon of judicial discrimination.

The following case (No. 46) may serve to illustrate a point: A woman, because of her sexual identity as a female, is not necessarily weaker, more defenseless, or less violent than a man. Yet it appears to be the assumption (certainly on the part of Houston grand jury members and trial juries who show a positive discrimination *for* female homicide assailants) that women are culturally characterized as weaker and less aggressive than men. The events of Case No. 46 are not very complicated. The couple, a Black man, age 46 and his common-law wife, age 40, had been living together for the past three to five years. The quarrel began in the late afternoon on November 10, 1969 and principally involved the woman's desire to terminate the relationship. She tried to get the victim to move his things out of the apartment and he apparently refused. She packed a suitcase with his clothes and placed it outside the door of their apartment. During the course of the argument she managed to kick the suitcase down the stairwell so that the clothes were scattered all over the place. After this, again only according to the woman, the fight began and as they were knocking each other around she retrieved her .38 caliber pistol from beneath the mattress and fired the first shot. The man was hit and ran out of the apartment. He turned once and shouted that he would kill the woman. She replied by firing another shot. So far the case has not departed radically from the previous cases involving a husband-wife domestic quarrel. Something about this case is different, however. The man did not die in the apartment and he was found walking around the streets by police officers who had been notified that shots had been fired. When they apprehended the mortally wounded man he stated to the police officers that he had been shot by an unknown assailant while walking down the street in front of his apartment. The police, with the assistance of witnesses who had observed what took place outside the apartment building, finally obtained a picture of what had really happened. The woman confessed to having fired two shots, she led the police to the spot where she had hidden the pistol, and she further directed police officers to the place outside their window where she at first had thrown the empty hulls. The police ran a routine check on the assailant and the victim and discovered that the victim had been shot by the same woman on previous occasions. Police records showed a case of aggravated assault in June 1967 involving her as assailant. In August 1968 she was again involved in two shooting incidents and an assault to murder case; the police further investigated a shooting at her apartment in May 1969, and once more had records of an assault to murder case in July 1969. The victim had been shot or shot-at in all of these previous incidents and he had consistently refused to file legal charges against his common-law wife. I will leave it to the reader to interpret his behavior as blinded by love or his judgment impaired by stupidity. The simple fact that the same person was permitted to possess and use the same .38 caliber pistol on successive occasions shows, more than anything else, what unsuccessful gun-control lobbyists have been trying to stop. Texans, generally, view it as a fundamental right that a person possess and use a personal weapon to defend his person and to prevent or avenge a personal injustice. In our 1969 cases, firearms were used 86 percent of the time as the principal weapon in killing, and 88 percent of these firearms were pistols, of varying caliber, 5 percent rifles, and nearly 7 percent shotguns. Need I add that the woman in the above case was no billed by a Houston grand jury?

In Case No. 53 the events leading to the killing of a 43-year-old Black man by his 47-year-old common-law wife were not known to the police. The wife notified the police of the shooting and simply stated that he "just kept coming at me and I shot him."

In Case No. 55, however, we again see a history of mutual violence in the relationship. The woman, a 26-year-old Black, said to the police that the killing occurred because her common-law husband, age 34, was trying to get even with her for a previous shooting. She had shot him, hitting him with four .32 caliber bullets, but he had not filed charges against her. The husband had killed a 25-year-old Black woman in 1965 and subsequently, in 1969, had committed aggravated assault against his common-law wife. She had also withdrawn charges against her husband. The killing took place in a lounge where husband and wife started to fight. He was armed with a pistol and she picked up a knife from a nearby table. According to eyewitnesses, the two had an exchange of "words," with each one threatening to kill the other. Amazingly, after the man fell to the floor bleeding fatally from several stab wounds in his chest, his common-law wife put a pillow under his head and comforted him as best she could. Although the wife was no billed for the homicide the police brought two other charges against her (it is not known what these charges were) and she was given a three-year probationary sentence for those offenses.

In reading these cases it is important to consider the socialization effect that these homicidal quarrels must have on children who have to cope with parents who live on and off with each other and who early in life witness how violence is defined by adults as an acceptable means of resolving interpersonal differences. In Case No. 120, the events were witnessed by the woman's 15-year-old son, his two brothers, and two sisters. The young boy reported to the police that he did not go to school and that he did not work. In the early morning hours on January 2, 1969, the young boy woke up to the sound of a parental argument. His mother, a

Black female, age 46, was telling her common-law husband, age 56, to leave the house. He was angry because she had failed to pick him up after work but she explained that the car had broken down. He left the house but returned to the front door (now locked from the inside) several times. He asked his wife for the car keys, went to the car to change tires, and returned to the front door carrying a tire iron in his hand. He began to beat on the door. The woman opened the door and he entered the house. He ran after her following her to the bedroom. She shot him with her .32 caliber revolver (legally, of course, since the woman was in the place of last retreat). The autopsy revealed a blood alcohol content of 0.25 percent in the assailant-victim's blood.

In Case No. 213 the couple, a Black female, age 25, and her common-law husband, age 24, were sitting together in their car outside of a lounge. They had visited several other lounges, spent some time drinking with friends, and were—according to the assailant—on good terms during the entire evening. They did not argue but began to "play around." The man asked where his wife was keeping his pistol and she took it out of her purse. He pointed it at her and said: "So you don't love me anymore, huh?" and she said, "You don't love me, why should I love you anymore?" They continued the verbal exchange along these lines and, according to the woman, began to "tussle" over the gun. It went off and killed the man. The woman was arrested, brought before a grand jury, and subsequently no billed.

In Case No. 134 we do not learn what the quarrel was about. All that is known from the police case file is that the couple, a Black woman, age 51, and her common-law husband, age 37, had been drinking beer with friends before the shooting occurred at 11 A.M. The couple had been sitting on the porch in front of their house, the woman had left and entered the house; when her husband followed she shot him in the doorway with a .22 caliber revolver. This occurred on May 17, 1969. The husband had filed assault to murder charges against his wife on November 28, 1968, just about six months before he met his death. When the husband was called by the police to testify against his common-law wife he refused to do so and that case was thus officially closed. Perhaps because of this earlier assault, and because the circumstances surrounding the killing were not at all clear, the case went before a jury. The jury found the defendant to be "not guilty" on the charge of murder without malice.

The principals in Case No. 195 were living together as a *trois de ménage* shortly before the killing. The two assailants, a White woman, age 25, and a Mexican-American woman, age 22, were both charged with the death of the elder woman's common-law husband, age 42. The man was the owner of a striptease club in which his wife worked as a stripper. They had a reputation for fighting. On August 2, 1969 the husband hired a new striptease performer–the 22-year-old woman. The new stripper had no place to stay and she was therefore invited by the club owner to stay with him and his common-law wife. Sometime after this arrangement was established the husband disappeared. Neighbors reported to the police that they had seen the two women remove a large steamer trunk on August 5 from the apartment and had become suspicious because the man had not parked in his assigned parking lot or told anyone he was going on vacation. Both women were apprehended by the police on August 7th and the younger woman submitted a written affidavit. The following excerpts from this affidavit express some remarkable views of life and human relationships:

> I went to work on Saturday, August 2, 1969 and after work I went to Carolyn's and Mike's apartment. . . . I thought the door was locked but all of a sudden it opened and Mike came into the apartment. I kind of gave him a dirty look and I told him I was not going to do it [relay a message from Mike to Carolyn]. He had sent Carolyn out to get some 7-Up before he told me this. . . . After [finishing my bath] I came out and a little later Carolyn and her small boy, who had a branch in his hand, came into the apartment. The little boy had been crying. I [saw] a bruise on the boy's face and asked what it was and she said that it was just a bruise. In a little while I left and went across the street to the drugstore in the shopping center. I left the shopping center and I started back toward the apartment. When I passed by the club I felt hungry and I went into the Mexican restaurant which is next door to the club. I had been in the restaurant for a little while and while I was eating Mike came in and sat down next to me. He just sat there and did not say anything until I told him, "You sure are quiet." He said, "I sure am." We didn't say much more and I finished eating and paid my bill and went back to the apartment. I went to work Monday. When I got off work Carolyn and I were supposed to take a new girl home. We had to go by the apartment to get my glasses and we found the door locked and could not get in. We tried the window and Mike came out and asked what was going on. I told him that I had to get my glasses and that we were going to take

this girl home. . . . He did not say anything else and I went in and got my glasses. It was close to 1 A.M. and we did not get back until about 3 A.M. and Mike had (again) locked the door and windows so that we could not get into the apartment. We went over to the club and stayed there during the night. We got up at 8 or 9 A.M. and went over to the apartment. Carolyn had to remove a glass pane to get into the apartment. After we got inside I went to the bedroom and shut the door. I then overheard an argument and a little later I heard the first shot. After hearing the first shot I went into the living room. I then heard another shot. Carolyn came running out of the bedroom and said, "Let's get out of here!" I ran with her and we went over to stay with her son's babysitter. On the way over she said that she had shot Mike and if I thought that he might be dead [they returned to the apartment and Carolyn threw her .38 caliber pistol away] . . . when we got back to the apartment and into the bedroom I looked at Mike and he appeared to be dead. Carolyn then felt him and said, "He is dead." We sat around for a while and it was then time for the club to open and we took the money over to the club and opened the club. We sat around for a while and I was so shook up so Carolyn said, "Let's go shopping!" We then went back to the apartment and checked on him again and he was still lying where we had left him. We then locked the apartment and were trying to decide how to get Mike's body out of the apartment. Carolyn just wanted to take him like he was and to drop him but I thought that a trunk would be better. We then went to some store and bought a large trunk. . . . We then went back to the apartment and brought the trunk inside. We sat down and fixed ourselves a drink and were trying to think how we could get him into the trunk. We placed the trunk beside him and Carolyn pushed him into the trunk. . . . Before we closed the trunk, Carolyn noticed Mike's face and she screamed and said, "Put something over his face." I got a towel and put it over his face. She closed the lid. We went back to work at the club and stayed there until closing time after midnight. We then went back to the apartment to discuss about the best time to take him out and dump him. Carolyn said about 3 A.M. We went outside the apartment several times and acted as if we were looking for Mike because we knew that people would begin to ask questions and to start looking for Mike. We tried to clean the place up and I used a sponge and a mop to clean up the blood. We first tried to place the trunk on

> Carolyn's son's toy wagon but it wouldn't hold. . . . We parked the car close to the apartment and dragged the trunk across to the car where we placed it on the back seat. We drove off to try to find a place to dump the body. . . . We . . . drove down a road until it came to a dead end [they returned briefly to a store where Carolyn left the car to buy some lighter fluid] . . . and we drove through a gate into the woods where we got out. It took us a long time to get the trunk out of the car. Carolyn tilted the trunk so that Mike's body fell out on the ground and I put a sheet over the body. We then pulled the trunk back away from the car and also placed our purses back away from the car. Carolyn then poured the lighter fluid over the sheet on the body. She lighted a match, started a fire and we grabbed the empty trunk and ran. . . . The only reason I helped Carolyn was because she said she would give me $1000 to help her.

Carolyn later led the police to the place where the body had been dumped. Autopsy revealed that Mike had died of a gunshot wound in the chest. Carolyn was arrested and indicted for murder. She was tried and found to be *not guilty* on June 22, 1970. Her assistant was charged and indicted for the same offense but there is no information about the outcome in her case.

The killer and her victim in Case No. 33 said their final goodbyes in the emergency room at Ben Taub Hospital. The couple, a White female, age 24, and her common-law husband, age 32, shared an apartment with another male tenant. His part in the family quarrel is unknown. In fact, acting on the complaint of the woman, he had left the apartment late in the evening to retrieve her husband from a nearby tavern. When the husband returned he entered the bedroom and, according to the tenant, the couple began to argue. A shot rang out and the husband crawled out into the living room. The wife followed, carrying a .38 caliber pistol, and she said that he wasn't hurt bad and that he didn't need any help. The woman said that she would shoot again if her husband ever "chipped on her again." The landlady arrived and the couple, together with their tenant, drove the wounded husband to Ben Taub Hospital. The police arrested the woman at the hospital, she was indicted, and sentenced to a five-year probationary term. When the police left the hospital to investigate the scene of the shooting they found the landlady in the apartment. She was busily removing a large amount of blood from the couch, stating to the police that she didn't see why a $300 couch should be ruined!

The final case in this category, Case No. 186, may serve to punctuate how the availability of firearms, of any caliber, by itself can mean the difference between a bruised ego and death. Two young Blacks, a female, age 19, and a male, age 25, had been living together for several years. On the night before the fatal shooting the man had come home drunk. The woman had not disturbed him but made up her mind that she would remove her husband's .22 caliber pistol from the house after she had observed one of her children playing with it. The next morning, at around 10 o'clock, the man awoke and the couple began to argue about the advisability of keeping a loaded gun around where the children could reach it. The woman was wearing an overcoat and her husband spotted his pistol in her coat pocket. He reportedly said, "You think that you are a smart S.O.B.!" and he jumped across the bed and grabbed for the gun. The couple struggled, the gun went off, with the man being hit with one bullet. He got up and walked out. He died on the sidewalk in front of their house. The police did not see this as a clear-cut case of self-defense and there was some doubt about the accidental element of the shooting as it was related by the woman. The judicial outcome of the case is not known.

Parent and Child Killings

When Freud first called attention to the implicit tensions between parents and children, in the so-called Oedipus and Electra complexes, his views were met with anger and scorn. Yet when Freud's detractors and critics eventually accepted the symbolic significance of his incest theory they, like Freud himself, overlooked the strengths of the essentially nonsexual bonds between parents and children. Anthropologists who have diligently searched for an explanation of universal nuclear family incest taboos have, like their colleagues in psychology, found more questions than answers. Parent-child bonds may be particularly strong because, as we have evolved as a species, the dependency relationship between adults and infants has been stretched farther than in any other species or, to put the matter differently, human survival requires strong ties between adults and their young. The realization of this, which is not to be confused with a scientific explanation of the bonding mechanism in humans, places parent and child killings in a very special category. To kill a parent or a child subverts, symbolically, one of the most basic principles of human survival.

It is not surprising, therefore, that parent-child killings occur less frequently than other kinds of killings and that the legal punishment for patricide, matricide, and filicide is the most severe. Four killings in the 1969 sample illustrate the interactional context of this very special killer-victim relationship.

Case No. 193 introduces a new dimensionality into the puzzle of homicide. A young Mexican-American couple, a male, age 21, and a female, age 21, were sharing their residence with the man's aging grandfather. The couple had a seven-month-old boy. The husband was employed. Homicide officers first became involved in the case when they were notified by officers from the Juvenile Division that the seven-month-old boy was in critical condition and judged unlikely to survive by pediatricians at the hospital. The boy's injury was believed to have been caused by a strong and direct blow to the stomach. The lacerations of his spleen could not have been the result of any self-inflicted injury. The parents, who both denied at first that any violence against the child had ever been used, became prime suspects. The couple stated that they had left the child with a babysitter and discovered, early the next morning, that the baby was barely breathing and that he looked as if he might be dying. They took the baby to the hospital where he died. Detectives from the Homicide Division took over the case from juvenile officers and they managed to piece together the circumstantial evidence that later led to the conviction of the father for the murder of his infant boy.

The infant slept in his parents' bedroom. The father, who occasionally helped with bottle feeding or diaper changing, had shown anger at the boy's lack of cooperation and, according to the young woman, he had been rather rough on previous occasions. The infant responded by manifesting dislike for being held by the father. One morning, at about 7:30 A.M., the infant began to cry and this so irritated the father that he got up, went over to the crib, and hit the baby once in the stomach with his fist. The wife had only noticed that the baby stopped crying after the father had "attended" to him and she did not see her husband deliver the fatal blow. The parents later took the baby to the hospital. Both parents pretended to be unaware of their role in causing their baby's death. After further questioning, the father told the police how he had become irritated with the baby and how he had punched it once to keep it from crying. The husband was indicted, tried for murder, found guilty on the basis of circumstantial evidence, and sentenced to serve a ten-year term in the Texas Department of Corrections.

Case No. 164 exemplifies a quite different kind of "irritational factor." The victim, a young White male, age 21, was killed by his mother, age 49, in the parking lot of one of Houston's large shopping centers. He was killed at three o'clock in the afternoon with a .22 caliber pistol, which was surrendered by his mother at the scene to the police. The victim's friend, together with a uniformed security guard, witnessed the shooting and supplied the police with affidavits. The mother told the police exactly how she felt and why she had shot her son: The son had been fooling around with homosexuals and drugs! On the day of the killing, the son was moving in with his male friend and the two of them were in the process of moving the victim's belongings from his apartment, which was also occupied by the victim's wife, to the apartment of his friend. The mother and son, and the son's friend, met by accident at the shopping center. This encounter, which openly acknowledged the son's situation, led to a final argument and his death. On their way out of the store the two men exited first followed by the victim's mother. She fired one shot at close range and hit her son in the head. The mother surrendered peacefully to the police and she did nothing at the scene that suggested either grief or regret. The jury trial was held almost one and one-half years following the shooting. The outcome: A five-year prison sentence for the mother.

Texas juries, following the abolition of the death penalty, gained national notoriety for imposing lengthy and successive prison sentences to ensure that the convicted felon would die in prison. The defendant in Case No. 99, a White male, age 22, was found guilty of the murder of both his father and his mother and sentenced to serve two 99-year prison terms. The victims, a male, age 55, and a female, age 52, were killed with a .22 caliber rifle sometime around 2 A.M. on November 30, 1969. When officers arrived at the scene they were met by the killer who stated that a burglar had shot his parents. There was no evidence at the scene to support this statement and the son was placed under arrest for the murder of his parents. He was brought to the Homicide Division and interrogated by different detectives. He gave conflicting stories of the events and even offered to help the police solve the crime by proposing different and alternative explanatory theories for the double homicide. The killer, upon further investigation, turned out to be a psychology major at the University of Texas. He viewed himself as a person of superior intelligence and explained carefully why he did not permit himself to express any grief over the death of his parents. His attorney did not convince the Houston jury of the young man's innocence. This case, together with a similar one that follows, focuses our attention and interest on the sentencing process. In Case No. 63 a young White male, age 25, shot and killed his 66-year-old father with a .22 caliber pistol. He was also found guilty and sentenced to serve 99 years in jail. But court records reveal that the sentence was reduced to a ten-year prison term at a later date. At the time of his arrest, the man surrendered his pistol to the police and was overheard to say: "I also robbed a store over on Fulton and I killed my father but wish that I had killed my mother instead." The mother's written affidavit summarizes the events leading to the killing as follows:

> Tonight, November 10, 1969, at about 5:30 P.M. my son came home. My husband was in the living room . . . my son . . . came into the house and I heard him cursing [sic] his dad about the trailer. I was in the kitchen fixing a pot of coffee. My son was standing in front of the bathroom door. I walked into the living room to see what was going on. I asked my son what was going on and he began to fuss at his daddy. I could see that he was mad. I asked what he meant talking to his daddy like that. My son told me it was none of my business and he hit me on the right side of my

> face and knocked me to the floor and he wouldn't let me get up. After he knocked me down, his daddy talked to him and asked him what was wrong with him hitting his mother like that. My son told us that we were driving him crazy about the trailer. About this time, he had a pistol in his hand. I saw a flash and heard a shot. I ran to my husband who had fallen to the floor. There was blood coming from his left cheek. I said, "Son, you have killed your own daddy." My son told his daddy to get up. Then he went to call an ambulance. He told me not to say a word to anyone. I waited until he left and called the police . . . [before he left the house] . . . he asked me if I had any money and I told him I didn't have any. Then he told me to get daddy's wallet and I told him I wouldn't get it. That is all he said and he then left the house. The trailer I have mentioned is the trailer that my son borrowed from his daddy on Sunday, November 9. My husband had told my son to be sure to return the trailer by Monday since he had to use it. . . . My husband is a cabinetmaker. I would like to say that I don't think my son meant to kill his father or that he meant to hurt me. I think my son needs to be under a doctor's care.

A statement by the killer's ex-wife provides some additional insight into the emotional state of the killer. He and his wife were divorced two months before the killing and since the divorce he had called his ex-wife on several occasions to effect a reconciliation and a remarriage. The couple had an infant daughter. The ex-wife, who was living with her parents and her daughter, told police that she had told her ex-husband that she viewed the divorce as final. We do not know how the difficulties of the marital relationship carried over to the parent-child relationship.

The Legal Disposition of Domestic Killings

In most killings within domestic groups it is known precisely who did what to whom and how. Although it cannot be known exactly why one person decides to take the life of another, one must acknowledge, in passing, the importance and recurrence in different cases of such motives as jealousy, anger, frustration, and passion.

To take the life of a close relative ought theoretically to be equivalent to taking the life of a stranger. Yet, as can be seen from the data summarized in Tables X, XI, and XII (Appendix E), the final legal disposition of a case, with very few and notable exceptions, varies directly with the killer-victim relationship. The closer, or more intimate, the relationship is between a killer and his victim the less likely it is that the killer will be severely punished for his act. Conversely, the more distant the killer-victim relationship is, as when the killer and victim are strangers, the more likely it is that the killer will be severely punished for his act. Although punishment may vary greatly from one case to another, within any given offender category, there is a certain uniformity to the outcome in similar and analogous cases. If this were not so the system of criminal justice would be wholly arbitrary.

Similar interpersonal relationships, or status equivalence, between killers and victims, and analogous situational contexts in which the final homicide drama is played out, generally evoke similar kinds of official response. An official response refers to the actions of the police in apprehending and processing a suspect together with the subsequent acts of attorneys, grand jury members, jurors, judges, and all other persons called upon to finally dispose of a homicide case. The decision on the part of these officials, individually and collectively, to formally disapprove the actions of a particular killer is governed by very complex cultural rules. It must suffice here to say that given certain kinds of homicidal acts (involving kinspeople, friends or associates, or strangers) and a limited range of judicial alternatives or outcomes (no bill, innocent, or guilty) we can infer how different cultural attitudes and values influence the decision-making choices of both killers and officials.

As a first step, 200 killer-victim relationships from 1969 have been classified into three broad categories that distinguish three principal kinds of killer-victim status relationships.

This procedure, which excludes cases for which the final legal outcome remains unknown, yields three broad categories: (1) *Kinspeople or Relatives*—those individuals who are related to each other by consanguineal or affinal ties; (2) *Friends or Associates*—those individuals who prior to the killing have known each other in some informal or formal capacity (e.g., paramour, neighbor, coworker, or roommate); and (3) *Strangers*—those individuals who prior to the killing have neither encountered each other previously or otherwise participated as reciprocals in a social relationship.

Because it proved impossible to categorize the relationships between some of the principals in a number of cases, we are left, for the purposes of statistical analysis, with a distribution of killer-victim relationships within each category as follows: 77 cases involving kinspeople, 68 cases involving friends and associates, and 55 cases involving strangers. The relatively even numerical distribution of cases among the three principal relationship categories provides a fair sample for proving whether the killer-victim relationship delimits the relative severity in the judicial outcome for individual homicide cases.

Hypothesis I: The killer-victim relationship does not affect the final legal disposition of a homicide case

This null-hypothesis, which in effect asserts that there is no significant relationship between the two variables, could be accepted as valid if the data displayed no significant differences in outcome for killers in the three offender status categories. The tabulated frequency data in Tables XIII and XIV clearly indicate that there is indeed a significant difference in the final outcome for killers in the three categories. The null-hypothesis therefore is rejected.

Hypothesis II: The killer-victim relationship significantly affects the final legal disposition of a homicide case

The tabulated data in Table XIII illustrate the relationships between the three major killer-victim relationship categories and 12 possible case disposition outcomes. The severity of outcome, which might be considered a continuum ranging from "no charge" to death or a literally enforced "life sentence," is unevenly distributed among the three offender categories. It must be noted and emphasized that the severity of the outcome correlates inversely with the degree of intimacy between killer and victim.

In other words, if a person kills a close relative he is more likely to escape punishment than if he kills a complete stranger. The most notable exception to this general rule is to be found in cases in the relative category where the relationship specifically involves two persons who are status reciprocals in a parent-child relationship. In parent-child homicides parents receive a disproportionately lighter sentence for killing their children than do children killing their parents.

The number of kinspeople, together with persons listed as friends and associates, who escape any form of negative sanctioning is *four* times greater than that of killers in the "stranger" category. To test Hypothesis II, therefore, it is necessary to look closely at those cases in all three categories that resulted in some kind of legal sanction. Yet even here, as summarized in Table XIV, the data fail to seriously challenge the explanatory power of the hypothesis.

The 1969 data show that there is a direct causal relationship between a killer's membership in a particular status category, the situational context in which the victim is killed, and the severity of official punishment applied to the killer.

The downtown area of Houston, Texas. (Photo courtesy of the Houston Chamber of Commerce.)

The headquarters of the Houston Police Department.

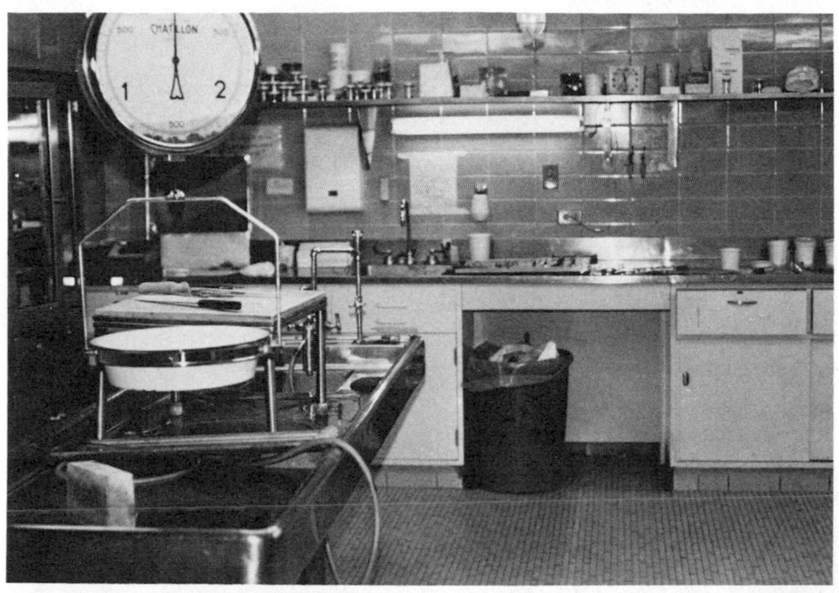

The autopsy laboratory at Ben Taub Hospital.

Homicide detectives and uniformed police officers at the scene of a killing. The victim has been shot twice with a small caliber weapon.

Bail bond agencies located across the street from the Houston Police Department.

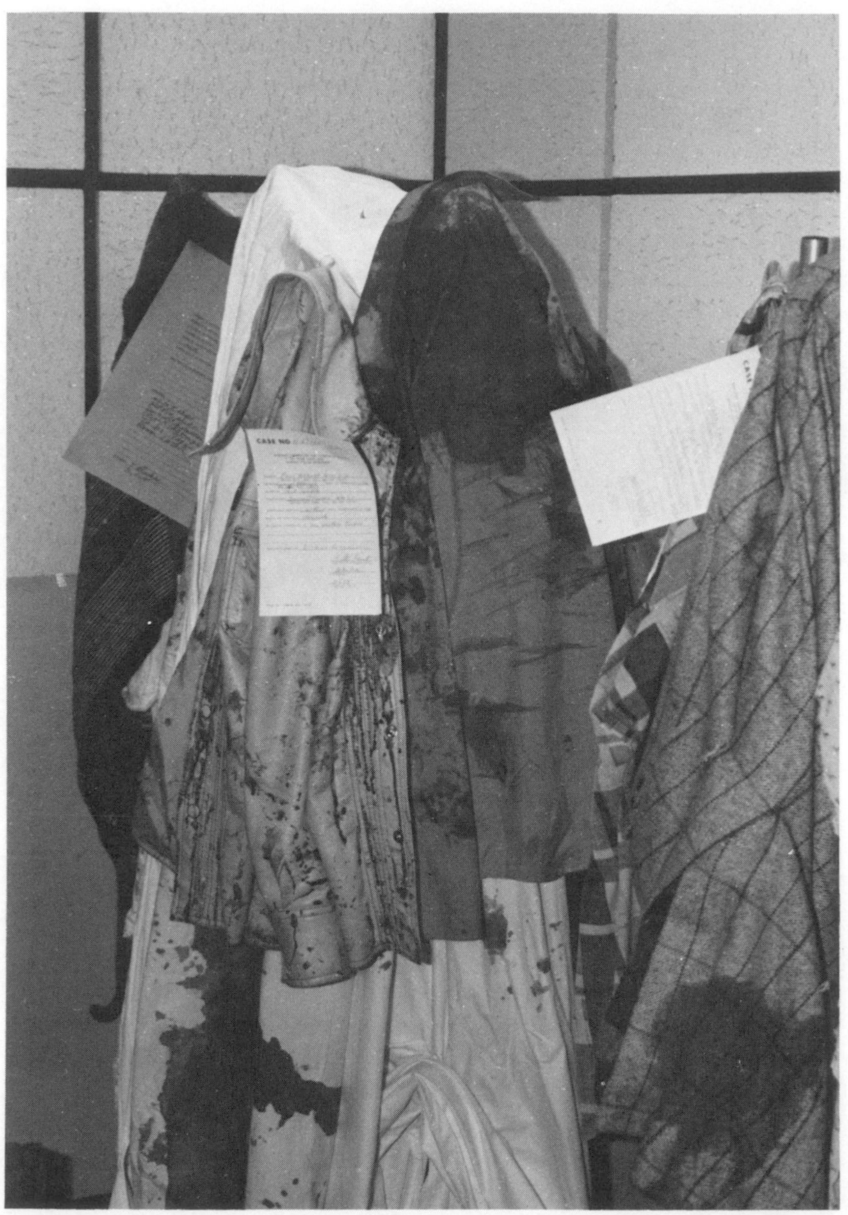

The "drying room" in the Homicide Division. The bloody clothes of homicide victims are left to dry before being taken to the crime laboratory for serological and other tests.

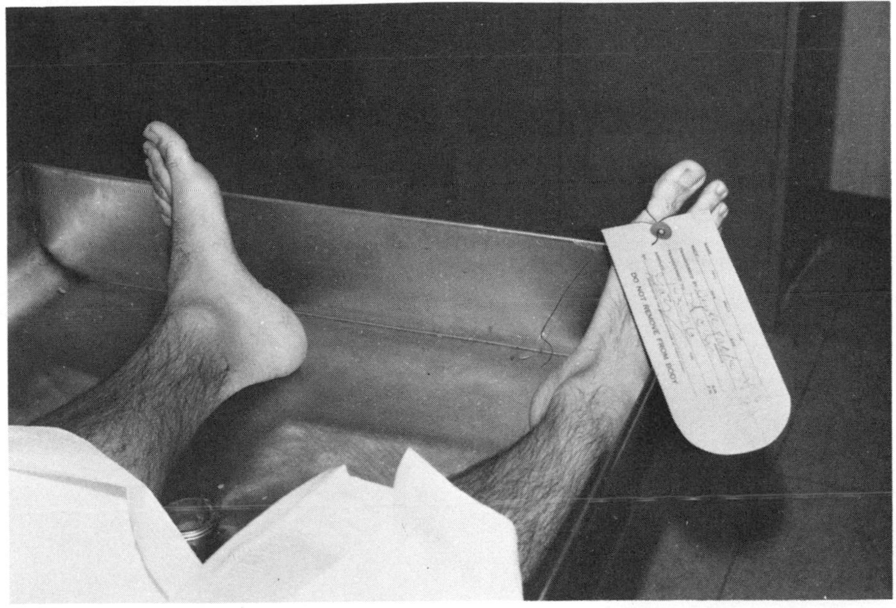

The victim of a homicide has been undressed, identified with an official tag, and is ready to be autopsied.

4 Homicide among Friends and Associates

Introduction

The official motto of the State of Texas is "Friendship." It is a high ideal to which many public and private citizens aspire. Public gruffness and surly behavior are only rarely witnessed in Texas. The overt and public friendliness expressed by the informal "How are y'all!" masks an individualism coupled to a strong sense of self-righteousness, however. Nemesis, the Greek goddess of retributive justice, might qualify Texas friendliness by adding *nemo me impune lacessit*–"no one attacks me with impunity." The transformation of personal friend or associate to killer/victim can partly be understood by a careful study of the social contexts and episodes that generate these seemingly incongruous relationship patterns.

Webster's dictionary defines a friend as a person who is "attached to another by esteem, respect, and affection," someone who is neither hostile nor a foe. By studying killings that involve friends and associates we can see connections and patterns in the episodes that precipitate the transformation from friend to foe and indirectly observe the interplay of different value orientations.

Friendship and colleagueship may be viewed as special kinds of relationships that imply the existence of dyadic or paired social positions. Social dyads, which for long have served as a focus of role theory and small group research, take many different forms. Dyads may be either symmetrical, as when the two persons view each other as equals, or asymmetrical. The parent-child dyad exemplifies the asymmetrical dyad in that the rights and duties of this special relationship, both by nature and cultural definition, are unequal. Friendship dyads normally involve a voluntary and mutual arrangement founded on status equivalence and reciprocity. An ongoing friendship may further be said to demand a wide variety of transactions in reciprocity that both define and sustain the dyadic relationship.

Some cultures stress the importance of friendship relationships whereas others so emphasize kinship ties that friendship alliances outside the kinship group may be rare or even nonexistent. Such expressions as "kith and kin" and "relatives and friends" in this culture signify a conceptual overlap or blurring between the vaguely defined categories of "family" and "friends." The expression "friends and strangers" denotes a further cognitive separation of personal relationship categories.

All persons in American culture interact dyadically with persons that can be defined as kinspeople, friends, or strangers. The basic difference between the categories of relationship appear to hinge on cultural definitions of intimacy.[1] Kinspeople form primary dyads that require intimacy and strangers may form dyads that specifically preclude intimacy as part of the relationship. Friendship dyads, which as a rule are symmetrical, can also be characterized as either familistic and intimate or distant and formal. Homicides that involve friends may occur among persons who have an intimate relationship or among persons who only interact regularly on a more formal basis. The kinds and degrees of intimacy and formality attached to the friendship dyad are more ambiguous than the forms of interaction found among kinspeople or strangers. Homicide among friends and associates not only terminates a particular relationship, but the act itself may help the killer resolve a conflict created by a lack of mutual trust or intimacy.[2]

A person, such as the assailant in Case No. 171 described below, may be prompted to kill his friend and coworker because the friend has "used" their relationship to obtain sexual access to his wife. In a different case (No. 185) a man kills because he suspects his associate violated the implicit terms of their colleagueship by reporting acts of dishonesty to their employer.

What appears so shocking, or understandable as the case may be, about many killings depends upon our personal understandings of and assumptions about the rules that "should" and "ought" to govern a particular kind of relationship. The mother-son dyad seems incongruous or incompatible with the killer-victim dyad whereas the jealous husband-unfaithful wife dyad more understandably transforms into a killer-victim relationship. The legal outcome for killers in 1969 fully supports these generalizations. It can therefore be stated with some certainty that the judicial outcomes for killers in the different categories probably reflect broad cultural judgments concerning both social dyads and situational contexts. Eight cases have been selected for discussion and analysis. These cases involve different dyadic relationships, but all of them involve face-to-face interaction. The social episodes that precede a killing add another dimension to our understanding of killer-victim relationships.

Eight Inimical Social Episodes

Each of the following cases has been selected, on the basis of their representation of killings within this category, to illustrate the kinds of relationships and social settings that often characterize killings among friends and associates. Relationships within this category generally include persons who regularly interact as friends, boy friends, girl friends, neighbors, employers, employees, colleagues, roommates, or social cohorts. The scenes of most of these killings are the places where friends and associates most frequently congregate, e.g., a place of work, a tavern, or a neighborhood. The residential distance between killers and victims is generally very short unless, of course, two persons have journeyed together to a place remote from either person's residence.

In Tables XV and XVI the 1969 homicide data are compared with analogous data collected on 489 criminal homicides in Houston during the interval 1945–1949. The similarities between the distributional data in the two periods are remarkable. Bullock, for example, found that the majority of homicide incidents took place within 0.04- and 0.9-mile radii of the homes of both killers and victims. His findings show a higher concentration of homicide incidents in the central city area than is evident in the 1969 data but that difference, which is not statistically significant, can be explained by differences in sample size (Bullock used the period 1945–1949 and I use the year 1969). It is also possible to explain other slight differences by the gradual shift in residential and commercial patterns within as well as between neighborhoods during the 20-year interval between the two data collection periods. The persistence of racial segregation well into and past the World War II era undoubtedly contributed to the concentration of violent crime in the most blighted and segregated areas of the city. Similarly, and as may be the case for the 1960s onward, the blurring of strict racial territorial boundaries has led to a greater city-wide dispersion of persons who use violence as a principal means of terminating an unsatisfactory relationship. Bullock's concluding comments suggest that he sees racial segregation as a principal, if not *the* principal, cause in the social forms of behavior that lead a large number of persons to resolve interpersonal conflicts by recourse to homicide. In his own words:

The process of segregation raises the probability of intra-group conflict not only by virtue of its power to generate proximity and intimacy, but also by virtue of its power to reduce respect for the areas that are segregated into deterioration. This is seen more clearly by those who, as inhabitants of these areas, experience the daily routine of such communal living. In Negro areas the relaxed pattern of social control is more obvious. It is reflected in the shuffle of unregulated traffic; the sharp odors of segregated theatres; or the sheer infrequency of uniformed police. In the downtown white area it is less obvious–more underground. Bell-boys of the cheaper hotels feel it; janitors of rooming houses feel and see it too, but the majority of this relaxed social control is behind the closed doors of places of cheap entertainment. The essence of it is that there has developed among many of the people who inhabit these areas a psychology of excuse. They often feel justified in breaking the general community code, or at least they have little conscience against it. They define community expectations in terms of their own deprivations. Probably this type of collective psychology is best illustrated through the case of a Negro man who sought to date a Negro woman, known to him only by the incident that they were both eating at the same segregated counter of a five and ten store [sic]. When the woman showed resentment of his advances, the man replied, "Don't get all het up, lady, we are all colored folks here together." The point we seek to make here is that many people of high homicide areas recognize that they generally fall below the city in terms of conventional concepts of social worth and class, and they merely act the part.[3]

Bullock's study exemplifies how sociologists generally use precisely quantifiable data to reconstruct social patterns. Yet his descriptive statements, as quoted above, are filled with insight, albeit subjective generalizations, that tell us more about the people and their views than is possible by statistical analysis.

A formal legal charge of adultery against a spouse is commonly accepted as sufficient grounds for granting a divorce. In Texas, as in some other states, a cuckold may legally kill his wife and her paramour if he can catch the pair *in flagrante delicto*. The terms *infidelity* and *cheating* properly denote a breach of trust or mutual obligation between husband and wife. The paramour, who may be either a lover or a mistress, adds a third, and frequently dangerous, dimension to the dyadic relationship. In Case No. 171 the relationships are further complicated by the fact that the wife's lover, the victim to be, is also a friend and colleague of the husband and killer. The killer, Mr. Jones, a 27-year-old White male, and his wife, age 32, had been very good friends of the victim, Mr. Russell, age 47, until the fatal episode that took place around midnight some time in October, 1969. When the police arrived at the scene of the killing they were met by Mr. Jones who calmly informed them that "I caught him with my wife and I shot him." The weapon, a .22 caliber rifle, was on top of the car in which Mr. Russell was shot. The relationships between the three principals, together with the final events leading to the homicidal episode, are vividly summarized in an affidavit submitted to the police by the principal eyewitness, Mrs. Jones:

> Last night, at about 11:30 P.M., I called Russell at his home. I called to ask if I could borrow some money from him to pay the rent and the utilities. He said that he would lend me the money and [that] he would let me have about $55. He said he would be over as soon as he found a service station open as his tank was nearly empty. I guess it was about five minutes to midnight when he got to my house. I opened the front door and told him to come in. He said, "No, it's late and I have to get on back home." After he said this he walked up on the porch and we were just standing there talking about different things and the troubles me and Jones were having. About this time Russell made some remark about my husband being down at some joint watching the go-go girls and that he could not stay as he had to work in the morning. About this time some cars passed [the house] and Russell said that I was going to be the talk of the neighborhood because I was standing out front talking to a bachelor. I said, "Let's go in the living room," but Russell said he wouldn't and that it wouldn't look too good so he said, "Let's just sit in the car for a few minutes." We got in the car and talked for a few minutes. After a little while Russell teased me about how my hair looked and he kissed me a few times and then I kissed him back a few times. I kidded him about wrinkling his white shirt and he said that he wasn't worried about his shirt and that it was his tight black pants that were bothering him. This is when he said he would get comfortable and that's when he pulled his pants down around his knees. His shorts were down too. When he said his pants were too tight, I told him to let me see and I felt and he had an erection. This is when he pulled his pants down and he took

his left leg out of his britches. He then reached over and kissed me. At this time I was sitting under the steering wheel and Russell was over on the passenger's side. This is when Russell told me "It's too late to send me home now!" He reached over and kissed me. About this time I looked over Russell's shoulder and saw my husband. He had a gun. I think it was a .22 caliber rifle and my husband said something and then Russell said "Now listen Jones" or "Wait Jones" and this is when my husband shot him. I jumped out of the car and ran around the front and my husband had the gun pointed at me. I asked him not to shoot me and to think of our daughter. Then he said he wasn't going to kill me and that I wasn't fit to kill and that he was just going to beat the hell out of me. He then hit me in the face and grabbed me by the arm. I pulled away from him and looked into the car and saw Russell. He was bleeding real bad from the back of his head and he vomited. I hollered for my husband to call an ambulance but he said "It's no use, he is dead." I ran into the house and called an ambulance but my husband jerked the phone out of my hand and said that he would call and that he would also call the cops. I grabbed a wet towel from the bathroom and went back to the car and started to wipe stuff off of Russell's face and then I put the rag behind his head. About this time the police arrived and I went back into the house to quiet my children. I told my son to keep the other children in the bedroom.

The follow-up police investigation revealed that Jones and Russell had worked for the same tool manufacturing company for several years. They worked different shifts, however. The adulterous relationship had started about two years before the killing and the Joneses were good friends with Russell as was made evident by their mutual get togethers for picnics and fishing. The couple also owned a houseboat together with Russell. According to Mrs. Jones, she and Russell managed to see each other privately and to have intercourse about three times a week. She had expressed a desire for a divorce but the couple had not separated or taken formal steps to dissolve the marriage.

Mr. Jones was charged with murder and brought before a grand jury. He was no billed and released from police custody. A letter from the assistant district attorney, addressed to the Homicide Division, informed the police of the outcome of the case and it further instructed the police to release the rifle to Mr. Jones. It must be added that Mr. Jones, who certainly must have been motivated by passion, had suspected his wife and his friend. On the eve of the killing he had told Russell that he was going up to Lake Houston and Russell, in turn, had told him that he was going home. The two men had been drinking beer together at a lounge. Mr. Jones changed his mind about his trip and as he returned home he spotted the car in his driveway. He drove his car past his house, parked it, and took his rifle from the car and walked toward the house. He looked into the parked car, saw the couple, and fired. The ready availability of the means to kill, the rifle, was not noted anywhere in the police report. But why should a loaded rifle in a personal car be raised as an issue, when as is generally known, it is a common and socially acceptable form of behavior to carry personal weapons?

Jones' early release from police custody certainly could not fail to signal the righteousness of his act to his children, his wife, their neighbors, and—as the story was disseminated by the news media—ultimately to the city populace at large. Those who argue that "law" and "custom" are separable realities or domains must, it seems, base their argument on semantic niceties rather than facts.

Case No. 148 exemplifies how aggressiveness and violence, combined with the strong sense of individualism and self-righteousness also noted in the above case, is reinforced by legal statutes and magnamimous public attitudes, as reflected in grand jury decisions, toward the armed citizen defending his manhood and "property rights."

The killer and victim, both Mexican-Americans, in Case No. 148 had little, if any, awareness of each other's existence before the shotgun slaying that took place in June, 1969. But the killer, a male, age 35, was the neighbor of the victim's nephew. This is why I choose, rather arbitrarily, to include this case in the friendship and associate category. The trouble began when the victim, a 50-year-old male, arrived together with his wife to visit his nephew and family. As they pulled up in front of the nephew's house they parked in such a way that the neighbor's driveway was blocked. The neighbor came to the house shortly thereafter and requested that they move the car. The car was moved to permit the neighbor to drive his truck out of the driveway. The victim's car, however, was again parked in front of the neighbor's driveway. This led to an argument between the two men. The killer went into his house, loaded his shotgun, and returned to the driveway where he openly stated that he would kill the 50-year-old man unless he moved his car away once and for all. The man unwisely chose to heed the advice of Nemesis and thus held his ground. He refused to acknowledge and respond to the verbal threat. One shot was fired and the victim fell over dead. The victim was not armed nor, according to several eyewitnesses, did he verbally or physically threaten the killer except, as noted, by holding his ground. An ambulance and the police arrived and the killer was arrested and charged with murder. Trial was set for October, and the killer entered a plea of guilty. He was judged and admonished by the court. He was then given a five-year probationary sentence!

In the previous discussion of killings within domestic groups, it became more or less evident that the final argumentative episode itself was preceded by an even earlier series of arguments, quarrels, and fights between the two principals. The temporal element in killings involving friends and associates appears to be shorter than in domestic killings. This lack of what might be called temporal depth creates some astounding and baffling examples of how seemingly trivial interpersonal differences, such as the perceived right to defend one's driveway, between two persons can lead to violence or death.

The killer in Case No. 209, a 43-year-old Black male (Smith), had given ten dollars to the niece of the victim (Hatfield). Smith understood this to be a loan, but Hatfield, a 40-year-old Black male, apparently saw the event differently. The two men, together with some of their relatives and friends, were standing outside a bar where they were barbecuing. Hatfield, according to eyewitnesses, told Smith that the ten dollars were not a loan to his niece but that Smith had "just bought some pussy from the girl." Hatfield escalated his verbal insult by handing Smith five dollars. Smith, in turn, left the barbecue gathering shouting something like "I am going and will be back and you had better not be standing in front of that barbecue pit when I come back because I will kill you!" The party left the barbecue area and entered the bar to drink beer. The incident was all but forgotten when 20 minutes later Smith entered the bar brandishing a loaded rifle. He walked straight over to the table where Hatfield was seated and shouted, "All right goddamn it, I am back like I told you. I am going to kill you, you mother fucker!" The unarmed Hatfield rose from his chair and was immediately shot in the stomach. It was Saturday in Houston and the Homicide Division could look forward to a busy evening. Smith was indicted on two charges. One of these charges, presumably relating to the illegal use of a firearm, was dropped. The other charge carried and led to conviction. The sentence: Four years imprisonment in the Texas Department of Corrections.

Case No. 230 unfolded at a cafe-lounge establishment. It is the kind of case that makes hardened homicide detectives shake their heads and philosophically ponder the limits of open disregard for the value of a human life. It is also the sort of case that first roused my curiosity and that eventually led to this study.

The killer, a 20-year-old Black male, and the victim, a 19-year-old Black male, were acquaintances. They had both gone to the same cafe-lounge late one Saturday evening. The melee started when the victim, Clifton, seated himself next to the killer, Crawley, who had just ordered a plate of barbecue. According to eyewitnesses and the signed confession by the killer, the victim provoked the fight. Part of Crawley's written confession reads as follows:

> Clifton came over and sat at the table where I was sitting. About five minutes later some food that I had ordered was served. Clifton asked for some of it and I gave him two pieces of meat and a slice of bread. We were sitting there eating together and he asked for another piece and I gave him another piece. He got through with that piece and he then reached over in my plate and got another piece [without asking]. I told him to put it back on my plate and he got mad and put it back. I got up from the table and was going over to another table when Clifton splashed hot sauce on my clothes. I asked him why he did that and he told me that he would do it again and about this time he got hold of the neck of the bottle like he was going to hit me with it. He came at me with the bottle and I pulled my knife out and as he grabbed me I cut him. His brother grabbed a chair and he was going to hit me with it. Some of the people in the lounge grabbed the chair from him and he then took Clifton to the hospital.

Clifton later died in the hospital from *multiple* stab wounds. Witnesses reported that the two boys had known each other most of their lives and that Clifton was well known in the neighborhood as a "tough guy." Crawley surrendered peacefully to the police at his home. The case went before the grand jury and was no billed.

Unlike consanguineal kinship relationships, friendships can be created and dissolved at will by either of the two reciprocals in the relationship. This element of "voluntary association" implies that persons who enter friendships can exercise considerable control over the kind and degree of intimacy that forms the basis of that relationship. In some friendships the persons choose their companions wisely by selecting persons who share their values and interests. In other instances, as exemplified by the relationship in Case No. 91, a person may indeed unwisely choose an incompatible friend or associate.

The killer Adams was, by anyone's definition, a violent person. At the age of 35, Adams was wanted by the police as a suspect in an armed robbery in which he allegedly had assaulted his victim. He was wanted by the police for burglary and theft and he was the principal suspect in yet another case involving aggravated assault. His latest victim, a Black male, age 68, had invited Adams to his house where the two men played a dice game for money. Adams lost $150 and then demanded the return of his money. The victim to be refused. Adams first knocked the elderly man down by hitting him with his fists. He thereafter procured a butcher knife from the kitchen and stabbed and slashed his victim to death. All in all, the victim received 16 stab wounds in the face, chest, neck, and in the back. His cervical spine was completely severed attesting to the force used to wield the knife. The episode in the kitchen was witnessed firsthand by the victim's 18-year-old stepson who told the police that his stepfather had nothing with which to protect himself and that Adams had continued to slash him after he had fallen helplessly to the floor. Adams was tried and sentenced to life in the Texas Department of Corrections. We must ask ourselves why, despite the obvious viciousness deployed by this particular killer, this man received a life sentence whereas the shotgun killer in Case No. 148 escaped with a probationary reprimand. It hardly suffices to say that one man probably was viewed as "protecting his territory" whereas the other man, Adams, was judged to be an undesirable character with an incorrigible "criminal personality!"

The killer and victim in Case No. 47, two Black males, age 33 and 40, respectively, were acquaintances. Both men lived in the same rooming house and both had been sexually involved with the same woman. It is apparent from the details of the killer's affidavit that the victim begrudged the sexual relationship between the younger man and his former mistress. According to the affidavit:

> About six weeks ago John [the victim] moved into the same house that I was living in. I had not been friends with John but just knew him when I saw him around the rooming house. My trouble with John started about two weeks ago when I was walking with a woman that lives in my area. I don't want to give her name because she is married. We passed John on the street and when I asked him how he was doing he told me not to be fucking with him and I could

tell that he was mad at me about something. I asked the lady if she was going with him but she told me that she wasn't. But I learned the next day that John had given her some money and this was what had made him mad at me. From that time on, every time I would see John he would try to start trouble with me and I would tell him that I didn't want no trouble. He has had run-ins with several people. Yesterday morning I got off work at 8:15 A.M. and went to a cafe on Lyons Street. John came in about 9 A.M. and he came over to the table where I was sitting with friends. John started messing with me, telling me that he was going to take himself some of my beer. I tried to ignore him and told him to quit messing with me. John then went back over to the bar. After a little while, I left the cafe and went to get a pack of cigarettes. When I got back to the cafe I found John standing in the doorway and he wouldn't move. He was standing there with his hand in his pants pocket and he looked at me like he was gettin his pocketknife open in his pocket. I just turned away from him and left. John had pulled his knife on me the time that he saw me with the lady that I told about in the first part of this statement. I went home and got my pistol. I was mad and tired of John messing with me every time I got out of the house. After I got my pistol, I left the house and saw John about half a block down the street. I walked down to him and I told him that I was tired of all the trouble and he then put his hand into his pocket and I pulled my gun and started shooting. I don't even know how many times I did shoot. I really didn't want to shoot the man but I just wanted to tell him that he was going to quit messing with me!

A woman standing on the front porch of her house witnessed the killing. She told the police that she saw the victim get hold of John and say, "Nigger, you are going to buy me a beer." John got away but the victim pulled at him once more. She heard the killer say, "I will just kill the mother-fucker and that will get him off of me," whereafter he fired five or six shots. The principle that holds here, it seems, is that if a man gives you a hard time you take direct action and remove him. There is only a hint in the case report that the two combatants were intoxicated. A jury found the killer guilty of murder and he was sentenced to serve three years in prison.

In Case No. 185 we see how two middle-aged Black coworkers in a funeral home failed to establish a workable colleagueship. The relationship between Connally, age 59, and Stevens, age 49, was perhaps doomed from the onset of Connally's employment at the funeral home. The owner of the funeral home suspected Stevens of embezzlement and he asked Connally to double-check on the accuracy of Stevens's records. Stevens soon discovered that he, together with other hearse drivers, was being watched. He went directly to Connally and informed him in no uncertain terms that he would kill him. Connally defended his "spying" by stating that he was acting on orders from their boss, the funeral director. The argument between the two men occurred in mid-August and Connally had assumed, until the night of October 29th, that the whole matter had been forgotten. Connally's job as night watchman in the funeral home, and Stevens's job as hearse driver, required them to cooperate. Connally would receive calls requesting their service and Stevens would then pick up the bodies in the hearse and bring them to the funeral home. When a call came in at about 11 P.M. on October 29th, Connally called and alerted Stevens who slept on a bed in the rear of the funeral home. Connally signaled Stevens by ringing a small bell. In his own words:

> I rang this bell and then in a few minutes Stevens came to where I was. I gave him the address and then he turned and left the office. I went back to bed and in about five minutes he came back and asked me where the god damn keys to the hearse were. I told him that I didn't drive the hearse and that I didn't know where the keys were. He then said, "You just want to be a bad S.O.B. don't you?" He then said that he had been wanting to kill me and then he hit me in the chest with his fist. He knocked me over on the bed and got on top of me while he kept hitting me with his fist. He asked me where my magnum was and told me that he was going to make me use it. He told me that he was going to his room and would get his rifle and kill me. He left the office and went outside and I got my pistol and went to the side door. I saw him heading for his station wagon and I know that he keeps his gun there. I told him there was no need for us to have this trouble and he told me that he was going to kill me. When he told me this, I pointed the pistol at him and shot him one time. I then went to the phone and called the homicide office and they sent an ambulance and a police car to the funeral home. . . .

Connally was no billed. Stevens was autopsied and, paradoxically, his remains were returned to and embalmed at the funeral home where he had been employed. May I remind the reader that the events of this case, as well as those of the previous ones, occurred in the city of Houston in the year 1969 and not in Dodge City, Kansas, at the time of Wild Bill Hickok's rule in the latter part of the nineteenth century!

Many Americans celebrate New Year's Eve by setting off rockets and firecrackers. Noisy parties are common, well-known ingredients of this calendrical rite. Many Texans celebrate New Year's Eve, and other similar events, by firing their guns into the air. It was a .38 caliber handgun used in this fashion that was to later fatally wound an intoxicated elderly man who worked as a dishwasher and janitor in a cafe. The episode unfolded in the early morning hours of January 1, 1969.

The killer, a 42-year-old Mexican-American male, had been manager of Lloyd's Cafe for some 12 years. On New Year's Eve he was working at the cafe. Around midnight he took his pistol and went outside to fire the pistol in celebration. Two other cafe employees joined in "the fun." They returned to the cafe and the manager put the pistol in his pocket and went on with his work. At around one o'clock in the morning they began to close the cafe. The victim, a 62-year-old White male nicknamed "Pops," was too drunk to perform his general duties as clean-up man. The manager told him to leave. Pops got into his car, but the manager went outside and told him that he was too drunk to drive. Pops, in the manner of drunk drivers, wanted to drive anyway. The manager first tried to deflate the tires with a drinking straw but that didn't work. Then he said to Pops that he would shoot the air out of the tires unless Pops got out of the car. At that very moment, Pops jumped out of the car and pulled the manager's arm. The pistol went off and Pops was dead.

The manager, with the assistance of his other employees, now lifted the old man's body into the car and left him there. He then closed the cafe and went home. He returned later that morning about 9 A.M. and told his cousin about his discovery. The cousin called the police and Pops was brought down to the morgue. The manager first said to the police that he didn't know what had happened to Pops but that he would gladly respond to the homicide detectives' request for a closer look at his pistol. Ballistics tests matched the bullet removed from Pops with the manager's pistol. The manager now said that he would tell all and that he didn't need a lawyer. He related the facts of the case to the police, was charged and brought before a grand jury, and subsequently released on a grand jury finding of no bill.

Two homicide detectives once accused me of attributing too much callousness to a group of young people who had been brought in following a killing that took place at an eighteen-year-old girl's birthday party. They said that the failure of these young people to express emotion was a show or a cover-up. The people who are surrounded by violence respond by acting tough or ignoring the disconcerting side of human nature that seems to accept homicide as an inevitable outcome if two people have "words," if they must fight, or if they, like Stevens above, get on each other's nerves. The detectives may be right and we must hope that they are. If the phenomenon of killing in Houston is more a concatenation of social and cultural variables, and not something that is intrinsically part and parcel of human experience, there is some hope for change. At the time of this writing, however, the homicide rate in Houston and elsewhere in the nation continues to rise.

Two facts may be inferred from the data that have been presented in this chapter. First, "normal" persons who become killers do not appear to be restrained by personal value orientations that demand either respect for the value of human life per se or by a feeling of accountability to an authority higher than the self. Second, the overall socialization effect of grand jury and court decisions on the community at large must serve as a mechanism that directly reinforces individualistic behavior and action.[4] There is no need here to argue over the effects of sanctions on individual behavior. Individual behavior is controlled and governed by sanctions whether they are positive or negative. If people believe, along with their officials in government and "law and order" advocates, that the principal issue is not *outcome* but motive, procedure, and means, then we may have found an important clue to the culture patterns that govern the frequencies of homicide in an urban modern community.

Killers and Victims in the Houston Populace

Violent behavior is in large part the product of learning and experience. How, when, and where violent behavior may be employed to achieve some goal, as is evident from the descriptive case material from Houston, is culturally determined. The well-established fact that violent behavior tends to occur more often among persons who, by virtue of their general socioeconomic status and relatively low educational and occupational levels of achievement, live near the base of the social pyramid does not negate the cultural hypothesis. It is at the bottom of the social class hierarchy that one sees the greatest discrepancies between what anthropologists traditionally have described as "ideal" versus "real" culture; that is, many people who early in life become exposed to such ideological premises as "all men are created equal" or "any person who applies himself can become a success" may witness, firsthand, how only a small percentage of those around them actually realize or even approximate these ideals in everyday life. The continuous exposure to contrasts between what "is" and what "ought to be" has, in the general literature, been conceptualized as relative deprivation. Deprivation–whether economic, social, or psychological–does not, of course, by itself lead individuals to pursue violent solutions to life's many problems. It is rather psychological, social, and cultural factors that combine to establish violent behavior as a viable and alternative strategy for survival and existence.

The cases discussed so far illustrate how many killers employ interactional tactics that result in some form of pure impulse gratification. Such tactics, when combined with the willingness and ability to use violence, also suggest that the dominant value orientation of killers resides with the present. Killers thus prefer to resolve problems immediately or they employ violence without much thought to alternative and future modes of conflict resolution. This value orientation, plus an emphasis on individualism and personal autonomy, has been extensively treated in Kluckhohn's and Strodtbeck's provocative 1961 study, *Variations in Value Orientations.* Attention to differences in value orientation leads to at least some understanding of why some individuals rely on violent and direct means of conflict resolution whereas others, if faced with analogous situations and problems, may withdraw, attempt some form of third-party intervention, or even seek to use formal adjudication as the principal means of conflict resolution.

The 1969 data indicate that recourse to personal and physical violence as a mode of conflict resolution is indeed concentrated among persons, both White and Black, who in terms of both educational and economic status can be characterized as lower class. Many of the Houston killers in 1969 share life-styles common to the lower class environment, and presumably, they share value orientations. The killing of relatives, friends, associates, coworkers, or so-called intimates predominate over killings that involve persons who are strangers. In the following chapter it becomes even more evident that homicides in the "stranger category" tend to represent persons from different socioeconomic classes and, in turn, represent individuals who may have very different personal views of how to cope with situational conflicts.

In this study it has been found that only 6 percent of the Houston killers in 1969 crossed racial categories. This finding, which is identical to Wolfgang's data from Philadelphia, supports the view that particular modes of conflict resolution are related to cultural experiences in a particular social milieu. The distributional data for Houston homicides show how the risk of victimization, together with the probability of becoming an assailant in a homicide case, is higher among Blacks than among Whites and how the risk is higher among the poor than among the affluent. When I speak of *Whites* and *Blacks* in the following paragraphs the reader should keep in mind that these are labels that only approximate the actual composition of different socioeconomic classes. It is quite evident, for example, that lower class Whites are much more similar to lower class Blacks than they are to upper class Whites. The boundaries between one social class and another are neither solid nor are they racial boundaries.

According to the U.S. census, there were 460,582 White and 110,151 Black males in the city of Houston in 1970. Together these two principal categories (81 percent White and 19 percent Black) comprised the total male population between 17 and 64 years of age. Of these, 185 died as the result of homicide. If, theoretically speaking, the frequency of homicide could be said to be equally probable for Whites and Blacks, the expected frequencies, for the year 1969, should then be proportionate to the size of each racial category. In other words, 81 percent (149) of the 1969 victims should be White and 19 percent (35) of the victims should be Black, *if there had to be 185 male victims in that year*. Actually, the number of Black males who became homicide victims is almost *four* times the expected number.

The distribution of females, between 17 and 64 years of age, in Houston in 1969 was 480,787 Whites and 114,984 Blacks. The percentage distribution here is identical to that of the male population. Since the actual number of Black female victims was 20, whereas the expected number of victims is six, the actual number of Black female homicide victims was more than *three* times the expected number.

It may now be stated, without further qualifications being necessary, that the probability of being killed is much greater for Black males and females than for White males and females. Within each of the two major racial categories, Black males were *seven* times more likely than Black females to become homicide victims and White males were *five* times more likely to become homicide victims than White females. In other words, the sex ratio of victims within the two population categories was 7 to 1 in the Black population and 5 to 1 in the White population.

Thus, in both racial categories the probability of becoming a homicide victim is higher for males than for females. It is also evident that males, in both racial categories, also are more likely than females to be assailants in a homicidal incident. The data tabulated in Table XVII again show that the number of White male killers outnumber the number of White female killers by a ratio of nearly 5 to 1. The ratio of Black males to Black females who became killers is nearly 4 to 1. The male-female killer ratio is lower in the Black than in the White population. The difference can be attributed to the large number of female Black assailants; that is, the number of female Black killers was *four* times the number of female White killers.

It remains for future studies to focus more closely on relationships between socioeconomic status and the propensities for expressions of violent behavior. Such studies, which undoubtedly will employ a historical analysis of intraracial and intraclass violence, will likely find correlations between lower class life-styles and violence.

5 Homicide among Strangers

Introduction

It is quite difficult to determine the exact number of persons who might be classified as assailants and victims within the third, and last, interactional category labeled "strangers." On the one hand, there is the always present problem of accurately determining killer-victim relationships on the basis of homicide reports that only incidentally include information that, as a matter of routine police procedure, is regarded as peripheral to the investigation of homicide incidents and the apprehension of offenders. On the other hand, we are here faced with a rather intriguing problem of defining *stranger*. Is a stranger an alien, a foreigner, or simply any other human being who does not share the traditions of one's own culture? Is a stranger a fellow citizen with whom we only interact within a strictly formal and impersonal format? Or, is a stranger somebody who quite literally falls outside one's network of personal relatives and associates? A stranger may be all or only a few of these. We need to narrow the scope of this relationship or interactional category if for no other purpose but to contrast and compare these particular killer-victim dyads with those described for kinspeople, friends, and associates.

Black's Law Dictionary offers an interesting definition of a "stranger in blood" as "any person not within the consideration of natural love and affection arising from relationship."[1] Wolfgang's study simply defines a stranger as a person "with whom no known previous contact existed."[2] These definitions help to focus the analysis of the status category of "stranger" by emphasizing: (1) the absence of affection or any degree of personal intimacy on the part of a person so defined and (2) the social distance between persons who view themselves as strangers. It should not be surprising, therefore, that most interactions between strangers commonly center on impersonal commodities or goods, services, and general economic transactions involving money. The assassin or the professional hired killer usually remains anonymous before he kills his designated victim(s). Either type of killer may, of course, be killing persons who are readily identified as members of a group—students, policemen, juvenile delinquents, or public officials—with whom the killer is acquainted. Anonymous strangers, such as for example criminals or policemen, may be slain much like an enemy in battle, i.e., without personal feelings of hate or enmity toward the individual target. The enemy is not seen as an individual, but as a depersonalized representative of a particular category of persons.[3] I mention these brief examples to illustrate a simple point: The killing of a stranger is not seen as principally motivated by previous interpersonal frictions in the killer-victim relationship but rather must be seen as the outcome of some other nonpersonal motive. The cases involving these kinds of killings, even more than killings within other dyadic relationship categories, illustrate that there is a principal cultural concern with motivational and materialistic factors rather than with the consequences to society of numerous homicides per se.

Although those parts of the Texas Criminal Code that address offences against the person, including homicide, do not discriminate between different kinds of killer-victim status relationships, the laws pertaining to homicide specifically distinguish between various motives in the assessment of a legal penalty. The legal outcome for a person who kills his wife's lover is, as we have seen, very different from the outcome for a person who combines killing with theft, robbery, or similar criminal or antisocial acts.

Homicide victims are not often compensated by society in the form of indemnities passed on to descendants or survivors. A business corporation, like a bank, can recover money lost through a robbery either through insurance or by a return of the stolen money recovered from the robber by the police. We must seek to understand, therefore, how the entire cultural bureaucracy simplistically labeled "the penal system"–which involves decisions by the police, the district attorney, the grand jury, the trial jury, the judge, etc.–may be connected to and influenced by general cultural value orientations that hierarchically rank motivational factors on a continuum from permissible to criminal. Although the statistical data tabulated in Table XIII (Chapter 3) support these working hypotheses, it is necessary once again to turn to individual cases for further insight into the probable connections between different kinds of homicidal dyads and the final legal outcomes for killers.

Homicidal Confrontations between Strangers

In the homicide cases discussed in Chapters 3 and 4, the final homicidal episode represented a final step in a long sequence of gradually disintegrating interpersonal encounters. In contrast to this, the homicidal confrontations between strangers conspicuously lack the cumulative elements that typify killings among intimates. The absence of a social relationship between a killer and his victim at first glance appears to introduce an element of randomness or chance that is uncommon in familistic killings. The chance factor, however, does not imply any absence of patterns of interpersonal and social conduct.

The behavior of a person who draws a pistol in a tavern and shoots the man at the end of the bar because his victim "was going for a gun or a knife in his pocket" exemplifies a very particular form of conduct. His behavior, which may be sanctioned either positively or negatively by "innocent" bystanders and members of society at large, is governed by complex and culturally defined rules for social conduct.[4] Similarly, the holdup man who points a gun at a cashier while shouting "Hands up!" is communicating that obedience to his command will neutralize the explicit threat to the cashier's own life. The cashier, by raising his hands, is signaling that he has understood the affirmative command. If either the holdup man or the cashier violates the culturally defined code of conduct for this interactional context, the robbery may easily escalate into a homicide. The slaying of a passive or compliant holdup victim is commonly viewed as brutal, legally premeditated, and perhaps even morally unforgivable. The passive victim, who suddenly turns against the holdup man, may similarly be labeled reckless, courageous, or perhaps even stupid. Homicide of this type thus involve complex understandings and definitions of appropriate and inappropriate behavior.[5] The following cases illustrate some of the cultural rules for conduct that help explain how an act of homicide simultaneously represents the response of an individual to a situation as well as the individual's interpretation and mediation of cultural norms. In the 1969 sample there were 55 killers who could be categorized as strangers, whereas 44 victims were known to have been killed by strangers. The discrepancy between the number of killers and victims in this category is accounted for by the fact that at least seven victims were slain by more than one killer.

In the cases that follow, I have followed a simple procedure:

Each case is reviewed for content and completeness of facts (cases for which the outcome for the killer is undetermined or unknown were omitted); cases that help link the details of the slaying with the final legal outcome for the killer have been chosen because they are of particular analytical interest. It must be noted that the actual cases in this category of killings, like killings in the other two general killer-victim categories, probably by far exceed the number of cases brought to the attention of the Houston Police Department.

The facts of Case No. 51 are uncomplicated. The killer, a 62-year-old Black male, left his place of work, a laundromat, at 8:30 P.M. and, as a matter of routine personal precaution, he walked cautiously toward his home in the middle of the street. He carried a considerable amount of cash and, as he told the police, he walked in this manner so as to be able to spot anyone walking up on him. A young Black youth, age 20, approached him and pulled a gun while shouting "Hold it!." The cautious would-be-killer was well prepared. He carried a .38 caliber revolver in his belt. He pulled the pistol and fired four shots at his assailant. The boy died on the street and, according to the cooperative citizen-killer, nobody came out into the street to see what had happened. The elderly man, who stated that he was carrying $150 in cash on his person, continued home to his house from which he called the police. The police recovered a loaded sawed-off .22 caliber rifle at the scene. The laundromat employee had defended his employer's property. He was no billed by the grand jury.

Case No. 128 also involves two Black males of disparate age. The killer, age 53, and his victim, a 29-year-old veteran of the Vietnam War, were complete strangers before the fatal incident. The killing occurred shortly before midnight before several eyewitnesses. One of these witnesses was a friend of the victim who perceived the probable outcome of the situation and attempted to prevent the tragedy. The killer owned a record shop located in a large shopping center. He returned to his store around 11 P.M. following his attendance at a local political rally. As he drove up to his store he noticed that another car was parked in his usual parking space. He got out of his car and, according to witnesses, "politely" asked the other driver to move his car. The man in the other car moved his car. The proprietor then went up to the door of his store and as he was letting himself into the store yet another man walked up to him and began to argue with him over the parking incident. The young man was overheard to say that he had a gun and that, as a war veteran, he was not about to take any abuse from anybody. The two men exchanged "words" and the victim's companion tried to get his friend to leave well enough alone. The good advice was not heeded and, as the young man followed the proprietor into the store, he was killed by shots from the proprietor's .38 caliber revolver. The autopsy showed that the victim's blood contained 0.162 percent alcohol. A grand jury no billed the proprietor who had killed the intruder in self-defense and, according to the letter of the law, had simply responded to a threat in fear of his life in his place of last retreat. The police report makes no issue of the fact that the proprietor, like his victim, was carrying a dangerous concealed weapon.[6]

The victim in Case No. 175, a White male, age 29, was killed with his own .32 caliber pistol. The killer, a White male, also 29, was visiting a tavern together with his brother and his wife. It was their first visit to this particular tavern. The two brothers were playing pool when, shortly after midnight, the killer briefly left the pool table to go to the restroom. As he walked toward the restroom a complete stranger stood up in front of him and held a gun to his head telling him to stop and that he didn't want any trouble in the place. The killer grabbed hold of the gun and in the struggle he was hit in the leg. He turned around and, with the assistance of his brother, walked out of the lounge where he managed to reach his car. The stranger pursued him and yet another scuffle broke out in the parking lot. According to witnesses, the aggressor-victim asked the wounded man in the car for the return of his pistol! The killer fired the stranger's own gun and quickly left the scene to get medical attention for his wounded leg at the hospital. The victim died in the parking lot. The police interviewed the killer at the hospital and the facts of the bizarre incident were reconstructed. The killer was no billed by a grand jury. The case report did not contain any information about the interesting and undisputed fact that only the killer had a gun during the scuffle in the parking lot. The probably intoxicated victim, who undoubtedly provoked the fight, promoted the termination of his own life or so, it seems, was the final public legal and moral view of this victim-precipitated homicide.

If somebody had related the details of Case No. 207 to me verbally I would undoubtedly have dismissed it as a fictitious tale. The facts of the killer's affidavit, which is supported in substance by written affidavits submitted to the police by both his wife and mistress, resulted in a no bill from a Houston grand jury. The affidavit reads as follows:

On March 15th, I went to Bob's Cafe and picked up my wife. She works at this cafe as a waitress and gets off work at 12:00 midnight. I had picked up my wife and we started home. I was driving south on Brewster Street when a car ran a stop sign and hit the rear end of my car. . . . I then followed this car. When we reached Collingsworth Street the man stopped his car and we stopped directly behind him. After we had stopped the car I got my knife. It was lying on the floor of my car and I picked it up and put it in my pocket. I then got out of my car and went up to the other car. . . . The man was still sitting in his car behind the steering wheel. I asked the man, "Mr. how come you hit my car and are taking off like that?" At this time the man started cussing at me and he got out of his car. He had his hand in his pocket and he continued to cuss me. After he got out of his car he still had his hand in his pocket and he backed up to the rear of his car. When he got to the rear end of the car he had his hand out of his pocket and there was an open knife in it. At this time I got my knife from my pocket. . . . The man started to swing his knife and he cut my left arm a little. . . . I then cut at this man and I think I cut him on the face. He staggered back and started to change hands with the knife. Then the man came at me again and knocked me down and knocked my knife out of my hand. Some way or another I managed to get the knife off the ground and then he came back at me and I had started getting up off the ground and I stabbed him. I don't know just how many times. After I stabbed him he staggered back to the side of his car and leaned over it. He was looking at me but he didn't say anything. . . . I told my wife "Let's go!" and we left. My wife had gotten out of the car a couple of times during the scuffle and we then got into the car . . . and went home. . . . After I got home I let my wife out of the car and I went and picked up Marilyn as she was at her aunt's house. I drove Marilyn to her house and I told her about the stabbing on the way to her house. . . . On my way home I drove down past the street where the incident had occurred and I looked to see if the car was still there. It was not. I thought that the man was all right and I went on home. . . .

The killer's wife corroborated the facts of the story. The girl friend's testimony, had it ever come to that, would of course have been viewed as hearsay and therefore inadmissible evidence in a criminal trial.

The case never did go to trial because the grand jury declined to indict the killer on the basis of the facts summarized in the preceding paragraphs. The weapon, incidentally, was a fair-sized hunting knife.

Case No. 207, described above, perhaps more than any other case in the 1969 sample, illustrates the ubiquity of fortuitous factors in every killing. But other cases, including Case No. 27 described below, serves to emphasize that killings tend to occur most frequently among persons who frequent the same places of business or recreation and who interact with strangers in accordance with an implicit but shared set of rules and mutual understandings. This patterning, which only reveals itself when individual cases are compared and contrasted, more broadly, with analogous cases, unmistakably signals the presence of behavioral responses that derive from the sharing of commonly held cultural values, attitudes, and beliefs. It is not sufficient, therefore, to simply say that at least 28 percent of the killings in Houston in 1969 occurred at neighborhood bars, taverns, or lounges. It is necessary to qualify such a generalization by pointing out that the kinds of persons who frequent these public "watering holes" only are strangers insofar as they do not know each other as individuals. Yet it is these same strangers who pull knives and guns on each other, who shoot to avenge verbal insults, or who know when to flee from a situation before it reaches a point of no return. The rules governing general tavern behavior, something which we know very little about, permit strangers to interact with each other since each participant is literally programmed to respond to situations in terms of quite complex rules for interaction. It is only the descriptive, and sometimes seemingly trivial, information culled from actual cases that, with effort and patience, permit an overview that places widely disparate homicidal incidents within an ideological framework of shared cultural patterns.

The victim in Case No. 27, a Black male, age 27, without question precipitated his own death. Although the incident took place in a small tavern along the Eastex Freeway, neither the victim's nor his killer's mental capacities were diminished by either alcohol or a barbiturate. The killer, a Black male, age 32, left his home shortly before 11 P.M. He entered the tavern and ordered a bottle of orange soda pop. He was standing at the counter when he noticed that two men at an adjacent table were looking at him and that one man in particular was saying something like "I don't like some mother-fucker standing over me. . . ." The killer's written affidavit further reads:

> I thought they were looking for trouble and so I put my drink down. I was going to leave but they moved over near the door and started in again. I asked them if they were talking to me and they stood up and said yes. One of the men put his hand in front of his shirt and I saw a pistol. I went outside and sat on the hood of my car. Both men came outside and one of them got a shotgun that was standing up against the building. He then pointed the shotgun at me and the other one pulled the pistol . . . they said that they were going to whip my ass before they got the guns. The man with the pistol shot at my foot and I turned and started to run around my car and he shot again. I reached into my car and got my pistol. . . .

The killer fired his .38 caliber pistol and killed the man who had shot at his feet. The other man, holding the shotgun, called for his friend to step out of the way so that he could get a clear shot at their target. The killer ran and miraculously escaped being hit by pellets from the shotgun. Several impartial eyewitnesses corroborated the killer's story and the case was closed when the grand jury failed to issue a true bill of indictment against the killer. None of the survivors of this episode were charged with violations relating to disturbing the public peace, assault and battery, or the possession, not to mention the use, of dangerous firearms.

The 19-year-old Black victim in Case No. 192 met his death in a tavern at 12:40 A.M. Two men, together with one of the men's wives, were at the tavern. One man was dancing with the wife when this young stranger walked up to him telling him to quit dancing with that woman. The woman's husband, who was sitting at a nearby table, quickly rose and got between the two men. Other men in the tavern helped throw the young man out. The woman's husband decided to leave after all the trouble, but as he got outside the young man fired his .22 caliber pistol at him from about ten feet away. The husband pulled his own .38 caliber pistol, fired it, and landed two shots in the young man's groin. The autopsy revealed that the deceased had a 0.189 percent alcohol level in his blood. The grand jury issued a no bill 11 days after the incident. To explain the homicide as "the outcome of a drunken brawl" would be tempting but somewhat inaccurate. It must be firmly kept in mind that there are city areas in Houston where this kind of incident only rarely, if ever, occurs. The affluent and undoubtedly less frustrated patrons in luxuriously decorated and apportioned public drinking establishments somehow manage to either sublimate or defer similar and aggressive impulses. The geographical distribution of homicides indicates that people more or less expect and anticipate certain actions and reactions from other persons who frequent similar, territorially defined enclaves. The fact that most, if not all, proprietors of city taverns are armed, and presumably ready to use deadly force, makes the occasional killing of a customer seem almost routine. Witness the events of Case No. 235.

A male Black proprietor, age 45, was watching a baseball game on the TV set in his liquor store. A woman customer was looking at the merchandise on the shelves. Three men, including the 26-year-old Black victim, walked into the store. One of the men looked at a pair of sunglasses and, according to the proprietor, put them in his pocket. The proprietor assumed that the three men had entered his store with the intent of robbing him. He claimed that he saw one of the three men pull a small .22 caliber pistol from his pocket. The proprietor responded by firing his .45 caliber pistol at the suspect. The pistol was not recovered from the scene but discovered to be in the possession of one of the survivors who fled the scene. Although the two friends of the victim admitted that the three of them had been drinking heavily before they entered the liquor store they denied that they had either known that their friend had had a gun or that they had seen him use it to threaten the proprietor. The details in the police report are not as complete as one might wish. Although the proprietor was properly charged with homicide he was nevertheless released, together with his .45 pistol, on his own recognizance. A grand jury later issued a no bill.

Several additional cases in the stranger category resulted in the dismissal of the killer. Only two cases (Nos. 231 and 174) were resolved by a public trial. Other cases, for which the charges were still pending at the time of this study, or the final outcome was undetermined, are inconclusive insofar as they cannot be used to either disprove or verify any working hypotheses. The focus now shifts to a consideration of a number of cases in which the killer was indicted following a grand jury investigation, brought to trial, found guilty, and sentenced to serve a prison term or to be executed. The study of these cases should facilitate by way of comparison to other previous cases a better understanding of some of the most critical factors that enter into the entire judicial decision-making process and, ultimately, determine the outcome for a killer.

Case No. 107 is of interest because the homicide illustrates the complex relationships between criminal statutes and the possible interpretations of the criminal law for each and every case. The killer in this case, a 36-year-old Black male who was the owner of a small store, not only pursued a person who had allegedly stolen money from the cash register in his store, but, after he had caught up with the alleged thief, forcefully detained him. The alleged thief attempted to escape. As he wiggled loose from his captor, the killer pulled out his .38 caliber pistol and shot him. These events, although briefly summarized, certainly illustrate how somebody "takes the law into their own hands." The police, who had been called in to investigate the theft on the previous day, were not told about the presence of suspects in the vicinity of the store; that is, a clerk at the store, who had seen the thieves, observed them in the neighborhood at the time the police came to investigate the complaint. The store clerk later told the police that he was afraid to tell the police officers about the suspects because he was afraid that they would come after him. The clerk's fear must have subsided after the police left the store because he had identified the suspects for the storeowner who, as we learned, gave pursuit and finally killed one of them. The case further calls attention to the sometimes limited role of the police in the prevention of serious offenses against the person. If private citizens learn that offenders can back their threats against individuals with uncontested force, and if such persons are freed on bail a few hours after being apprehended by the police, it is the exceptional person who will seek direct help from the police when other community or personal resources may be both safer and possibly more effective.

The grand jury found enough problems with the facts of this case to issue an indictment. In his trial, the killer was found guilty of homicide and he was given a five-year probationary sentence. A slap on the wrist one might say.

Case No. 133 could well be labeled "Saturday Night on the Town." It involves a number of White men, all in their early 30s, who were shooting pool in a run-down neighborhood tavern located near the University of Houston's main campus, drinking heavily (beer and vodka mixed!), and who concluded their Saturday evening by brawling and fighting with pool cues and barroom furniture. As the police sorted out the details of the case, from statements of witnesses and from verbal testimony volunteered by the killer who surrendered to the police the following day, it became clear that only one man would be charged with the killing of the victim. The victim, a 39-year-old White male, was killed with a 12 gauge shotgun the killer had brought to the tavern for the purpose of showing it to a friend who had expressed an interest in buying the gun. The killer had a police record. He was indicted and charged with both aggravated assault and homicide. The two charges applied to two different complainants, and the defendant pleaded guilty to both charges separately. He received a nine-month sentence for conviction on the charge of aggravated assault and a five-year probationary sentence for murder. It is evident that the victims of the assault and the homicide both precipitated the defendant's violent responses. Why the defendant's willingness to escalate the fight from one with pool cues to one with pool cues and a shotgun apparently failed to impress the particular judge who issued the two sentences is not clear, however. Texas law does not require a person to flee from an attack. He may retaliate. The problem, then, is to draw a fine legal distinction between avoidance, self-defense, and overreaction to an attack by means more powerful than that exerted by the assaulterer.

Another Saturday night drinking spree, this time involving a Black female, age 28, as the assailant, points to the inherent dangerousness of some Houston taverns as places to congregate or visit. The details of Case No. 229 are obscured by the intoxicated state of the material witnesses at the scene and, all in all, the behavior of the principals at first glance seems to defy rational explanation. The 22-year-old Black male victim died because he had the misfortune to be at the same tavern as his completely anonymous killer. The woman was sitting at a table when, suddenly and for no particular reason, she began to shout loudly and wave her .22 caliber pistol in the air. Several persons attempted to restrain her but the weapon went off and the young man was killed. Upon formal indictment, the woman was charged with three offenses. Two of these were dropped, but she was charged with murder, found guilty, and sentenced to five years in the Texas Department of Corrections.[7]

The facts of this case serve to remind us that any satisfactory explanation of the connection between an act of homicide and its legal sanctioning, if there is any, must be sought in the total culture rather than in specific social institutions. We have seen time and time again how the absence of any "malicious" and "conscious" intent generally results in a comparatively light punishment for the killer. On the other hand, if we shift from a psychological to a sociological interpretation, and thus change the emphasis from a concern with motive to one with consequence, we can ask how the cultural system applies different sanctions to homicidal behavior. It seems clear at this point that the governing mechanism of the sanctioning system regulates conduct in accordance with motive rather than overall consequence. The actual act of killing, therefore, is subject to sanctions, but the consequences to society of permitting individuals (i.e., not sanctioning individuals) to enter a tavern with a loaded and dangerous weapon fall well outside the scope of real public concern.

Case Nos. 8 and 222 both involve multiple killers and robbery. The victims in both cases were shot because they got in the way of the robbers. Although the exact details of Case No. 8 are unknown, it is evident from the police investigation that the victim, a 17-year-old White grocery clerk, was shot while five Black men robbed the drive-in grocery store. In Case No. 222, a 50-year-old Black man was shot and killed by two White men at 6:15 A.M. The two White men were holding several employees of a small peanut processing company at gunpoint while they were robbing the main office. The would be victim, as he arrived at work, saw what was happening. He turned his pick-up truck around and attempted to escape from the scene. He was hit with a .38 caliber bullet as he drove off. The police found the dead victim resting on the steering wheel in his truck. These killings, evidently, were incidental to the execution of another crime. The long-term prison sentences, up to 50 years for two killers, may be attributed to the juridical juxtaposition of robbery and homicide rather than homicide per se. This fact brings up the question of the relative magnitude of a crime; that is, does the actual or potential value of the stolen goods in terms of economic cost alone influence, or in any way correspond to, the severity of punishment for the thief and robber? The formulation and testing of a hypothesis on this subject, however, would require more detailed data than are now available. The difference between the 50-year sentences imposed on two defendants involved in the homicides and robberies at a small grocery store (Case No. 8) and at a food distributor company (Case No. 222) and the ten- and 15-year sentences imposed on two defendants, in Case No. 7, who killed a pushcart vendor with a few dollars on his person, strongly suggests that there is a relationship between the economic value of the stolen goods (or the socioeconomic status of the victims) and the sentence imposed on the robbers.[8]

In Case No. 7, for example, three Black youths in their late teens were driving around Houston seeking an opportunity to rob anybody for the purpose of obtaining money to buy an accessory for one of the youths' car. At about 9:40 A.M., the young men spotted an old man, a 67-year-old White male, who was standing next to his small pushcart selling ice cream, candy, etc. They parked the car and walked up to the old man and, according to several nearby eyewitnesses who overheard the conversation, demanded at gunpoint that the vendor hand over his money. The old man reached for his money but one of the young men fired his .22 caliber pistol three times before the victim could hand it over. The robbers took the vendor's money but for some unknown reason they put the money back into the victim's pocket before they fled the scene. The man died in the street and the three young men were apprehended by the police several days after the brutal slaying. The ten- and 15-year prison sentences clearly would take the killer and his associates off the streets for a long time, so the problem here is not to evaluate the appropriate length or kind of punishment for such an act. The problem rather is one of comparison. If the killers in the cases mentioned previously (Nos. 8 and 222), who incidentally were also in their late teens, had received similar prison sentences we could correlate the act of killing a stranger with a predictable degree of punishment.

The differences between a 15- and a 50-year prison sentence is a significant one. What factors can explain the difference? It may, of course, be argued that the circumstances of the various cases were such that different sentences were warranted. The singlemost discriminant factor here, however, appears to be the relative magnitude of the "property offense" rather than the absolute finality of the outcome for the victims. This interpretation should not be mistaken for a cultural rule that might specify that the penalty for killing the affluent person is greater than the penalty for killing persons at the lower end of the socioeconomic scale. Persons, or their status, may have relatively little to do with this problem. It is the "property offense" plus the "offense against the person" that appears to increase the magnitude of the penalty. The "property offense," which can be expressed absolutely in terms of monetary value, lends itself to objective measurement. In a materialistic technocratic culture like ours it would indeed be surprising if things were otherwise. But it is also evident from a review of the cases in this category that it is not necessarily the amount of money stolen in connection with a homicide that affects the severity of the penalty for the robber-killer. The potential monetary value also seems to play a significant role in determining and predicting the final outcome. How else does one explain the much shorter sentence in the killing of the old pushcart vendor by comparison to the sentences in Case Nos. 8 and 222? The following case may help provide an explanation.

In Case No. 45 the victim was a 19-year-old White gas station attendant who was working, together with the older station manager, on the graveyard shift. The killer, a 20-year-old Black male, drove up to the station requesting a fill-up. The killer, and his companion who later was apprehended but not prosecuted, left their car at the gasoline pumps and went into the station. One of them suddenly pointed a gun at the two gas station attendants. He demanded all the money in the cash register. As the younger man began to open the cash register he accidentally broke off the handle. He put the handle in his back pocket and that action was taken by the killer to mean that the attendant was going for a gun. The killer fired his .22 caliber pistol and the 19-year-old gas station attendant fell over dead. The killer and his companion, a 19-year-old Black male, emptied the cash register and left the station with their haul, which amounted to $80. Both men were later apprehended by the Houston police. The killer, who only briefly contemplated fleeing Houston, told his mother what he had done; they had decided together that he should give himself up and called the Homicide Division. In the killer's affidavit he stated to detectives that he had been drinking heavily the week before the robbery and that he had taken a strong eight-hour cough syrup on the morning of the robbery. When asked if he had any money, the killer produced a check in the amount of $149, which he said was his paycheck for the previous week. He had no other money and, having assumed that the gas station attendants would refuse to cash a check that large, he proceeded with the robbery and escalated matters further by killing the apparently non-compliant victim.

This 20-year-old Black was tried and convicted of murder. He was sentenced to serve 40 years in the Texas Department of Corrections. As deliberate, premeditated, and selfish as this murder may appear, it hardly seems more calloused than the murder of the old pushcart vendor. Could it be that somewhere in the judicial system there may be a rule that places the murder of a self-employed street vendor at one end of the economic scale and an employee of a major oil firm at another? Such a rule is not articulated in the Texas Penal Code. But the economic variable, together with the biased sentencing patterns of individual judges, does seem to influence the degree of punishment.

It might be added that just about this time in 1969 the number of gas station holdups in and around the City of Houston had become epidemic. Some gas station owners refused to keep their stations open at night when they were the most likely to be hit by robber-killers. The situation eventually grew to such serious proportions that most gas and service stations posted very explicit signs that they would accept only exact change, deposited in a strongbox, or credit cards from customers after 6:00 P.M. Gun control laws were not even mentioned as a possible alternative to the widespread threat to the business community from young robbers who, as we have seen, would kill to obtain small amounts of cash.

The 24-year-old Black male in Case No. 218, who held up a 20-year-old grocery clerk and killed him, can probably attribute part of his 99-year prison sentence to a growing public resentment of these random killings. He exchanged his freedom for an amount not exceeding $100 in small change.

The killer in Case No. 39, a Black male, age 19, typifies what many citizens probably regard as a vicious criminal or a person who completely disregards the rights of other members of society. Allan, as we might call him, had recently left prison and moved in with a girl friend. One day he encountered a former inmate friend of his and he suggested that the two of them hold up a tool manufacturing company. His former prison associate only reluctantly agreed to go along and it is from him that the police reconstructed the crime and built the case against Allan. The two men entered the tool company and held up two men in the main office. They got about $80 in cash to split between them. As they were about to leave the office, Allan turned toward one of the men and asked him to take his watch off. The man complied with the request. Allan then fired his .32 caliber pistol at the man for no apparent reason. When his friend asked him why he had done it, Allan replied, "I do not like for people to laugh at me and he thought that I was bull shitting!" Allan further said that he hoped the man would die from the wound. The two accomplices then went their separate ways. Allan joined a dice game where he lost most of the money he obtained in the robbery. He was later apprehended, charged, and convicted of murder. He was sentenced to death. His reluctant friend was also apprehended, charged, and convicted. Since he had not pulled the trigger or initiated the robbery itself, he was spared a death sentence but was given a 30-year prison term.

This was not the first and only time that Allan and his friend appeared in the homicide statistics. Both men were involved in other robbery and murder cases (Nos. 59 and 237). The three robbery and murder cases (Nos. 39, 59, and 237) occurred within the same week. None of the robberies could be said to have significantly enriched the two men, but they nevertheless chose to risk a murder charge to steal a little cash.

In many of the cases described earlier there has been a recognizable element of bravado, desperation, impulse for self-destruction, or what might even be called a frontier element; that is, some sort of challenge and response between victims and killers. In the cases that combine robbery and homicide there is an undisputed element of raw violence. In Case No. 136, for example, we clearly see a touch of viciousness. A Chinese grocery store owner was surprised by a 23-year-old Black youth who walked into his store, pointed a .32 or .38 caliber pistol at the grocer and asked him to turn around. The grocer complied and was immediately shot in the back. The killer then emptied the cash register and fled the store. All this took place before several eyewitnesses. These witnesses reported to the police that they were quite sure that the killer shot his victim before saying or doing anything about the grocer's money. This was, in other words, a homicide *followed* by a robbery. The killer, who was identified by one of the three eyewitnesses at the store, was quickly apprehended. He was wanted by the police on a previous charge of robbery by firearms. A Houston jury found little difficulty in reaching a verdict of guilty and recommending a death sentence.

Case No. 81 adds a novel dimension to the robbery-murder type of killing. In this case, a Black male, age 22, sought employment at a chemical company. He arrived at 7:10 A.M., was briefly interviewed by the White 65-year-old owner of the company, and hired. The owner of the company was sweeping the floor and, as the event was related by the owner's son, told the man that as soon as he had finished he would get the new employee started on the job. The elderly man was still sweeping the floor when, according to his son, the young Black shouted "Hey!" As the man turned around, he faced the barrel of a .45 pistol. The "employee" at the point of the gun forced both men into their private office and demanded money. The elderly man was overheard to say something like "Now, that isn't necessary." The owner jumped the robber and his son rushed into the office. While the three men struggled over the gun it discharged and the owner fell to the floor. After the owner had hit the floor the killer fired a bullet at close range into the victim's back. The son, who had managed to grab a broom, tried to defend himself with the broom and, surprisingly, the killer ran from the office. The would-be robber left without any money. He was apprehended by the police at a later date in connection with another robbery. A jury found the killer guilty and recommended a death sentence.

It is appropriate to close the descriptive and analytical study of individual homicide episodes with Case No. 150. In this case, a 37-year-old police officer was killed while answering a burglary call at a local high school. The killer, a White male, age 32, was later apprehended and sentenced to life in the Texas Department of Corrections.

The police officer's death, taken together with the fact that at least 32 other Houston police officers were shot in 1969, attests to the dangerousness of police work in any community where citizens are personally armed. The point to be made is simply this: Despite the availability of personal weapons for self-defense, and the technical know-how in the effective use of such weapons, the individual's personal safety is far from being secure.

Order and Disorder

The killer who chooses a stranger as his victim overtly threatens the preservation of social order. This generalization is supported by two sets of facts: the empirical data from 1969 on judicial outcomes for apprehended killers and the renewed emphasis in Texas and other states on more severe penalties for crimes against "strangers."

Section 19.03 of the 1974 Texas Penal Code, which may be challenged on grounds of its unconstitutionality, specifically states that persons who are found to be guilty of murder of particular persons (i.e., some "strangers") must be punished by a mandatory death sentence or life imprisonment. The "Capital Murder" statute applies to the killing of peace officers, firemen, and incarcerated prisoners. More importantly, however, the statute specifies that a person who intentionally commits murder in connection with an act of kidnapping, burglary, robbery, aggravated rape, or arson, also must be given a mandatory death sentence or life imprisonment. This section of the 1974 Texas Penal Code, which in effect reinstitutes the death penalty for certain crimes, was enacted *after* the U.S. Supreme Court (in a 5–4 decision in the 1972 case of *Furman v. Georgia*) found that the death penalty was unconstitutional on grounds that it violated the eighth amendment to the constitution protecting citizens against "cruel and unusual punishment." The final outcome, which may be determined by a test case, could result in a new interpretation by the U.S. Supreme Court of an unenforceable capital murder statute in the Texas Penal Code. The point to be made here, of course, is not whether the death penalty is a deterrent to crime or if its application by the state is cruel and unusual. The problem is to explain why one kind of killing is punished more harshly than another. The answer must reside with the overriding concern of any organized society to maintain order.

Social order, by definition, implies that public forms of interaction must depend upon the observance of basic rules. These rules, which may range anywhere from optional courtesies to mandatory regulations, enable persons in society to predict the behavior and actions of others. Predictability in social relations is taken so much for granted by most of us that we tend to forget that social relations would become anarchical if such predictability did not exist. Lyn Lofland's sociological study, *A World of Strangers* (1973), appropriately subtitled *Order and Action in Urban Public Space,* illustrates how citizens in the public world of the city learn and transmit rules that enable strangers to coexist and minimally cooperate.[9]

Social cooperation requires that two or more persons observe the same rules. Such rules, which may take the form of reciprocal rights and duties, create a network of what might be termed symmetrical social relationships. Both parties in a symmetrical relationship are aware that one person's actions affect the other and that sustained reciprocity requires some form of bilateral exchange. An asymmetrical relationship, however, does not have any common ground from which to establish, continue, or terminate mutually recognized obligations. This is a roundabout way of saying that the person who kills along with some other form of antisocial behavior customarily lacks any sense of what might be called reciprocal altruism.[10] Such a person does not see that, minimally, his actions ought to take into consideration the simple fact that other persons may not share his views or, in the case of robbery, notions concerning the transfer of property.

Killings among intimates, as previously noted, are generally viewed by society at large as less problematical than are killings that involve strangers. This is true in part because intimates form symmetrical social relationships that insulate them within a series of obligations subject to enforcement by social and psychological sanctions. The robber, rapist, killer, or even the self-styled terrorist is not restrained in his behavior by anything other than criminal sanctions.

Asymmetrical contacts between an individual and society at large have the greatest potential for disruption, chaos, and social disorder. The killing of police officers, firemen, and public officials generally and symbolically threatens the social order and public sanctions against killers in this category must therefore be particularly explicit and severe. The social commentator, Vance Packard, has suggested that U.S. society is becoming a nation of strangers.[11] His thesis, which is well supported by carefully researched information, is that social mobility has created social situations and communities that place much less reliance on primary group relationships and temporal commitments to specific neighborhoods. This will, of course, lead to a future in which the principal sources of social control may reside in public institutions. These institutions may, as adumbrated in the findings of this book, be the least effective means of defining, suppressing, and sanctioning undesirable forms of human behavior.

6
Homicide as Custom and Crime

Introduction

Nullem crimen sine lege is a basic and universal premise of criminal law. Homicide, accordingly, is only properly viewed as criminal behavior if and when an act of killing is defined as unlawful. In this chapter we will consider and apply those criminal statutes from Texas that discriminate between different kinds of lawful and unlawful homicide pertaining to the judicial outcome for known killers. The high number of Houston homicides, together with the finding that most of the apprehended killers escape any form of legal sanction, will be considered relative to various legal distinctions between murder (with or without malice), homicide by negligence, and justifiable and excusable homicide. The complex connections between social custom and judicial process, as adumbrated in the previous chapters, may be clarified, if only partially, by a careful analysis of the official legal sanctions that apply to an act of killing.

Although nearly 90 percent of all reported homicides in 1969 resulted in the apprehension of the alleged killers, fewer than 50 percent of the suspects were negatively sanctioned for their acts. These notable discrepancies between apprehended suspect and convicted offender can, in part, be explained by pointing to the differences between lawful and unlawful homicide. It is the initial purpose of a criminal proceeding to determine whether a particular act fits into one or the other of these two general categories.

The more general social ends to be served by criminal proceeding are, according to the eminent jurist William L. Prosser, "to protect and vindicate the interests of the public as a whole, by punishing the offender or eliminating him from society, either permanently or for a limited time, by reforming him or teaching him not to repeat the offense, and by deterring others from imitating him."[1] Prosser further notes that a "criminal prosecution is not concerned in any way with compensation of the injured individual against whom the crime is committed, and his [the victim's] only part in it is that of an accuser and a witness for the state. So far as the criminal law is concerned, he will leave the courtroom empty-handed."[2] The victim of a homicide is always a silent and fictitious witness for the state. The separation in modern American law of criminal and tort liability has not only made it exceedingly difficult for a victim's survivors to seek damages from a killer, but it may actually have eliminated a potentially powerful deterrent against homicidal behavior. A tort, which defies precise definition, is generally viewed as a civil wrong. It is an offense against a private individual, as opposed to an offense against the public at large, for which the law may provide a remedy in the form of restitution or financial compensation for damages. Several recent studies of victim compensation programs illustrate both the opportunities for and obstacles against further innovation in this important area of criminal justice. The increasing rate of crimes against the person at the same time reminds us that, as a society, we cannot afford to suppress innovative approaches that may improve the system of criminal justice.[3]

The observation to be made here is that the Texas Penal Code explicitly emphasizes the legal rights of killers. A victim has no rights and his survivors acquire or exercise no rights whatever. This is perhaps best illustrated by the fact that the law of homicide carries no provision for survivorship indemnity or compensation. This is almost the exact opposite of early Anglo-Saxon and English law, and many non-Western legal systems as well, in which the victim's survivors, legal heirs, or relatives received compensation in different kinds of homicide. The modern criminal law has completely transformed the ancient view of homicide as a wrong against a victim and his family to its modern version that views homicide as an offense against the state. The prevalent view of crime as strictly a "social problem" therefore holds no surprise.

The substantive criminal law of Texas is the product of a long common-law tradition that dates back to and is derived from Anglo-Saxon and early English law. The first Texas Penal Code was enacted in 1856 and, except for some minor recodifications, it has survived 117 years without substantial change. The public recognition in 1965 that the Penal Code ought more closely to reflect the changing ideological and socioeconomic conditions of the twentieth century resulted in the enactment of a new Texas Penal Code. This new code (hereafter referred to as the 1974 Code) was enacted by the 63rd Legislature and became effective on January 1, 1974. Charts 2 and 3 in Appendix D outline the differences between the homicide statutes that were in effect before and after the enactment of the 1974 Code. The most perceptible differences between the old and the new codes pertaining to offenses against the person basically amount to minor semantic changes in terminology and the introduction of Capital Murder as a special category of homicide. It must be noted and emphasized that the 1974 Code, if applied to the 1969 cases, would have produced minor differences, if any, in outcomes for apprehended and convicted killers.

A comparative study of the old and the new penal codes does not reveal any major and significant differences in the homicide statutes other than a change in wording or contextual organization. The 1974 Code, for example, eliminated some 67 different usages associated with the *mens rea* doctrine—which alludes to the medieval notion of an evil-meaning or guilty mind—and substituted four terms to categorize a person's culpability and state of mind. An act is thus deemed lawful or unlawful on the basis of the actor's mentality. Criminal culpability implies that a person behaves *intentionally, knowingly, recklessly* or that he is simply *criminally negligent*. These concepts are graded in terms of their relative magnitude. A person who commits an act *intentionally* is penalized more heavily than a person who is *negligent*. The criterion used to measure the seriousness of a particular act in this scheme is the behavior of a fictional entity characterized as "an ordinary person."[4]

Professor Charles P. Bubany's law review article, "The Texas Penal Code of 1974," illustrates how the new conceptual system may be applied in a homicide prosecution:

> Assume that a defendant strikes a pregnant woman in the abdomen and as a result the baby dies shortly after birth. In a homicide prosecution the evidence might show any of the following: (1) if he struck the woman knowing she was pregnant and for the purpose of killing the child, his conduct was *intentional;* (2) if he knew she was pregnant and that his blows were likely to cause the death, his conduct was *knowing,* even if his only purpose was to cause her pain; (3) if he knew she was pregnant and knew that death of the baby might result, but he did not care, he was only *reckless;* (4) if he knew she was pregnant but did not think his blow was hard enough to hurt the baby, or he did not advert to the fact that she was pregnant although it was plainly observable, he acted with *criminal negligence;* or (5) if he did not know she was pregnant and to the ordinary observer she did not look pregnant, he did not have any culpable mental state, at least with respect to the baby's death as a result (ibid., 1974, p. 306).[5]

The distinctions between lawful and unlawful homicide that emerge from the grading of offenses in accordance with the degree of mental culpability call attention to a basic premise and a fundamental weakness in the criminal law: The classification of an act of killing requires the sanctioning agent—whether a legislature, a district attorney, or a trial judge and jury—to infer *motivation* and *intention* from the killer's behavior. The criminal law is thus almost singularly directed toward the determination of culpability on the basis of psychological variables. The social and cultural implications of a particular act for society at large also are only of tertiary interest to lawyers and judges who are charged with prosecuting and defending killers. The system of criminal justice thus fails to either remedy or in any way resolve "the problem of crime" because it only processes individual offenders in terms of what, at best, must remain uncertain psychological factors resulting in legal culpability or innocence.[6] If a Houston killer can demonstrate the slightest element of "self-defense" (i.e., he did not set out to kill the victim but his response was precipitated by a stimulus from his victim) he downgrades the act to either justifiable homicide or murder without malice. The excessive reliance by the classificatory scheme on such factors as "malice," "state of mind," "intent," and "motive"—which take its ultimate meaningless form in the legal fiction of "the reasonable man"—derives less from the findings of psychology and psychiatry than from prescient and lay presumptions about human behavior.[7] It is, in part, these commonly held presumptions about human behavior that anthropologists and behavioral scientists generally label "custom." Consider for a moment, by way of example, why jurists in Western cultures emphasize such factors as motive and intent rather than stressing the social consequences of an act. A homicide victim is just as dead whether his killer intended to kill him or not and his survivors are just as parentless or childless whether the state absolves the killer of criminal culpability or executes him. Permit me to stretch the example further by contrasting the common-law view of homicide with killing in Eskimo society. The eminent anthropologist E. A. Hoebel has suggested that the Eskimos only developed a form of "rudimentary law" and that they did not collectively punish a killer unless his act, and especially if he repeated it, visibly threatened the survival and welfare of the social unit as a whole. Whether the killer was motivated by passion, wife-stealing, megalomania, or the sadistic pleasure of inflicting pain and suffering upon others was not a deciding factor. The behavior of killing per se, and its social consequences, such as loss of social cohesiveness and cooperation in the interest of survival, were principal factors used to determine the degree of lawfulness or unlawfulness of a killer's homicidal act or acts.[8]

Sir Stephen's distinction between murder and manslaughter squarely demonstrates how psychological rather than sociological considerations dominate the Anglo-Saxon view of relative criminality. He says: "in murder the act or omission by which death is caused is attended by one or more of the states of mind included under the description of malice aforethought, whereas in cases of manslaughter malice aforethought is absent."[9] Justice Holmes (1881) cites an earlier work by Stephen and elaborates the argument for accepting the manslaughter definition that resolves itself into the formula: Murder minus malice aforethought equals manslaughter.[10] Other jurists, who are called upon to develop legislative measures to alleviate many human and social problems, often completely ignore the insights and findings of modern science. If, for example, "the principal end of the law of homicide is the prevention of behavior which may cause death"[11] it should be asked whether simplifying the homicide statutes in fact reduces the number of killings. The following statement from the Foreword to the 1974 Code shows that the legal community is aware of these problems but that significant reforms insofar as the control of interpersonal violence is concerned must await the passing of time.

> The 1856 Penal Code was of course designed for a state much different from the Texas of today. The Texas of a century ago was a rural society with an agricultural economy. The civil war and two world wars had not been fought, the automobile and airplane had not been invented, and no one had heard of Sigmund Freud or Karl Marx. It should come as no surprise, therefore, that the old code punished horse theft more severely than murder without malice, made forgery of land titles a more serious offense than forgery of government bonds, and justified killing the wife's lover (but not the husband's mistress) if taken in the act of adultery. . . . Not all of the new code is appropriate for the 21st century [sic]. Chapter 46 in particular, which deals with weapons, retains too much of the frontier in its treatment of firearms. Chapter 9 (justification), although significantly reducing the amount of violence lawful under the old code, still permits too much force on too many occasions. But these defects pale beside the achievements of the new code in making our penal law responsive and respectable.[12]

In Chapter 3, I stated a hypothesis concerning the relationship between the killer's social status and the final legal disposition of a homicide case. It was found, in the case data presented in Chapters 3, 4, and 5 (with few notable exceptions), that there is a statistically significant correlation between the degree of killer-victim intimacy and the severity of legal punishment for the killers. Let us now reformulate the earlier hypothesis and state it in its broadest possible terms. First, however, it is necessary to restate the killer-victim relationships in terms of positions on a hypothetical continuum; that is, killers and victims who are relatives, friends, or associates occupy one end of the continuum and killers and victims who are strangers occupy the other end. The relationships, at the two extremes, respectively, fall within either "private" or "public" domains. Killings among intimates fall in the private domain and killings among strangers fall in the public domain. This hypothesis can be restated to incorporate both notions: *The severity of penalty for an act of homicide varies directly with the placement of an offense within domains on a continuum.* A corollary of this hypothesis holds that the severity of punishment for the killer depends directly on the place assigned to a particular offense along the private-public poles on that continuum.

We are now returning, full circle, to the beginnings of the common-law tradition, which, according to Stephen and others, shifted the emphasis from the compensation of a victim's survivors to the collective interests of the state. The state, as previously noted, transforms the ancient rights of indemnity from survivors to a right by the state to punish the offender. The data indicate that the most public forms of killing (i.e., "public" in terms of the social distance in the killer-victim relationship and not the physical setting) meet with the greatest concern by the state and its official representatives. It is assumed, generally, that the greater severity of punishment for the most "public crimes" somehow helps reduce the volume of crime whereas the state, more often than not, views itself as quite powerless to prevent crimes of passion within the four walls of a home. The Texas law of murder, manslaughter, assault and battery, and justifiable homicide amply documents these simple points.

Murder and Manslaughter

The Texas State Legislature passed its first murder statute on February 12, 1858. The wording of this statute derives directly from English common-law tradition. The statute, in part, reads as follows: "Whoever with malice aforethought shall kill any person within this State shall be guilty of murder. Murder is distinguishable from every other species of homicide by the absence of circumstances which reduce the offense to negligent homicide or manslaughter, or which excuse or justify the homicide."[13] This statute was subsequently amended and repealed by successive legislative acts in 1913 and 1927. The homicide statutes that apply to all the cases for 1969 largely represent minor revisions of the 1927 murder statute.

Article 1256 of the Texas Penal Code defines murder simply as the *voluntary killing* of any person in the absence of any additional circumstances that may reduce the offense to negligent, excusable, or justifiable homicide. Although this statute has eliminated any distinction between different degrees of murder, together with the common-law distinction between murder and manslaughter, it has not preserved the distinction between the element of "malice aforethought" and "without malice" as part of the instructions to a jury.[14] Subsequent efforts in the new and revised 1974 Code to eliminate the ambiguous element of malice aforethought do not, as indicated previously, affect the judicial findings in the 1969 cases.

Article 1257 of the Texas Penal Code states that the "punishment for murder shall be death or confinement in the penitentiary for life or for any term of years not less than two." The jury, which acts upon instructions from the trial judge, can recommend punishment within these broad limits. In his instructions to the jury, the trial judge is bound by a duty to define the difference between malice aforethought and murder without malice. Unless the jury believes that the guilty defendant in a murder case acted with malice aforethought, it cannot assess a punishment longer than five years. The distinctions here are therefore of critical importance for assessing the severity of the penalty, called constructive interpretations in legal language, that may be appropriate for a particular crime. The definitions of malice in the Texas Penal Code may serve as worthy examples of semantic muddling. Malice, generally, refers to a quality or state of mind that can be inferred from observation of an individual's behavior. Since a jury cannot have the events of a homicide recreated for it in the courtroom, they must rely on verbal descriptions of the act and then, on the basis of this evidence only, make a prescient inference about the state of mind of the defendant in a murder case.

Various subsections of Article 1256 may be excerpted to illustrate the subjectivity of any finding that purports to discriminate between malice and its absence. Section 6, for example, describes malice aforethought as "all those states of mind under which the killing of a person takes place without any cause which will in law justify, excuse or extenuate the homicide. It is the doing of a wrongful act intentionally, without just cause or excuse. It is a condition of the mind which shows a heart regardless of social duty and fatally bent on mischief, the existence of which is inferred from acts committed or words spoken."[15] Interestingly enough, another subsection reports: " 'Legal malice' does not have its popular meaning of hatred, ill will or hostility towards another but includes all those states of mind in which a killing takes place without any cause which in law justify, excuse or extenuate the act, and may exist without any former grudge or antecedent menace."[16] Compare this to: " 'Murder without malice' is not a degree of the crime of murder but is a murder committed under the influence of sudden passion arising from an adequate cause. . . ."[17] Malice may arise from a long nurtured grudge or be activated in the mind immediately before killing. This eliminates much of the concern with motive and such factors as intent and premeditation. "It is not necessary that any length of time should intervene between the formation of the intent to kill and the killing."[18] This statement, interpreted at face value, allows for the simultaneity of intent, motive, and act. It is no longer a mystery why a person who arms himself with a handgun before attending a social gathering is said to lack the motive and intent to kill before he might be provoked by his victim. In case after case we have observed how the act of carrying a gun is not interpreted as "generalized malice," but may it really be debated whether a person who arms himself with a loaded and dangerous weapon completely lacks any intent to use it and, further, whether he cannot be provoked into using his gun? This question, i.e., inferring malice on grounds that the defendant carried and used a deadly weapon to execute the killing, is left entirely for the jury to decide. In a community in which it is customary for many people to carry personal firearms allegedly for the protection of self, it is not unreasonable on our part to assume that a jury drawn from that same community would not a priori equate being armed with a person's motive and intent to kill.

The 40th legislature repealed Article 1244 of the Texas Penal Code in 1927. This act eliminated manslaughter as a category of homicide and thus broke with common-law tradition effective up to this date. The 1927 murder act thus merged murder and manslaughter under one single offense. A person found guilty of murder, however, is significantly affected by the jural distinction between malice aforethought and murder without malice. In either case, the judge must instruct the trial jury to decide the question whether the person found guilty of murder could be said to have acted with or without malice. Article 1257c contains the statutory instructions for issuing a charge of murder without malice:

> In all cases tried under the provisions of this Act it shall be the duty of the Court, where the facts represent the issue of murder without malice, to instruct the jury that murder without malice is a voluntary homicide committed without justification or excuse under the immediate influence of a sudden passion arising from an adequate cause, by which it is meant such cause as would commonly produce a degree of anger, rage, resentment, or terror in a person of ordinary temper sufficient to render the mind incapable of cool reflection, and in appropriate terms in the charge to apply the law to the facts as developed from the evidence.[19]

The most critical distinction between the two charges to a jury appear to be the presence or absence of an intent to kill. This criterion is so fraught with ambiguities that only extreme acts of murder, such as premeditated assassination or killing in response to a personal provocation or threat, can be rationally categorized as belonging to one or the other of the two penal categories.

Article 1258 enlarges the grounds for lawful killing by including consideration of threats and the victim's character as ameliorating circumstances contributing to removal of malice from the act. The article reads as follows:

> Where a defendant accused of murder seeks to justify himself on the ground of threats against his own life, he may be permitted to introduce evidence of the threats made, but the same shall not be regarded as affording a justification for the killing unless it be shown that at the time of the homicide the person killed by some act then

> done manifested an intention to execute the threat so made. In every instance where proof of threats has been made, *it shall be competent to introduce evidence of the general character of the deceased.* Such evidence shall extend only to an inquiry as to whether the deceased was a man of *violent or dangerous character,* or a man of kind and inoffensive disposition, or whether he was such a person as might reasonably be expected to execute a threat made (italics added).[20]

This article, among other things, specifically illustrates the role of the deceased victim in a murder trial. Here it appears that the victim's character, reputation, personal disposition, or personality can be resurrected for presentation before a judge and jury. The point to be made is very simple: The issue in the judicial decision-making process is not one of dealing with homicide as a wrong against a particular individual and his survivors. A victim characterized as dumb, illiterate, and quarrelsome is unlikely to find much sympathy from jurors who are instructed that the victim's character may be considered an important factor in reducing the penalty for the convicted murderer. Although it is easy to become sympathetic to the underlying considerations of fairness behind the wording of Article 1258, it must not be forgotten that the whole legal system, founded as it is on cultural definitions of both morality and justice, nominally purports to treat all citizens as equals before the law. This view is at best a metaphor.

Suppose, to use a different example, that Texans generally take pride in their tradition of friendliness, forthrightness, and sense of setting things right without too much fuss about what the lawbooks might have to say about their behavior. If this reputation is believed by strangers or visitors to the State of Texas would that lessen the penalty if the outsider killed a Texan? I personally doubt that any Texas jury would accept such a defense based as it were on the outsider's general assumptions about typical behavior patterns among Texas citizens. The court and the jury generally would undoubtedly conclude that such a defense was based on just so much sociological nonsense. I would personally agree with such a view but must add that the assessment of a victim's character, unless a psychiatric record were available, similarly is based on faulty psychological inference. Does it make any difference if the deceased victim never saw himself as "a man of violent or dangerous character," should his mother define him as such to establish the fact beyond a doubt, or would it be sufficient to bring in a previous police record, if any? The reader can predict with reasonable accuracy what a jury will do if a defendant's attorney explains that his client simply shot first because he knew of the killer's reputation as a tough character. An observant visitor to a criminal trial in Houston cannot fail to notice the well-dressed and groomed defendants who almost appear "out of character" as one listens to the prosecutor outline his charges. But what defense attorney would be foolish enough to ignore the subjective impression on the jury of his client? The victim can too readily be verbally described as "one of those toughs" who made life difficult for everyone around him, including that of the killer.

Articles 1266 and 1267 further define the conditions and limitations of threats: "it is necessary that the threat be seriously made, and it is for the jury to determine whether the threat, if made, was seriously made or was merely idle and with no intention of executing the same" and a "threat that a person will do any act merely to protect himself, or to prevent the commission of some unlawful act by another, does not come within the meaning of this chapter."[21]

Assault and Battery

In Chapter 1 it was noted that the ratio of homicide to aggravated assault, for the nation as a whole, approximated 1 to 20 as a ten-year average. The number of assaults, and especially aggravated assaults and battery, thus by far exceed the number of homicides. All or most of these assaults were associated with the use of deadly weapons and, save for the availability of excellent emergency medical services, many more assaults might have resulted in death.[22] The violent behavior that ultimately leads to injury and death is therefore quite similar although, in principle, the victim's condition–whether dead or alive–conveniently and legally serves to categorize the offense. The possible punishment, however, for assault and battery, by comparison to the punishment for murder, seems almost trivial. Article 1145 of the Texas Penal Code provides that *"The punishment for a simple assault or for assault and battery shall be a fine not less than five nor more than twenty-five dollars."*[23] Any assault, in theory, that falls short of homicide is viewed with the same seriousness as a minor traffic violation! Any jury in a murder case is therefore faced with a terrible dilemma. Jurors must decide on grounds of the aggressor's psychological motive and intent only whether the homicide resulted from a simple assault or if it was perpetrated from the beginning with an unlawful intention to take someone else's life. The problem here, as I see it, is a classical one; that is, any theory and system of criminal law must continually seek to balance the overall social desirability of maximum personal freedom with the necessity of limiting such freedoms by various kinds of restraints. Any offense against the person, therefore, must be weighed on a scale calibrated to measure degrees of "offensiveness." Brief examination of the statutes pertaining to assault and battery inform us on the intervals and marks on the public scale designed to measure criminal culpability. I intend to show how the interval between aggravated assault and battery and murder is indeed very large, whereas the interval, or degree of separateness, between an assault and a killing in reality is very small. It is not necessary for our purposes to describe and discuss different kinds of assaults (such as assault with a motor vehicle or hazing) but simply to look briefly at those aspects of the Texas Penal Code that concern various technical distinctions between lawful and unlawful violence against the person.

Article 1138 of the Texas Penal Code defines assault and battery as the "use of any unlawful violence upon the person of another with intent to injure him, whatever be the means or the degree of violence used, is an assault and battery. Any attempt to commit a battery, or any threatening gesture showing in itself or by works accompanying it, an immediate intention, coupled with an ability to commit a battery, is an assault."[24]

Article 1139 of the Texas Penal Code clarifies the meaning of "intent" by stating that an injury caused by violence presupposes an intent to harm unless the aggressor can positively demonstrate his innocence of intention or otherwise excuse his act by defining it as accidental. Article 1142 provides an assailant with substantial grounds for defending his act as well within the scope of lawful violence.

> Violence used to the person does not amount to an assault or battery in the following cases:
>
> 1. In the exercise of the right of moderate restraint or correction given by law to the parent over the child, the guardian over the ward, the master over his apprentice, the teacher over the scholar [sic].
> 2. [Omitted.]
> 3. To preserve the peace, or to prevent the commission of offenses.
> 4. In preventing or interrupting an intrusion upon the lawful possession of property.
> 5. [Omitted.]
> 6. In self defense, or in defense of another against unlawful violence offered to his person or property.
> 7. Where violence is permitted to effect a lawful purpose, only that degree of force must be used which is necessary to effect such purpose.[25]

A citizen of the State of Texas thus may use violence to defend his person and property, to defend other persons and their property, and, generally, to help preserve the peace. These rights clearly derive in part from the conditions of a frontier society where men and women often had to combine the role of judge, jury, and executioner.

The criterion of "aggravation" escalates the offensiveness of an assault and battery and, in accordance with Article 1148 of the Texas Penal Code, can result in a legal punishment of a fine anywhere between $25 to $1,000 and/or imprisonment in jail from one month to no more than two years. It may be recalled that the penalty for murder without malice is imprisonment in jail for a period between two and five years. The difference between a serious aggravated assault and battery and murder (without malice) quite literally depends on whether the victim is alive or dead. The penal code is silent on the question of damages for the victim of an assault. It is unlikely that any person with only modest financial means at his disposal will be able to obtain the services of an attorney who can bring suit for damages under various civil laws that concern damages for torts. An aggressor, of course, would view the situation from a different perspective if he knew that his act of violence might result not only in a prison sentence, and a relatively light financial penalty paid to the state, but also a tort action resulting in very heavy financial obligations toward his victim. If an aggressor ever did think this out, he might reasonably conclude that it would be better to kill his victim than simply assault him. In this way the murderer would answer solely to the State and face a comparatively lighter penalty than would be possible if the victim were alive to sue him for personal damages. These, and other similar views, imply a certain rationality of mind on the part of aggressor-killers that probably is not there. The importance of this discussion, however, is to consider the legal sources of criminal law of persons.[26] It appears that social tradition, as reflected in publicly expressed views on individual rights and freedom, is firmly embedded in both statutes and court decisions involving violence and killing.

Two additional articles from the Texas Penal Code individually address the question of the unlawful use of weapons and the penalty for combining assault and battery with an unsuccessful but intended act to kill.

Article 1151 of the Texas Penal Code states that "If any person shall willfully commit an assault or an assault and battery upon another with a pistol, dirk, dagger, slung shot [sic], sword cane, spear or knuckles made of any metal or made of any hard substance, bowie knife, or any knife manufactured or sold for the purposes of offense or defense, while the same is being carried unlawfully by the person committing said assault, he shall be deemed guilty of an assault with a prohibited weapon and upon conviction shall be punished by a fine not to exceed two hundred dollars or by imprisonment in jail not to exceed two years, or by confinement in the penitentiary for not more than five years."[27] The reader may recall that no less than 86 percent of all 1969 killings involved the use of firearms. The Houston Homicide Division reported that guns were used in no less than 1,151 separate offenses involving assault and battery during 1969. Although I do not have any firsthand data on how many persons were charged with carrying or using a prohibited weapon, as applicable under the authority provided by Article 1151 quoted above, it seems conservative to estimate that fewer than 10 percent of all police cases included a charge for the violation of this Article.

At first glance this may seem highly incongruous: We have here a statute that specifically prohibits the unlawful carrying and use of prohibited weapons and also a seeming lack of vigorous prosecution of persons under the criminal statute that provides the police with this authority. The problem, of course, is not that simple. How, for example, should one interpret the intent of Article 1151 against the intent of Article 1, Section 3, of the Constitution of Texas which reads: *"Every citizen shall have the right to keep and bear arms in the lawful defense of himself or the State"?*[28] To some, no doubt, it is a constitutional right to own weapons. Since many assaults with weapons and most homicides involve first-time offenders, it seems almost a moot point to include the constitutional provision of Section 23 that limits the right by stating "the Legislature shall have power, by law, to regulate the wearing of arms, with a view to prevent crime."[29] As applied to the data for 1969, the right to bear and use dangerous weapons by far outweighs any corresponding and opposite duty on the part of the citizenry to refrain from exercising this right in all but the most life-threatening situations.

Article 1160 takes us back to the question of "how to measure the seriousness of an offense." It is not, as we have seen, the use of violence per se, the use of a deadly weapon per se, or the victim's condition that critically discriminate between lesser and greater forms of offenses against the person. The wording of Article 1160, as with the articles pertaining to murder, discriminates among offenses on the basis of the assailant's motives, intentions, mental capacities, and the context or social situation in which the killing episode unfolds. If "the situation" involves acts that are part of the assault or homicide–such as rape, robbery, or burglary–the outcome for the assaulter or killer is gauged in relationship to the seriousness of his auxiliary crime.

Article 1160 reads as follows:

> If any person shall assault another with intent to murder, he shall be confined in the penitentiary not less than two nor more than fifteen years; provided that if the jury [sic] find that the assault was committed without malice, the penalty assessed shall be not less than one nor more than three years confinement in the penitentiary;

> if the assault be made with a bowie-knife or dagger, or in disguise, or by laying in wait, or by shooting into a private residence, the punishment shall be double.
>
> Sec. 2. Upon the trial of any person for assault with intent to murder, the Court, in its charge to the jury, shall define malice aforethought and in a proper case murder without malice, and instruct the jury touching the application of the law to the facts.[30]

The penal clause attached to this Article clearly implies that the law distinguishes between what might be called the "forthright" element of an assault and battery and its opposite element of "slyness." Perhaps this is an example of the tenacity of custom and social tradition. The assailant who squares off with his victim in face-to-face combat is not viewed in the same way as the assassin who shoots or stabs his victim in the back! These brief comments must suffice as background for the following discussion of justifiable homicide.

Justifiable Homicide

The Texas Penal Code provides that it is lawful and therefore justifiable to kill a human being under any one of the following circumstances: (1) Killing a public enemy, (2) executing a convict, (3) acting in response to a lawful order or directive by a police officer, (4) aiding a police officer, (5) preventing the escape of a person legally apprehended or captured, (6) suppressing a riot, (7) preventing the successful completion of a criminal or felonious act, (8) responding by a husband to provocation by an act of adultery, (9) defending a person or property, (10) defending oneself against an unlawful attack, and (11) defending or upholding property rights.

These 11 justifications can be divided into two general subcategories of justifiable homicide. In one we can include all those killings that result from some form of official law enforcement (1 through 6 above) and, in the other, we include all those killings that result from the act of private citizens who kill in a lawful manner (7 through 11 above). The category of justifiable homicide, which principally concerns killings by private citizens, is, of course, of primary interest in this study.

The statutory problems with those articles that provide individuals great latitude in the use of deadly force are aptly summarized in a comment by William M. Ravkind. He says:

> The provisions of the Penal Code concerning justifiable homicide and their judicial interpretation do not reflect the tempo of our modern-day society, but rather are representative of the code of the "old west." Much of the Penal Code has remained unchanged since the date of its enactment in 1856. Specifically, in the area of justifiable homicide, no significant attempt on the part of the legislature has been made to modernize our law. Our courts have not facilitated the difficulties, but seem to have placed more emphasis upon technical rules of statutory construction than upon the development of a law to meet an everchanging society. Certainly, the legislature could perform no finer service than to reconsider the laws which shelter the violent elements of our society and which were outdated several decades ago.[31]

A quick glance at Table XVIII shows the number of justifiable homicides reported for 1969. None of these have been used in any of the statistical analyses presented in the previous chapters. These cases, all of which were thoroughly investigated by the Homicide Division, were of such a clear-cut nature that the district attorney could dismiss each case as lawful, or non-criminal, and therefore not subject to any further legal action by the State. Other cases, subsequent to the investigation by the police and evaluation by the grand jury, also resulted in findings of justifiable homicide. It must suffice to say that the decision to bring a case before a grand jury or to dismiss it outright as justifiable homicide is a discretionary right that is exercised by the district attorney. One can guess, from the list of circumstances tabulated in Table XVIII, that the majority of cases involving robbery, burglary, or hijacking (and official police response to distress situations) almost automatically result in a finding of justifiable homicide.

We now must look more closely at those articles of the Penal Code that provide private citizens with wide discretionary powers to kill their fellows legally and with impunity. Here we recall the data for the 232 homicide cases summarized in Table XIX, which describes the motives or facts leading to an act of killing. Of these cases or episodes, 50 (22 percent) developed from a quarrel, 28 (12 percent) were the result of victim provocation, 26 (12 percent) were motivated by self-defense, and 47 (22 percent) evolved from domestic quarrels or quarrels over sex. The majority of the homicides in 1969 may therefore be said to qualify for consideration as justifiable homicide. How can this be? The answer, or certainly part of the answer, is to be found in the Penal Code.

Article 1220 of the Texas Penal Code explicitly allows a husband to kill his wife and her paramour if caught in the act of adultery. Although the statute narrowly specifies that the right to kill prevails only as long as the adulterous couple is engaged in intercourse, or while they are still together, it is evident that few if any courts in Texas have interpreted the right to kill *in flagranto delicto* this narrowly. Interestingly enough, a wife does not have the same statutory right to kill her husband and his mistress under similar circumstances.[32]

A man does not forfeit his right of self-defense if caught in the act by a woman's husband. If courts and juries stretch the intent of the statute to include "knowledge of adultery," as opposed to witnessing the spouse in the act of adultery, the way is cleared for husbands to exercise considerable discretion in their treatment of wives. The statute, and the court decisions upholding a husband's right to kill under these circumstances, undeniably finds broad support in the social mores and values of the society. It is of further interest to note that justifiable homicides in this category do not require any legal consideration of intent; that is, whether a husband shoots his wife and her lover in "cold blood" or "in the heat of passion" does not matter. The reader may recall Case No. 171 described in Chapter 4. In that case the husband quite brutally shot his friend, who was his wife's paramour, without also killing his wife. Since he had suspected that his wife and friend were involved in an adulterous relationship he literally trapped the couple and coolly decided to kill his friend but merely beat his wife. In other states or jurisdictions the husband could conceivably be charged with murder because he manifested not only intent to kill but also his actions were premeditated with malice aforethought. If the events and outcome of this case had been slightly different—if, for example, the wife's lover had seen the husband walking up to his car with a rifle and shot the husband before he shot him—the lover would face a murder charge, but the instructions to the jury, if the case was ever held over by the grand jury for formal indictment, would have necessitated a lesser charge of murder *without malice*.

Professor Stumberg's review of the Texas Penal Code articles on justifiable homicide introduces a phrase that puts the problems in bold relief. He says *"The Texas point of view* is set forth in Articles 1221, 1222, 1224, and 1227 of the Penal Code . . ." (italics added.)[33] The "Texas point of view" is, of course, another way of saying Texas custom or Texas culture. It is in these Articles that we see the formalization or institutionalization of cultural values and beliefs. If certain kinds of homicide are culturally defined as lawful it matters very little whether some people more than others benefit or take advantage of the existence of such laws.

Article 1222 makes it justifiable homicide if a person attempts to prevent murder, rape, robbery, maiming, disfiguring, castration, arson, burglary, and theft at night. Of particular interest in this Article is a paragraph that states "If homicide takes place in preventing a robbery, it is justifiable if done while the robber is in the presence of the one robbed or *is flying* [sic] *with the property taken by him*" (italics added).[34] This paragraph, as we can see, permits a person to pursue a fleeing burglar or robber. To kill a fleeing person may be, and here is, viewed as an act in defense of property but it is clearly not a killing precipitated by fear of life or necessitated by self-defense.

The wording of Article 1224 makes it quite explicit that justifiable homicide applies equally to the protection of one's person and property. The reader may recall the facts of Case 51 described in Chapter 5. In that case a man "defended" his employer's property ($150) when asked to "Hold it" by a 20-year-old youth who backed up his verbal threat with a .22 caliber pistol. The killer was no billed by a grand jury. If the case had gone to court the killer's attorney would undoubtedly have moved for a dismissal of the case on grounds that the act was excused by Article 1224. He, after all, had not only acted in self-defense but had actually defended the property in his custody.

Article 1225 helps explain why so many persons kill and get away with it under circumstances that in other states would lead to a murder conviction. *"The party whose person or property is so unlawfully attacked is not bound to retreat in order to avoid the necessity of killing his assailant"* (italics added).[35] In Texas a person can stand this ground and, if he deems it necessary, kill a person who attacks him. In the descriptive case material we witnessed time after time instances in which both killers and victims could easily have de-escalated the seriousness of the situation by retreat. But then, of course, the coward has never been held in very high esteem by frontiersmen or anyone for that matter who equates *macho* with wisdom. The student of Western jurisprudence cannot help seeing the discrepancies here between, say, contract law and the "eye for an eye" element in the Texas Penal Code. Contracts, for example, are negotiated, validated, and subject to arbitration and mediation by third parties. The Texas laws pertaining to justifiable homicide practically eliminate the need for police, judges, juries, and any form of third party authority as long as one can convincingly establish that the killing was a response to a threat against person or property. The qualification added by Article 1226 only truncates the right to kill: "The attack upon the person of an individual in order to justify homicide must be such as produces a reasonable expectation of fear of death or some serious bodily injury."[36] The reader may again recall the facts of Case No. 27 where a man was provoked by two other men in a cafe. He left the cafe but remained outside. When the two men came out, the provoked killer, who had retreated as far as sitting on the hood of his automobile, had armed himself and was ready to fight off the armed attacks by the two men. The killer certainly had more than a reasonable expectation of being hurt or killed, but why didn't he drive off and call the police?

Article 1224 confers a rather broad privilege to take a human life in defense of person and property. Article 1227 more specifically defines the conditions that must be met if a person exercises his privilege to kill somebody in defense of his property. The brilliant jurist W. W. Hohfeld would have scoffed at the imprecise and muddled language of Article 1227. Hohfeld, as early as 1913 and again in 1917, helped clarify the concept of property by calling attention to the symmetrical nature of all legal relations in terms of jural opposites and correlatives.[37] In brief, one cannot speak of property as either corporeal or incorporeal or of legal relations between people and objects or material possessions. Only people have legal relations, and "things," if you will, merely symbolize these relations. Notice the wording of Article 1227:

> When under article 1224 a homicide is committed in the protection of property, it must be done under the following circumstances:
>
> 1. The possession must be of corporeal property, and not of a mere right, and the possession must be actual and not merely constructive.
> 2. The possession must be legal, though the right of the property may not be in the possessor.
> 3. If possession be once lost, it is not lawful to regain it by such means as result in homicide.
> 4. Every other effort in his power must have been made by the possessor to repel the aggression before he will be justified in killing.

The wording of Article 1227 reflects a parochial understanding of legal concepts–such as confusing the manifestation or exercise of legal rights (possession) with what is called a "mere right"–and it is therefore not surprising that the citizens of Texas generally assume that they simply have a legal right or even a kind of license to kill anyone who tries to take away some of their material belongings. It may be recalled that the killer in Case No. 107 (Chapter 5), on the basis of hearsay evidence provided by his employee, tracked down the alleged thief and killed him when the man refused to submit to his custody. The employer had clearly lost possession of his money and his killing was not classified as justifiable. He was tried and found to be guilty of homicide *but* released from police custody with a five-year probationary sentence serving as a warning.

The final point to be made is simply this. A variety of statutory provisions exist whereby individual citizens may be justified in the taking of a human life. Few citizens are aware of the legal technicalities that separate criminal from non-criminal homicide. What many Texans do learn as part of the growing-up and socialization process is something closely akin to the principle "a lot of people need killing but no property needs stealing." The person who fails to learn that many people value their "property rights" over a basic human "right to life" is likely to find himself in trouble with "the law." You may justifiably kill because of money or property, but you cannot kill to acquire money or property. If, however, you do kill somebody and the circumstances warrant a trial by judge and jury the probabilities for being penalized and legally punished depend upon cultural views of acceptable and unacceptable homicidal behavior. That killing only rarely is viewed as an unacceptable mode of conduct is shown by the disproportionate number of killers who receive no penalty for the taking of a human life and, generally, in the number of acquittals for the minority population of killers who actually are convicted.

Punishment

Punishment, some people say, is a primitive form of inflicting pain and suffering to satisfy a need for revenge. The "primitive element" supposedly is removed when the State rather than the victim's survivors administers the punishment. Other persons, inspired by humanitarian motives, condemn the senselessness of legal punishment on grounds that they find it arbitrary, barbaric, and unjust. The juvenile delinquents in *West Side Story* symbolize how punishment of the individual fails to discriminate between individual shortcomings of character or in behavior and the broader responsibility of a society that produces its own delinquents. The blame may be thus distributed among inadequate parents (crime as a psychological disease), peers and associates (crime as a sociological disease), and limited social opportunity (crime as a political disease). The old-fashioned and admittedly barbaric view of criminality places similarly the blame directly on the perpetrator of crime and not on the multiple factors, such as the ready availability of firearms and an array of legal rights to use violence, that produced the criminal personality and made inevitable his behavior in the first place.

The wide discrepancies observed in the legal sanctioning of killers in 1969 are sufficiently documented to call into question the meaningfulness of the term justice. Any account of prison life in America could document and disprove the notion that imprisonment is an institutional means for rehabilitating persons who have done wrong.[38]

It is difficult to be sympathetic with anybody who kills another human being. Yet it is also difficult to see any rational grounds for extending the most severe punishment to those who combine killing with various crimes against individual or corporate property rights. Violation of property rights could and should be shifted to that part of the law concerning contractual liability, insurance, and indemnity. A man who kills his wife, or vice versa, is depriving other significant people like children of the benefits of a parent. A man who robs a gas station, and kills the gas station attendant as part of his robbery, can be made to pay back the money stolen. Can he compensate the widow and children for the economic benefits deriving from his victim's employment? Can he compensate the aggrieved family for the loss of an important relative? Surely, we can all agree that the victim, or even his role equivalent, cannot be resurrected to fill an important gap in the family. In most of the so-called primitive societies of the world it is quite evident that survivor compensation is the principal motive for punishment. In our modern nation-state the government simply punishes offenders without compensating victims. Why? Part of the answer is to be found in our present system of criminal justice, which, for purposes of convenience and efficiency, sweeps bodies off the streets and places the most serious and dangerous criminals in "penitentiaries." How else can the discrepancies in penalty and sentencing practice observed in the 1969 data be explained?

The killer who is indicted by a grand jury and bound over for public trial is the exception rather than the rule. At first glance this would at least suggest that quite a few killers end up as wards of the state. That is not the case, however. In a review published in 1947, a University of Texas Law School student addressed himself to this very same question. He studied the relationship between the number of convictions and the number of acquittals in Texas Criminal Courts for the years 1924 through 1944. His finding: "the rate of convictions in the trial courts are extremely high [and] the reversals from the appellate court are also extremely high."[39] The data collected and analyzed in this study suggest that this is still true. In other words, of those killers who actually have their cases brought to trial only slightly more than 50 percent actually go to jail. The probability of being punished for homicide in Texas is to this day less than a 50-50 proposition (more accurate data on sentencing practices in Houston would have to be made available in order to calculate precisely the mathematical probabilities of legal punishment for homicide). Surely these attributes of the criminal justice system cannot be said to be equivalent to any official indifference to the taking of a human life. What, then, accounts for the high rate of nonculpable homicides in Houston and in Texas generally? Part of that answer is to be found in various statutes, which, as we have observed, provide the individual citizen with wide discretionary powers to defend his person or property. Statutory regulations notoriously have very little influence on actual conduct so one cannot conclude that "it's the fault of the Penal Code." The behavior of police officials, district attorneys, judges, and all types of judicial authorities balance and interpret the statutory regulations promulgated by the legislature by such pragmatic considerations as the time, money, and manpower that must be marshaled if the state is to have an even chance against a good defense attorney. Finally, and perhaps most important of all, one must look to the people themselves. The values, attitudes, and social norms shared by the majority of taxpaying citizens ultimately permeate the system of criminal justice, but the elements of frontier justice exemplify the existence of a cultural lag. In Texas the people simply value their freedom and so-called property rights highly, and their representatives in government share the prevailing attitudes that killing is at times perhaps regrettable but certainly necessary. It is, as is seen in the statistical tabulations of the 1969 data, equally fair to conclude that social norms sanction killings among intimates and directly discourage killings that involve acts of abnormal behavior, unfair advantages (as in the killing of innocent and unarmed persons), or violations of property rights.

Toward the conclusion of this study, I read an extremely important article, "The Harris County Grand Jury–A Case Study," by Professor Robert A. Carp (1974). The article is of particular interest because (1) it represents a participant-observer's analysis of the activities of a particular grand jury; (2) it is written by a political scientist who was aware of the unique opportunity to collect and publish data on *actual* grand jury proceedings, which are not open to the public; and, finally, (3) the article suggests that the grand jury is a key to an understanding of why such a relatively large percentage of apprehended homicide suspects are no billed and subsequently freed from police custody and further legal prosecution. It must also be noted that the members of the grand jury, who may be said to act as "brokers" between the private citizen charged with the commission of a crime and the district attorney and his staff, who are the technical experts on matters of formal law, interpret cases in terms of their own apperceptions of "the system." These apperceptions are what I have referred to as implicit cultural patterns.

Carp first characterizes the members of the grand jury in terms of their socioeconomic and ethnic status within the Houston community:

> The typical Harris County grand juror is an Anglo-Saxon male college graduate about fifty-one years of age who is quite likely to earn about $25,000 per year while working either as a business executive or as a professional. How does this profile compare with what the 1970 census data indicates about the "typical" citizen of the county? A brief summary of the data reveals the following information about the residents of Harris County: 49 percent are male and 51 percent are female; the median adult age is thirty-nine; 69 percent are Anglo-Saxon, 20 percent are black, and 11 percent are Mexican-American; the median education is twelve years (a high school diploma); and the median family income is $10,348. These

figures clearly demonstrate that even by rudimentary standards Harris County grand juries do not meet the judicial criterion of a fair cross section of the community's human resources. Grossly under-represented are women, young people, Negroes, Mexican-Americans, the poor, and those with less extensive educational backgrounds. . . .

A typical civil libertarian might ask how are the young people, the minority groups, the poor, and the oppressed to be accorded due process of law when they are not proportionally represented among those who administer the laws. Such a critic would do well, however, to consider what numerous investigations reveal about the attitudes of high-status persons toward dissident and minority factions in American society. Studies by Stouffer, Lipsett, and Hyman and Sheatsley, for example, reveal that higher-status people (those with at least a college degree and who are in the professions or who are business executives) are significantly *more* likely to be solicitous toward the rights of ethnic minorities and social dissidents than are those who come from the lower end of the social and economic spectrum (ibid., p. 96).

Carp's study also reveals that the members of the grand jury often are presented with very incomplete information on specific cases. I assume that the district attorney at times must present a case to a grand jury without as much information available to him as indicated in the police case reports cited in this book; that is, a case may be brought before a grand jury before the police have developed all of the evidence necessary for a prospective court trial. The reader may now want to reconsider the descriptive case material and reflect on how one could reach a fair decision for or against indictment of the apprehended killer. If, as indicated by Professor Carp's study, cases are presented in short five-minute summaries, the decision-making process almost reaches a point of absurdity.

Although the data suggests considerable variation in the amount of time spent deliberating on the various categories of cases, the evidence reveals that the typical grand jury spends only five minutes per case. (In 1971 twelve Harris County grand juries spent an estimated 1,344 hours deliberating on 15,930 cases.) This average time of five minutes includes the assistant district attorney's

> summary of the case and his recommendation as to how the case should be decided (about sixty seconds per case), the hearing of testimony, and the actual secret deliberations by the grand jury. By anyone's standards, justice is indeed swift (ibid., p. 100).

The final quotation from this important study does not significantly alter the findings of my own study. On the contrary, I feel that Professor Carp's interpretations demonstrate the links between general cultural values and the institutional channels through which cultural values and value orientations apply directly to collective approval and disapproval of individual modes of social conduct.

> In addition, the never-ending flow of cases with which grand juries are daily bombarded places another obstacle in the path of a full and fair hearing for all those accused of felonies. Given the generally vague and inaccurate nature of the police reports and of the district attorney's file on the accused, five minutes per case is certainly not enough time to spend on the determination of probable cause.
>
> Besides the fact that only a small percentage of cases (probably no more than 5 percent) are examined with any care at all by the grand jury, the evidence suggests that even the selection of that 5 percent is an arbitrary process reflecting the bias of the upper-middle-class grand jury composition. The evidence reveals that the vast majority of these cases includes the bizarre, unusual, or "important" cases that are covered by the news media and that frequently involve the names of well-known local personages, businesses, and organizations. Murder of a prominent socialite, corruption in the local fire department, and alleged immoral conduct by professors at a local state university have all been subjects of extensive grand-jury investigations in Harris County. Such cases are regarded as significant by upper-middle-class grand juries, because the subject matter has a special appeal to the moral, ethical, or even salacious instincts of the middle-class mentality. On the other hand, the robbery of a liquor store, the stabbing death of a derelict in a ghetto bar, and the forgery of a credit card tend to be regarded as routine, boring cases by most grand jurors. As one grand juror said in candid jest, "*We kind of looked forward to the rape and sodomy cases and stuff like that because they broke the routine. I mean*

if you've heard one bad check case, you've heard them all. But the unusual cases were a little more interesting, and we kind of took our time with them."

The result of this bias may be that the more bizarre, infamous, or salacious the case, the greater the likelihood that it will be among the small percentage of cases in which the grand jury carefully performs the investigation. Conversely, the more routine and uninteresting the case, the greater the likelihood that it will be hastily concluded in reliance on the district attorney's advice that any mistakes will be corrected at trial. Since 46 percent of all Harris County grand-jury indictments since 1950 have ended in either dismissals or acquittals, one may well assume that many mistakes are indeed passed over by bored, unresponsive, and overworked grand juries (italics added) (ibid., p. 119).

7
A Cultural Perspective on Homicidal Behavior

The emphasis of this study has been to focus attention on killers and victims in different social situations. The killer and victim relationship has been described and analyzed in the situational context of the homicidal episode, but no conscious attempt has been made to explain homicide in terms of psychological or motivational attributes of the actors in the homicide drama. This, of course, is just another way of saying that different theoretical and explanatory approaches to the study of homicide result in different emphases and conclusions. My approach, which focuses on persons, dyadic killer-victim relationships, and social situations, is essentially a conjunctive theoretical perspective designed to derive cultural patterns from a series of separate incidents. Although all or most of us like to think of ourselves as free agents, individualists, and perhaps even nonconformists, it is an inescapable fact that behavioral similarities in any culture by far overshadow behavioral differences. If this were not the case, human beings would not live in societies, and we would not be a species of cultural animals. The distributional patterns in the homicide data from different cases cluster into categories and seemingly unique actors and situations do fit into well-defined empirical categories.

Colombia, Mexico, and many other countries have higher homicide rates than the United States. Houston, however, has maintained a volume of homicide well above that of the United States generally. The volume of killing in Houston is similar to that in countries in which the highest per capital death rate is due to homicide. The frequency data depicted in Figure 1, which was provided by the Homicide Division, dispels several myths about homicide but generates new questions for which answers are scarce.

The categories of killer and victim relationships, together with the kinds of social situations associated with homicide, do not appear to have changed significantly over the past 40 years. Additional interviews with homicide detectives in 1976 suggest that there has been a slight increase in the number of killings involving strangers since 1969. A rise of killings within this category may be attributed in part to an overall increase in narcotic-related crimes. It is also evident from official police statistics that the clearance rate for homicides, which in previous years reached nearly 90 percent, has shifted downward.

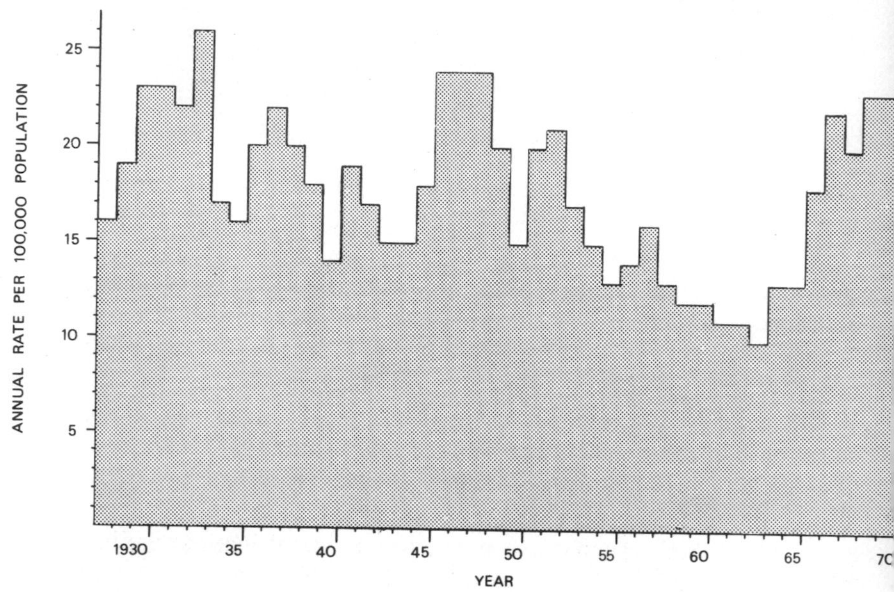

Figure 1. Reported homicide rates per 100,000 population (to nearest whole number), Houston, Texas, 1928–1970. (Source: Homicide Division, Houston Police Department.)

Future studies may also attempt to explain why the annual rate of homicide fluctuates. The problem here, however, is not one in which it may prove of interest and importance to explain the high and low years of homicide in relationship to such external variables as, for example, national depression, global war, or changes in city government. The problem rather is to try to understand two things: (1) The volume of homicide has remained high and changes, up or down, represent fluctuations within patterns rather than changes in fundamental patterns; (2) the annual rate of homicide itself can be questioned in terms of empirical accuracy. The rates depicted in Figure 1, which are similar to rates produced by the F.B.I. Uniform Crime Reports, are inaccurate. That is, the statistics reflect homicides that have come to the attention of the police in any given year. The rate does not accurately reflect the number of actual homicides in any given year. Consider again what would have happened to the 1969 data base if the 27 victims of the torture-murder conspiracy uncovered in 1973 had been included in the calculation of the homicide rate for 1969. What can be said, and what should be said emphatically, is simply this: The homicide rate for any city, any state, or any country is undoubtedly higher by an unknown x factor than the rates produced by police officials, government statisticians, and others. The discrepancies for 1969 between the police homicide records and the county health department, which is supposed to tally all alleged and actual homicide victims autopsied by the medical examiner, is sufficiently large to call into question the accuracy of the numerical base used to calculate the rate of homicide in Houston and, probably, the calculation of homicide rates elsewhere.

The behavioral scientist who is upset over the inaccuracy, or rather inconsistencies, of numerical data will undoubtedly view this as further evidence that he is a practitioner of a "soft science." Such a person must regrettably be viewed as the brainwashed child of the statistical laboratory. If he had talked to a physicist or a mathematician he would have learned that science, largely, is concerned with theory and that probabilistic prediction is a form of engineering.[1] Notice that the *rate* of homicide per 100,000 in the City of Houston never, in the recorded 40-year interval, fell below ten. Death from homicide, therefore, is as predictable as death from cancer, heart failure, or industrial accident. The problem now is to narrow the scope of our inquiry so as to see, if possible, when, where, and how homicide as a cause of death is most likely to occur.

Figure 2 shows that the highest frequencies, and therefore the greatest probability of victimization, of homicides occurred in May, August, September, and October. It would be a matter of pure speculation to say that these months, because of some special calendrical attributes, affected the homicide rate. One cannot correlate the data in Figure 2 with any other significant variable. This is not the case for the data summarized in Figure 3, however. It is an undisputed fact that most homicides occur on weekends. The volume of killing accelerates on Friday night, picks up on Saturday night, and peaks in the hours immediately before and after midnight on Sunday. Saturday night affords most people an opportunity for interaction over the weekend, which contributes to the high rate of homicide during this interval. The weekend is a time when people are released from many chores of work and may, in the lower as well as the upper income groups of the city populace, seek escape from the pressures of the work week.

Why, in the whole year, should most killings occur on the 27th day of every month? Figure 4 shows that this particular day, and no

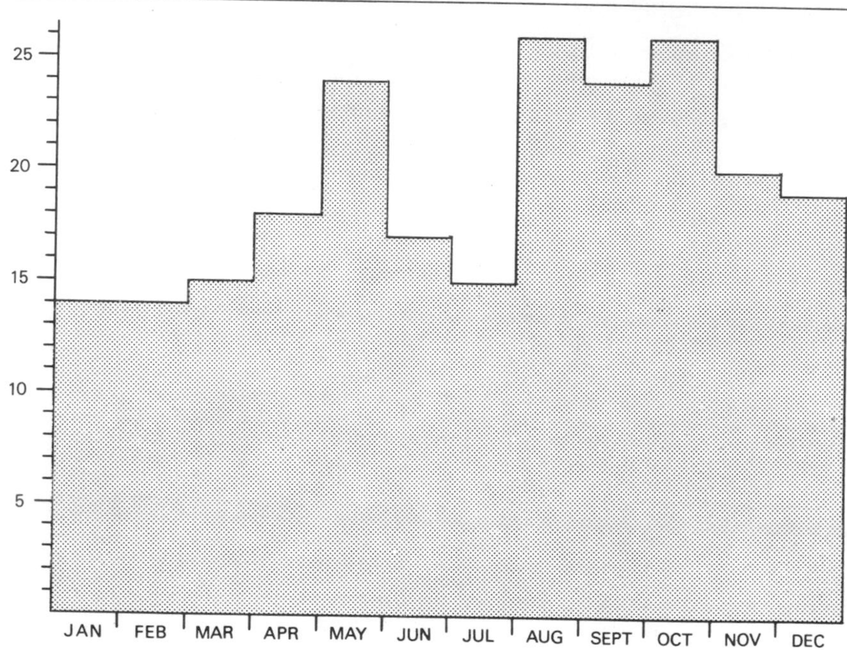

Figure 2. Number of Houston homicides in each month, 1969.

other day except perhaps the first day of the month, "produces" more victims than any other day in any other month. The first day of the month, which coincides with "payday" or "welfare check day" as the case may be, would have been more logical. People have more money, they may fight over how to use it, or they may go to places of public entertainment where alcohol plus frustration generates the fight that all too often results in the death of one of the combatants. It might, of course, be argued that the 27th day of the month falls just before payday when many outstanding bills may be due and that frustration with the world is at its zenith. But such an assertion is negated by the relatively low incidence of homicide on both the 28th and the 29th day of the month.

It is safe, therefore, to dismiss both "day of the month" and "month" as insignificant. Neither variable helps explain the phenomenon of homicide. The data represented in Figure 5, however, suggest that both "day of the week" and "hour of the day" can be used to predict the volume of homicide. Homicides most frequently occur on weekends and between the hours of 6:00 P.M. and 2:00 A.M. These are the times when,

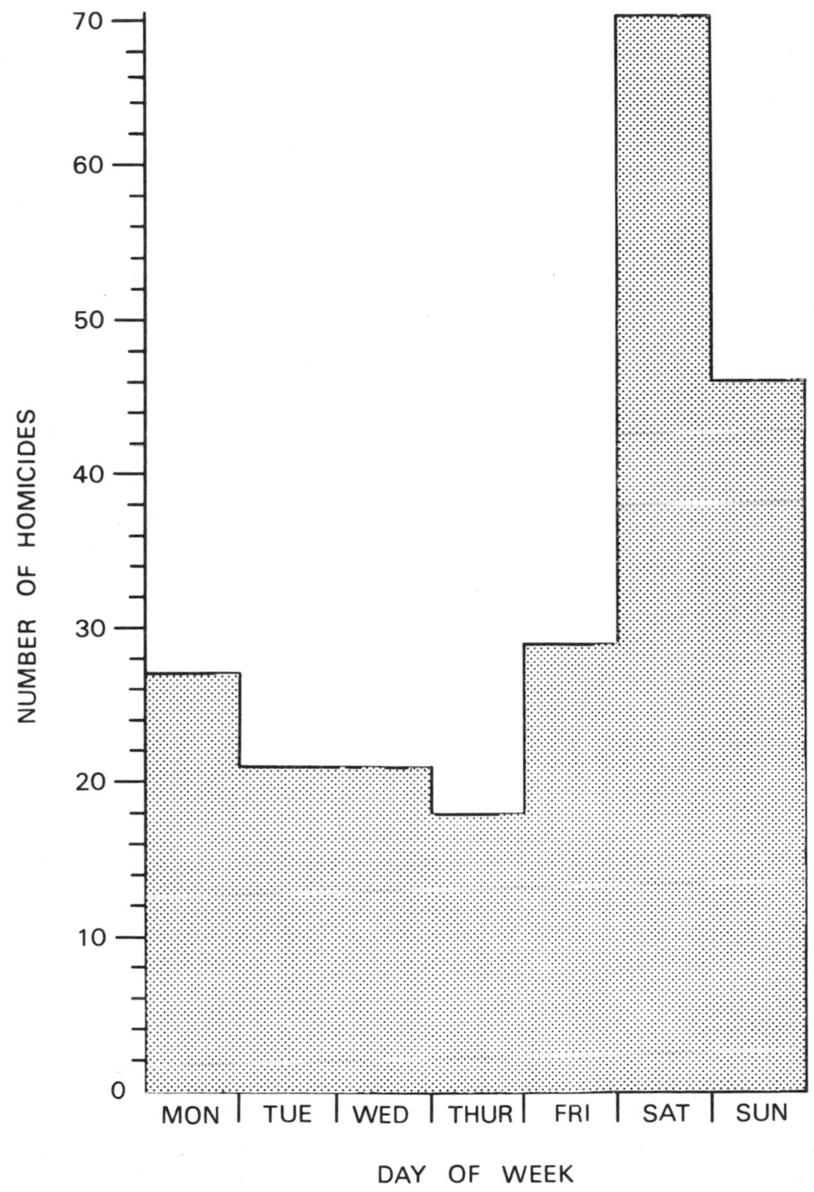

Figure 3. Number of Houston homicides in each day of the week, 1969.

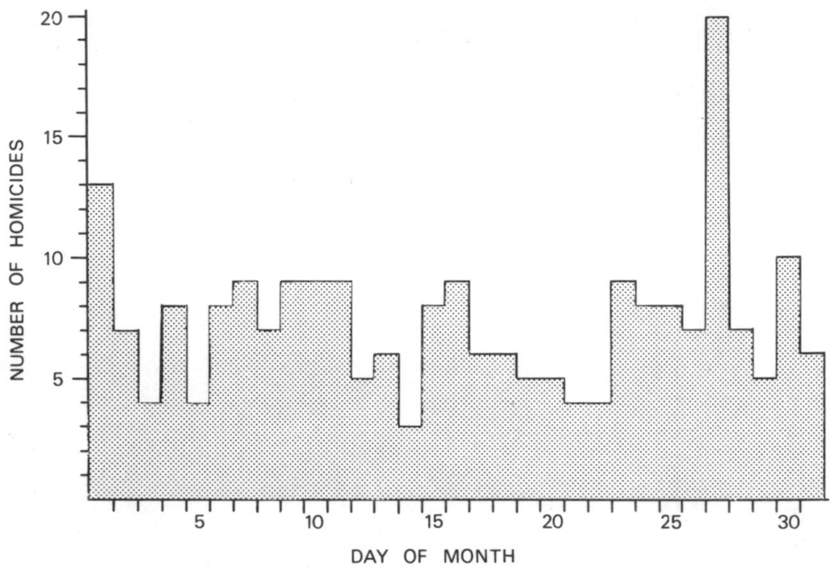

Figure 4. Number of Houston homicides on each day of the month, 1969.

as has been observed in the homicide cases cited, most people find opportunities to congregate and interact socially. National and three-day holidays produce the same results as the ordinary weekend. If we, by way of emphasizing these points, state a null-hypothesis that postulates that homicides are equally probable on each day of the week, it is possible to test the hypothesis against the 1969 data. Since there were 232 cases of homicide in 1969, we would expect 33 homicides to have taken place on each day. The difference between the expected and observed frequencies can be seen in Table XX. Since the critical value Chi^2 here for 6 degrees of freedom equals 22.46, we reject the null-hypothesis and conclude that there was a significantly larger number of homicide episodes on certain days than on others. That most homicides occur on Fridays, Saturdays, and Sundays may not come as a surprise to anyone. A Martian anthropologist, however, who could take nothing for granted about American culture, would naturally be puzzled by these behavior patterns. He might even be confused if he heard natives define the purpose of the Sabbath as a period set aside for rest and peaceful worship of the supernatural.

Figure 6 illustrates that homicide strikes young and old alike. The youngest victim is an infant and the eldest victim is almost an octogenarian. The youngest killer is a teenage and the eldest killer is in his late 70s. The age distribution depicted in Figure 6 only includes killers whose exact age is known. Data omitted because of incomplete information do not alter the general picture significantly. What is amazing is the relatively large number of killers and victims who fall into the broad age range from 18 to about 50 years of age. It is clear that homicide is not another form of juvenile delinquency and it is not, insofar as the present data indicate, an act that is in any way exclusive to psychopaths or professional criminals. Most killers are first-time offenders who, with relatively few exceptions, are not principally motivated by economic gain. The data summarized in Tables XIX and XXI suggest that motivational factors, insofar as they may be inferred from the descriptive data, must be sought in the interpersonal relationships of intimates and that the places where homicides occur correspond closely to places where intimates congregate.

We finally come to the question of the role of weapons. Guns, obviously, do not kill people by themselves. They are simply efficient tools used by people for the killing of people. Tables XXII and XXIII show the distributional frequencies of the kinds of weapons employed in the 232 Houston homicides. Firearms make up 86 percent of the weapons used and firearms, more than any other form of weapon, remove such factors as age, sex, physical strength, or killer-victim contact from consideration. A 15-year-old boy can kill a street vendor with a .22 caliber pistol just as easily as a 78-year-old woman can slay her disagreeable husband with the family shotgun. It is not firepower, or the relative sophistication of the weaponry employed, that makes the critical difference between wounding and killing. More people in 1969 lost their lives to .22 caliber "toy" bullets than to sophisticated pistols and rifles that fire high velocity large bullets. Any Houstonian who is 18 years of age, and who has a valid Texas driver's license, can purchase a handgun legally. It is sometimes easier, and even cheaper, to buy a gun from an acquaintance or, for that matter, from almost anyone on the street.

In the 232 homicide cases analyzed in this study, 86 percent of the killings resulted from the use of firearms. Nearly eight times as many handguns as rifles and shotguns were used in these killings. Handguns, obviously, are readily concealed and transported. They are as deadly as any other weapon at close range. These facts cast serious doubt on the general applicability of Wolfgang's statement "that few homicides due

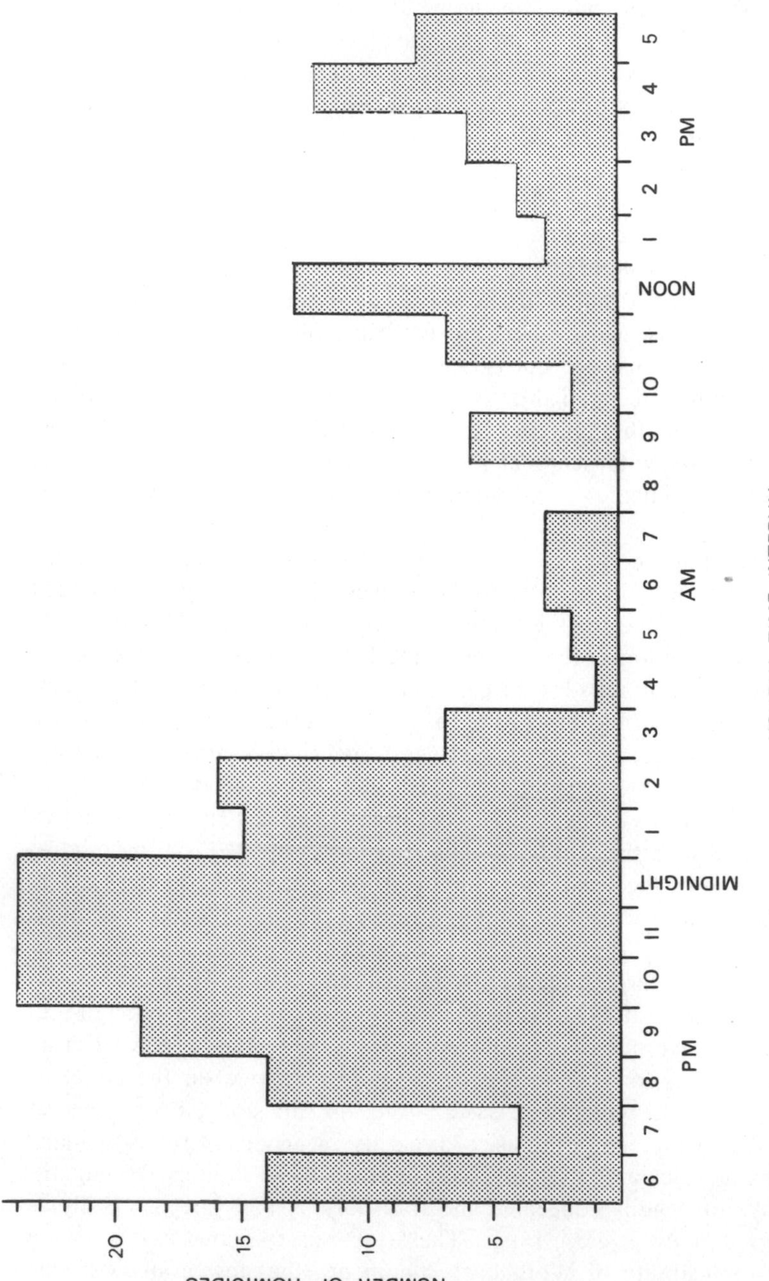

Figure 5. Number of Houston homicides in each hourly interval, 1969.

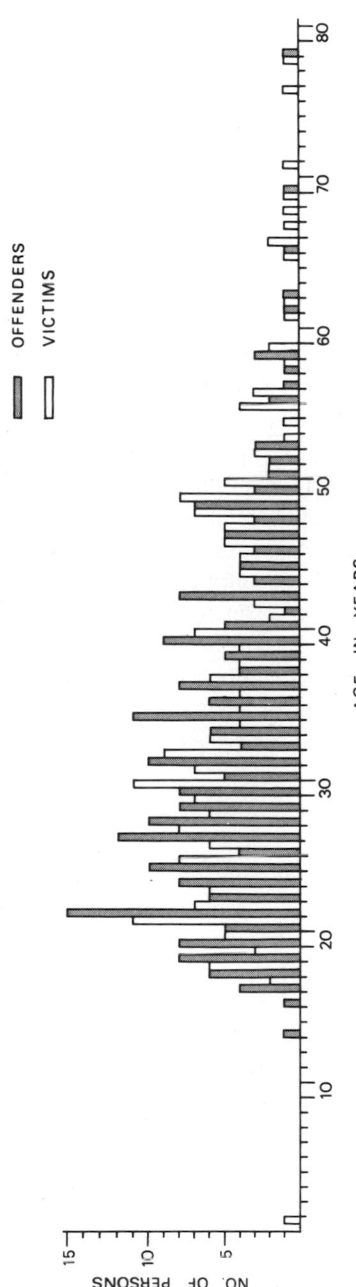

Figure 6. Age distribution of Houston homicide offenders and victims, 1969. Tabulation excludes offenders whose exact age is unknown.

to shootings could be avoided merely if a firearm were not immediately present, and that the offender would select some other weapon to achieve the same destructive goal."[2] It may very well be true to say that the person who sets out with the single-minded intention of killing somebody else may avail himself of any weapon to achieve his goal. The descriptive case-by-case data presented in this book suggest that the majority of killers often have ambiguous rather than clearly defined motives and that many killings evolve from ambiguous circumstances and myriad different social situations.[3] The only sensible way to determine whether firearms significantly contribute to high frequencies of homicide would be to eliminate all firearms for a specified length of time! The objections to such a test, however, would very likely be as irrational and intellectually stultifying as an editorial comment in the October 1974 issue of *The American Rifleman:*

> More than a few of those who minimize the menace of Communism are loud in their alarms over legitimate gun ownership in the U.S. If you doubt it, just read your daily newspapers and make out a checklist of the public figures who are: (1) soft on Communism and; (2) tough on firearms. . . . Few if any moderates or conservatives, of whatever political party, favor firearms confiscation or anything approaching it. Nearly all of the clamor for more gun control or gun bans comes from those who take a soft attitude toward Communism, toward marijuana and other drugs, and to what many old-time Americans regard as moral laxity. . . . The purpose of such people ought to be painfully obvious by now.

But in a carefully controlled experiment on the role of weapons as aggression-eliciting stimuli, Berkowitz and LePage confirmed their hypothesis that the presence of weapons serves to elicit and escalate aggressive responses in experimental subjects.[4]

The problem is to discover how private and public sanctions, or acts of approval and disapproval, sustain the patterns of interpersonal violence in an urban community. We have looked at many examples of interpersonal violence and our emphasis now must shift to a concern with the conceptual and ideological parts of the culture that ultimately define the phenomenon of killing as either permissible or as a problem that must be brought within the boundaries of social control.

Although far from having explained fully why thousands of Americans annually are homicide victims, the data and findings of this study imply that anything short of a general cultural perspective inevitably fails to explain why so many ordinary citizens find it necessary to use violence against others. The differential treatment, both unofficial and official, accorded known killers shows how a variety of cultural sanctions precipitate and resolve one of the most fundamental problems of social life: the continuous balancing of individual freedoms with the necessities of social order or restraint. The great latitude accorded Texans by statutory law in responding to threats from fellow citizens unquestionably precipitates more violence in the populace than might otherwise be the case. By scaling official sanctions in response to the private and public interest in a particular act, a society manages to negatively sanction aggressive and violent behaviors that directly threaten overall public welfare or that interfere directly with the individual's right to enjoy property. Although various psychological and psychiatric, biological and ethological, or historical and sociological explanations expose many of the variables that correlate with violent behavior (such as intelligence, personality, social environment, and even life-style) none of these has heuristic theoretical value. Killing, as we have seen, when defined in terms of social relationships and punishment, if any, can be explained by referring to cultural values deeply embedded and reflected in formal legal institutions.[5] The cultural perspective, as clumsy and defective as it may appear at times, enables us to incorporate many different explanatory hypotheses into a general and heuristic theoretical framework.

The anthropological and scientific concept of culture is of particular value because it is all-inclusive and neutral. The concept simply refers to "all those historically created designs for living, explicit and implicit, rational, irrational and nonrational, which exist at any given time as potential guides for the behavior of men."[6] The shooting of an innocent victim for "kicks" is as complicated a cultural event as is a carefully planned and executed assassination of a political opponent. The culture concept forces us to shun such tempting ethnocentric and a priori categorizations of killers as hardened criminals, social misfits, psychopathic personalities, or delinquents. The concept allows us to see interpersonal violence as a form of behavior that is not only learned but one that is shaped in many different and subtle ways by cultural values, value orientations, beliefs, attitudes, and everyday norms for interpersonal conduct. The simple fact, so evident in the Houston data, that killers and their victims, in the majority of cases, have a great many things in common should suffice to caution us against the indiscriminate use of labels, such as murderer, that connote psychological attributes and impose a unidimensional perspective on our thinking about different forms of antisocial and anti-life behavior. The critical point here, and the one I shall be principally concerned with explaining, is how cultural guidelines for behavior actually shape the behavior of persons who employ violent means to achieve some personally defined goal.

The principal link between cultural rules, as abstract guidelines for personal conduct, and individual behavior resides in sanctions. On this point, it is difficult to improve upon Radcliffe-Brown's description of how sanctions, both positive and negative, provide the individual members of every culture with a set of prescriptive and proscriptive rules for social interaction:

> In any community there are certain modes of behavior which are usual and which characterize that particular community. Such modes of behavior may be called usages. All social usages have behind them the authority of the society, but among them some are sanctioned and others are not. A sanction is a reaction on the part of a society or of a considerable number of its members to a mode of behavior which is thereby approved (positive sanctions) or disapproved (negative sanctions). Sanctions may further be distinguished according to whether they are diffuse or organized; the former are spontaneous expressions of approval or disapproval by members of the community acting as individuals, while the latter are social sanctions carried out according to some traditional and recognized procedure. . . . The sanctions existing in a community constitute motives in the individual for the regulation of his conduct in conformity with usage.[7]

Radcliffe-Brown further clarifies, as Malinowski concluded in his study, *Crime and Custom in Savage Society* (1926), how sanctions function to ensure a high degree of social conformity and why it is even possible to speak of human behavior as governed largely by cultural norms. Radcliffe-Brown proposes that

> [sanctions] are effective, first, through the desire of the individual to obtain the approbation and to avoid the disapprobation of his fellows, to win such rewards or to avoid such punishments as the community offers or threatens; and, second, through the fact that the individual learns to react to particular modes of behavior with judgments of approval and disapproval in the same way as do his fel-

> lows, and therefore measures his own behavior both in anticipation and in retrospect by standards which conform more or less closely to those prevalent in the community to which he belongs. What is called conscience is thus in the widest sense the reflex in the individual of the sanctions of the society (ibid.).

The truly antisocial and deviant person is somebody who either fails to comprehend the rules of his social universe or who consciously rejects community standards in favor of self-defined guidelines. The person who lives outside the normative framework of his society will, if his behavior is defined as threatening or unacceptable to others, be labeled and treated as a misfit and deviant.[8]

It follows that homicide, or any form of interpersonal aggressivity and violence, not only can be viewed as a category of cultural phenomenon but can be studied and analyzed by applying general sanctioning theory. We therefore need to know, for every level of social interaction, how cultural guidelines define and redefine acceptable and unacceptable ways to employ violence in interpersonal relations.

Many Western scholars have come to identify sanctions with the negative organized sanctions of criminal law. This view has led some anthropologists to dispute the applicability of the concept of law to primitive stateless societies and political scientists and jurists to debate whether international relations, which typically lack the sanctioning powers of municipal law, can be effectively regulated with legal rather than economic or military sanctions.[9]

Although the criminal process does indeed represent a very explicit form of sanctioning behavior, it is theoretically unsound to limit the study of sanctions to those situations that most closely represent the criminal process. The general purpose here is to show how almost any kind of well-defined institutionalized sanction, such as the negative sanctions made explicit by criminal law statutes, derive their effectiveness from the complementarity between sanctions and rules of social conduct. The failure of Houston grand juries to indict a sizable number of homicidal offenders must be viewed as public evaluations of some forms of killings as acceptable.

The Danish jurist and sociologist Verner Goldschmidt has conceptualized the distinction between sanction and crime, as follows:

> The term sanction *behaviour* is used instead of merely *sanction* in order to emphasize the fact that sanction constitutes a special type

> of behaviour characterized by authority and disapproval. In this connection it is important to bear in mind that the deprivation of life implied by a death-penalty, the deprivation of liberty implied by imprisonment or the deprivation of economic values implied by a fine are not in themselves sanction behaviour. Considered separately these interferences might equally well be elements of respectively murder, criminal deprivation of liberty and theft. It is the symbolically meaningful reference to authority combined with disapproval, that makes the decisive difference between sanction and crime.[10]

Similarly, most economic sanctions are ineffective without complementary political or military sanctions and psychological sanctions may be equally ineffective without ritual, moral, or religious sanctions. The analysis of human interaction in terms of sanctions and sanctioning behavior promises to resolve some basic problems relating to cultural stability and change, the maintenance of order together with the protection of individual human freedom, and the resolution of cultural conflicts without recourse to destructive forms of human violence. In these concluding paragraphs it is my purpose to reflect on the Houston data in order to enlarge our perspective on social control.

In the mid-1960s, American society turned "law and order" into a potent political issue. Two major presidential crime commissions, and several new federally supported state crime fighting programs, were established to seek new solutions and to combat the disruptive activities of various protest groups and the "un-American" life-style patterns of hippies and of the drug counterculture. In the 1970s, our society is facing crises of morality, political accountability, and white-collar lawlessness. It is in this rather frantic atmosphere of never-ending crises that the remedies of organized criminal sanctions seem so promising. Yet, the Watergate scandal, which we have all seen or read about, called our attention above all to the relativity of law, as an instrument and source of power, and the profound influence of different values and beliefs on conflicting guidelines for personal and public conduct. The stress placed on the criminal justice system, as a direct result of our desire to cope with presidential misbehavior and ordinary criminality, suggests that some cultural institutions actually have reached a state in which it is possible to speak of an institutional overload.[11]

The treatment of known homicidal offenders in Texas shows us how a society manages to sort out so to speak the "trivial" from the serious. A husband-wife killing, except for very exceptional cases, is not viewed with the same seriousness as the killing of a police officer or gas station attendant. Here, no matter what else one may think of the criminal justice system, the system has a built-in governance mechanism that keeps many potential law cases from clogging the courts and ultimately perhaps generating constitutional issues (and crises) from every unique trespass against law and common morality. These points apply to the current and ongoing debate about the desirability or undesirability of punishing so-called victimless crimes (i.e., prostitution, homosexuality, etc.).

The study of sanctions represents a significant step toward creating a more balanced view of social control and cultural stability. Legal sanctions cannot and should not be expected to perform feats for which they were never designed, feats that tend to ignore the positive side of sanctioning behavior, i.e., the reward of individuals and groups for performance of valued societal duties. These so-called diffuse positive sanctions, although admittedly more illusive than the organized negative sanctions of criminal law, are extremely important to the functioning of a viable social system. The anthropologist and lawyer A. L. Epstein has summarized the relationships between sanctions and social control as follows:

> The sanction is, of course, a concept of fundamental importance in jurisprudence and has played a paramount role in different legal theories. But there seems no good reason why its use should be restricted in this way. The legal sanction, manifested in the form of the penalties, remedies, and modes of redress of the law, represents only one particular means of enforcing conformity to norms and restating their validity when they are breached. Each group and subgroup within a society tends to develop its own distinctive pattern of usages and the means of maintaining them without necessary recourse to the municipal law. Sanctions therefore come to operate within every conceivable set of group relationships: they include not only the organized sanctions of the law but also the gossip of neighbors or the customs regulating norms of production that are spontaneously generated among workers on the factory floor. In small-scale communities, or within segments of a large-scale society, informal sanctions may become more drastic than the penalties provided for in the legal code. Thus the concept of sanctions is not merely of jurisprudential interest; it also has immediate sociological relevance to the analysis of the problem of social control.[12]

We also should examine why it is felt to be necessary to punish a marijuana smoker more severely than a killer and why low income workers often pay higher income taxes than many millionaires. These brief examples may serve to illustrate how criminal sanctions have become the source of what I term the institutional overload. The Houston data illustrate how a large community can effect social control through a variety of sanctioning processes. One such process, so clearly evident in the cases presented in this book, demonstrates how a community positively rewards private citizens who defend their rights, personal honor, or their property by taking the lives of those who threaten them. The data further show that homicides that result from unsatisfactory interpersonal relationships are not viewed in any way as threatening to the maintenance of social order. Because the vast majority of Texas homicidal offenders are "first offenders," we must acknowledge that the low frequency of punishment for killers effectively pushes "the problem" out of the overloaded criminal justice system and back into the community.

We should clarify the basic conceptual problems here. Sanctioning behavior must be conceptually and analytically separated from other forms of social interaction. The sanctioning concept must be heuristic and universal. It must apply to interpersonal interaction and social group relations. Equal attention must be directed toward clarification of positive or negative and diffuse or organized sanctioning behavior. A general model of this sanctioning process must simultaneously make operational the sanction concept at different levels within each society and be cross-culturally applicable, for scientific purposes only.

Our model specifies that sanctioning behavior, and in turn the sanctioning process, begins with some form of interaction. The interaction involves a sanctioning agent and any number of members of the social system. Systematic description of the kinds of interaction that result in the application of some kind of sanction will, in part, depend on the quality and richness of the ethnographic data. A homicidal episode, an economic transaction, a contractual agreement, or an involved and difficult negotiated settlement between two parties all represent behavioral events leading to empirical inputs into the sanctioning model. The data or interactions, which are essential to a description of how the sanctioning process applies at different levels, and at different historical time intervals, within each society, yield information on different sanctioning thresholds. The sanctioning threshold, which varies between different levels within one society, represents that point in an interaction at which the sanctioning agent either approves or disapproves, overtly or covertly, of a specific act or behavior.[13] The homicides described in this book illustrate how private and public agents decide on the relative seriousness of a particular act. Witnesses to a killing give the police their views on the interactional context of a killing. The police, and in turn the district attorney, make further judgments that affect the outcome for the killer. If, as demonstrated by eyewitness statements and the official interpretation of the homicidal episode, a victim has participated in the release of a sanction against himself, the official response will be quite different from cases in which a killer attacks persons and property without victim provocation.

Once the situation that triggers the release of the sanction has been described, it is possible to observe not only the different kinds of sanctions used within the society but to see the overall sanctioning process at work. The task here is to categorize and understand the particular kinds of sanctioning mechanisms actually in use relative to the context of specific situations and, further, to study the range of sanctioning mechanisms invoked by sanctioning agents (e.g., legal, social, political, economic, religious, psychological, military, ritualistic, moral, or customary). It is not immediately important to classify the different kinds of sanctions as either organized or diffuse or positive or negative. The essential problem is to collectively characterize the kinds of sanctions in relationship to the kinds of situations that invoke the sanctioning processes. This much has been accomplished in earlier chapters.

The study of homicide as a form of social interaction permits us to narrow the data base line down to manageable proportions. The study of homicide allows us to scale different sanctions in terms of relative importance, seriousness, and general frequency of expression. It is neither difficult to shift the focus from the analysis of a particular sanctioning subsystem, such as the sanctions that specifically pertain to homicide, to other forms of violent interaction (such as rape, assault, child abuse) nor impossible to extend the analysis to other kinds of social relationships that involve persons in different but less lethal transactional episodes.

We have seen indirectly how such variables as technology or the level of socioeconomic complexity may fail to affect the general outline of sanctioning behavior. It is suspected that cross-cultural differences in sanctioning behavior will reside with individual and cultural usages of different kinds of sanctioning mechanisms rather than with any inherent complexities between simple homogeneous societies and complex heterogeneous ones. Sanctions are clearly more than reactions to breaches of conduct or expressions of approval for conformity. Sanctions must, in some real sense, be part of the cultural ideology and values so that human social action is integrated and coordinated to serve cultural rather than individual ends. Social integration, and in turn cultural stability, must to a large extent result from a compromise between the allocation of authority and social privilege and the preservation of individual choice and action. Societies change, and individuals constantly adjust their motivations and decision-making choices, in response to internal as well as external pressures for change. A clear understanding of sanctioning processes can help us understand how and perhaps even why total cultural systems both sustain and modify their behavioral and ideological guidelines in response to the changing demands of human existence. It is impossible to predict *when* Americans will view the social and private costs of interpersonal violence as parallel in seriousness to the loss of life and happiness to cancer, heart attack, alcoholism, or any form of human experience that prevents the individual, and ultimately society, from maximizing personal and collective achievement. Professor Schneider's insightful study of the punishment for incest in a small Pacific Island society concludes with an important observation that supports the notion that the definition of crime and punishment is relative to the general cultural values and traditions found among the members of any human society. According to Schneider, "The Yap data suggest that it may be useful to separate the problem of why an act is deemed wrong from the question of what is done about it and by whom. It seems that what is done about a particular crime depends very much on who has the right to do something about it. This is essentially a political question and depends on the manner in which the right to use force is distributed throughout the social structure."[14] It is evident from the data presented in this book that Houstonians in particular and Texans in general have maintained a working equilibrium between the rights of private citizens and public officials to negatively sanction disapproved forms of social behavior with death.

APPENDIX A

Houston Police Department Homicide Report Outline

HOUSTON POLICE DEPARTMENT
HOMICIDE REPORT OUTLINE

INTRODUCTION:

A. Your location when you received call.
B. From whom you received call.
C. Time you received call.
D. Time you arrived at scene.
E. First officer or officers at scene.
F. Immediate findings at scene.
   1. Type offense. (Shot, stab, direct violence.)
   2. Victim still at scene or moved by ambulance.
   3. Offense committed by whom.
   4. Defendant arrested–still at scene–fled scene.

SCENE SUMMARY:

A. Description of scene.
B. Position of body.
C. Identification of victim, by whom or how.
D. Dress of victim.
E. Wounds or apparent wounds of victim.
F. Disorder of scene, room, etc.
G. Signs of struggle.
H. Exit–entry.
I. Recovery of weapon or instrument used, if found at scene.
J. Weather conditions.
K. Lighting conditions.
L. Visibility.

REAL EVIDENCE:

A. Movable.
   1. Guns recovered at scene.
   2. Knife recovered at scene.
   3. Other instruments used and recovered at scene.
   4. Hulls picked off of floor, etc.
   5. Articles dropped or lost by fugitive. (Hat, pants, pen, pencil, lighter, etc.)
   6. Articles dropped by victim.
   7. Broken bottles used in crime.
   8. Pieces of torn clothing.
   9. Notes.
   10. Poison containers.

B. Immovable.
   1. Bullet holes in wall, door, floor, etc.
   2. Broken furniture, doors, windows.

C. Scientific aids.
   1. Fingerprinting of body. (by whom)
   2. Investigator examining scene.
   3. Fingerprints.
   4. Photos.
   5. Measurements.
   6. Sketches.
   7. Footprints.
   8. Blood (to be typed).
   9. Hair.
   10. Tool marks.

CORONER:

A. Personal effects.

B. Disposition of body.
   1. Ambulance.
   2. Driver.
   3. Place of removal.

C. Information regarding autopsy.

HOSPITAL INVESTIGATION:

A. Attending physician.

B. Pronounced dead by whom.

C. Chart of wounds.

D. Physical condition (if living).

E. Alcoholic condition or content.

F. Manner and condition of dress.

G. Attitude (if living).

DETAILS OF OFFENSE:

A. Summary of facts leading to commission of crime.

B. How committed.

C. With what committed.

D. Motive of why committed.

INTERROGATION OF WITNESSES AND DEFENDANT:

A. Oral statements.
   1. Statement of the deceased before death.
   2. Dying declaration of deceased.
   3. Statement of victim if living.
   4. First statement by defendant after arrest.
   5. Any Raes Gestae [sic]* statement by the defendant.

B. Written statements.

* Correct form: Res gestae.

1. List statements on report, giving full name, age, address, telephone number, and place of employment.

PERSONS WANTED:

A. Full description.
B. Address.
C. Place of employment.
D. Place of previous employment.
E. Relatives.
F. Place of birth and previous residence.
G. Mode of escape or flight.
H. Description and license of car.
I. Names and addresses of associates.
J. Places where he frequents.

DISPOSITION:

A. Arrest.
    1. Where.
    2. By whom.
    3. When.
    4. Assisting officers on arrest.
    5. Other details of arrest.

B. Unfounded.
C. Cleared due to lack of prosecution on the part of complainant.

EVIDENCE TAGGED:

A. In whose name tagged.
B. Complete description of articles tagged.
C. If gun tagged as evidence, check with Records for stolen.

PROGRESS REPORTS:

APPENDIX B

Census Tract Distribution of Homicide Incidents

CENSUS TRACT DISTRIBUTION OF HOMICIDE INCIDENTS

Census tract	number	Census tract	number
121	8	318	3
122	2	319	2
123	2	321	2
124	8	325	1
125	1	328	2
126	9	329	3
174	1	330	2
201	11	339	2
202	1	342	1
203	1	358	1
204	2	401	2
205	14	402	1
206	2	403	1
207	1	407	1
208	3	410	1
210	4	416	1
215	3	419	1
216	2	420	1
217	2	423	3
218	2	425	1
219	1	502	5
225	3	503	1
227	1	504	3
232	1	505	4
301	4	506	2
302	3	507	1
303	6	508	1
304	17	509	3
305	8	510	3
306	8	511	1
307	5	514	1
308	1	515	4
309	3	516	2
310	1	518	3
311	3	519	1
312	4	521	1
314	1	523	3
316	1	524	1
317	3	525	2

APPENDIX C

Residential Location of Homicide Offenders and Victims

RESIDENTIAL LOCATION OF HOMICIDE OFFENDERS AND VICTIMS

Census tract	Offenders					Victims				
	Subtotal	White	Black	Mexican-American	Oriental	Subtotal	White	Black	Mexican-American	Oriental
121	3	3				4	1	2	1	
122	2			2		1			1	
123	1		1			2		1	1	
124	8	6	2			9		9		
126	6		6			9	1	8		
174	—					1	1			
201	6		6			10		10		
202	2	2				1	1			
203	—					4	1	2	1	
204	4		4			2		2		
205	12		12			8	1	7		
206	2		2			1			1	
207	1		1			1		1		
208	5		3	2		3		3		
210	3		2	1		5		5		
212	—					1	1			
215	4		4			4		4		
216	—					3		3		
217	2		2			—				
218	3		3			2		2		
219	1		1			3		3		
220	1	1				—				
223	—					1	1			
225	3	2	1			3	2	1		
301	3	1	1	1		3	3			
302	1	1				2	1		1	
303	5		5			4	4			
304	18		18			17		17		

RESIDENTIAL LOCATION OF HOMICIDE OFFENDERS AND VICTIMS (Continued)

Census tract	Offenders					Victims				
	Subtotal	White	Black	Mexican-American	Oriental	Subtotal	White	Black	Mexican-American	Oriental
305	6		5	1		6		6		
306	6		6			2		2		
307	4		4			3		3		
308	2	2				1		1		
309	3	3				1	1			
310	1	1				—				
311	2	1		1		3	1		2	
312	2			2		3		1	2	
314	1	1				1	1			
315	1		1			3	1	2		
316	—					3		3		
317	4		4			6		6		
318	5	1	3	1		1		1		
319	—					1	1			
320	1	1				2	2			
321	3		2	1		4	1	2	1	
324	—					1	1			
325	1	1				1	1			
327	2	1	1			—				
328	3		3			2		2		
329	3		3			4		4		
330	2		2			1		1		
334	—					1		1		
335	—					1		1		
339	2		2			—				
340	1		1			—				
342	—					1	1			

360	1	1			—				
401	3	1	2		1	1			
402	1		1		3	2		1	
405	—				2	2			
407	1	1			1	1			
408	—				1	1			
415	—				2	2			
416	1	1			1	1			
420	1	1			1	1			
423	3	1	2		2	1	1		
425	1	1			1	1			
501	1	1			—				
502	6	1	5		6		6		
503	—				1			1	
504	3		3		3	1	2		
505	1	1			4		4		
506	2	1	1		2	2			
507	—				2	2			
508	1		1		—				
509	1		1		2	1	1		
510	2		2		2	1	1		
514	—				2	1	1		
515	1	1			6	4	1		1
516	2	1		1	1			1	
518	2	1	1		3	3			
519	1		1		—				
520	2		2		—				
521	1	1			1	1			
522	—				1	1			
523	2	1	1		2	1	1		
524	—				1		1		
525	2		2		2		2		
531	—				2	1	1		

APPENDIX D

Critical Events in a Houston Homicide Case
Texas Homicide Statutes

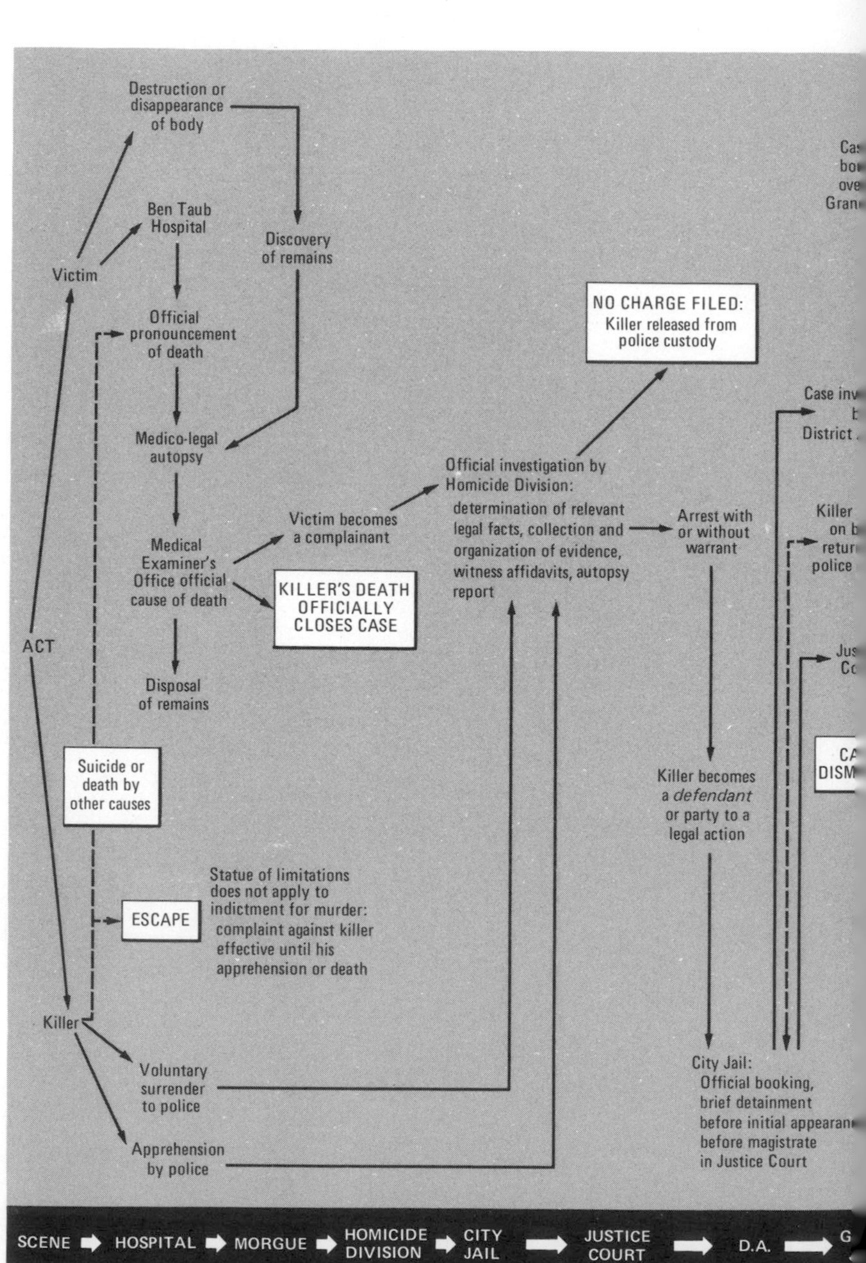

Destruction or disappearance of body
Ben Taub Hospital
Discovery of remains
Victim
Official pronouncement of death
Medico-legal autopsy
Medical Examiner's Office official cause of death
Victim becomes a complainant
KILLER'S DEATH OFFICIALLY CLOSES CASE
Disposal of remains
ACT
Suicide or death by other causes
ESCAPE
Statue of limitations does not apply to indictment for murder: complaint against killer effective until his apprehension or death
Killer
Voluntary surrender to police
Apprehension by police
Official investigation by Homicide Division: determination of relevant legal facts, collection and organization of evidence, witness affidavits, autopsy report
NO CHARGE FILED: Killer released from police custody
Arrest with or without warrant
Killer becomes a *defendant* or party to a legal action
City Jail: Official booking, brief detainment before initial appearance before magistrate in Justice Court
SCENE
HOSPITAL
MORGUE
HOMICIDE DIVISION
CITY JAIL
JUSTICE COURT
D.A.

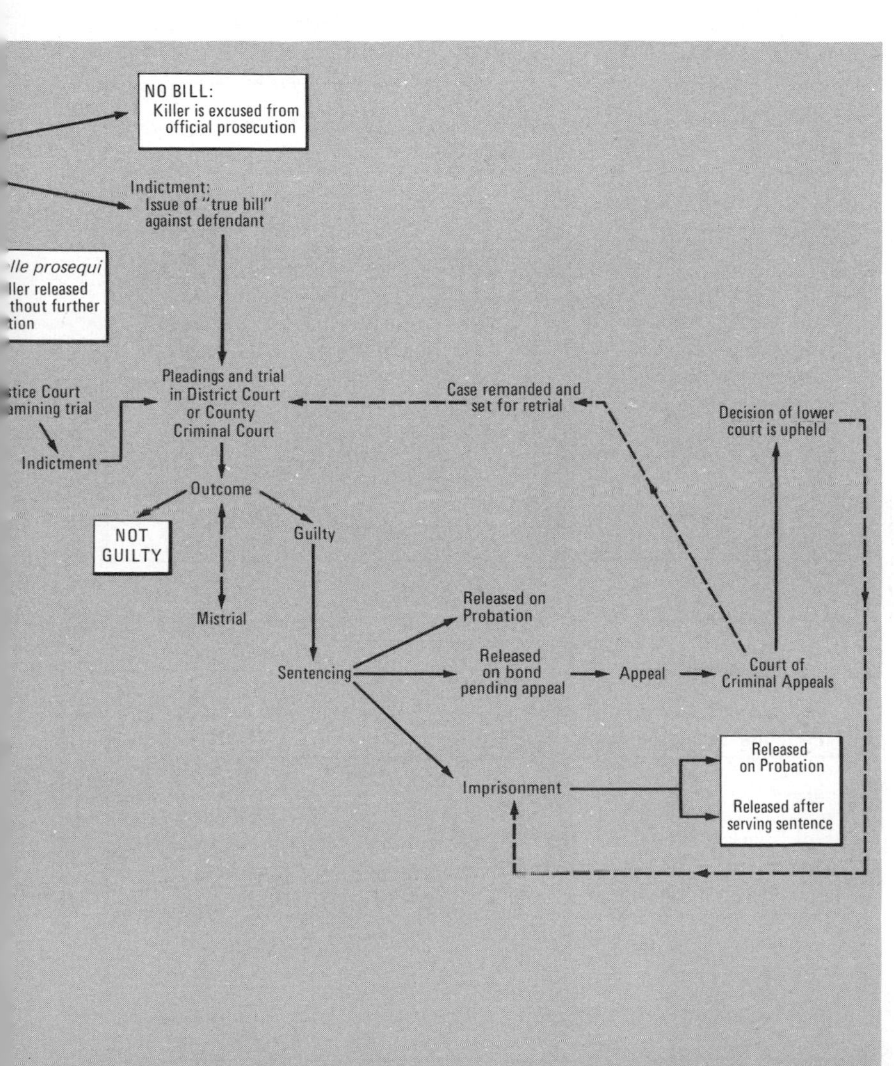
NO BILL:
Killer is excused from official prosecution
Indictment:
Issue of "true bill" against defendant
lle prosequi
ller released
thout further
tion
stice Court
amining trial
Indictment
Pleadings and trial in District Court or County Criminal Court
Case remanded and set for retrial
Decision of lower court is upheld
Outcome
NOT GUILTY
Guilty
Mistrial
Released on Probation
Sentencing
Released on bond pending appeal
Appeal
Court of Criminal Appeals
Imprisonment
Released on Probation
Released after serving sentence
TRIAL COURT
APPELLATE COURT
PENITENTIARY
RELEASE OF KILLER
CASE OFFICIALLY CLOSED

CHART II

A SCHEMATIC VIEW OF TEXAS HOMICIDE STATUTES APPLICABLE TO ALL ACTS COMMITTED BEFORE 1974

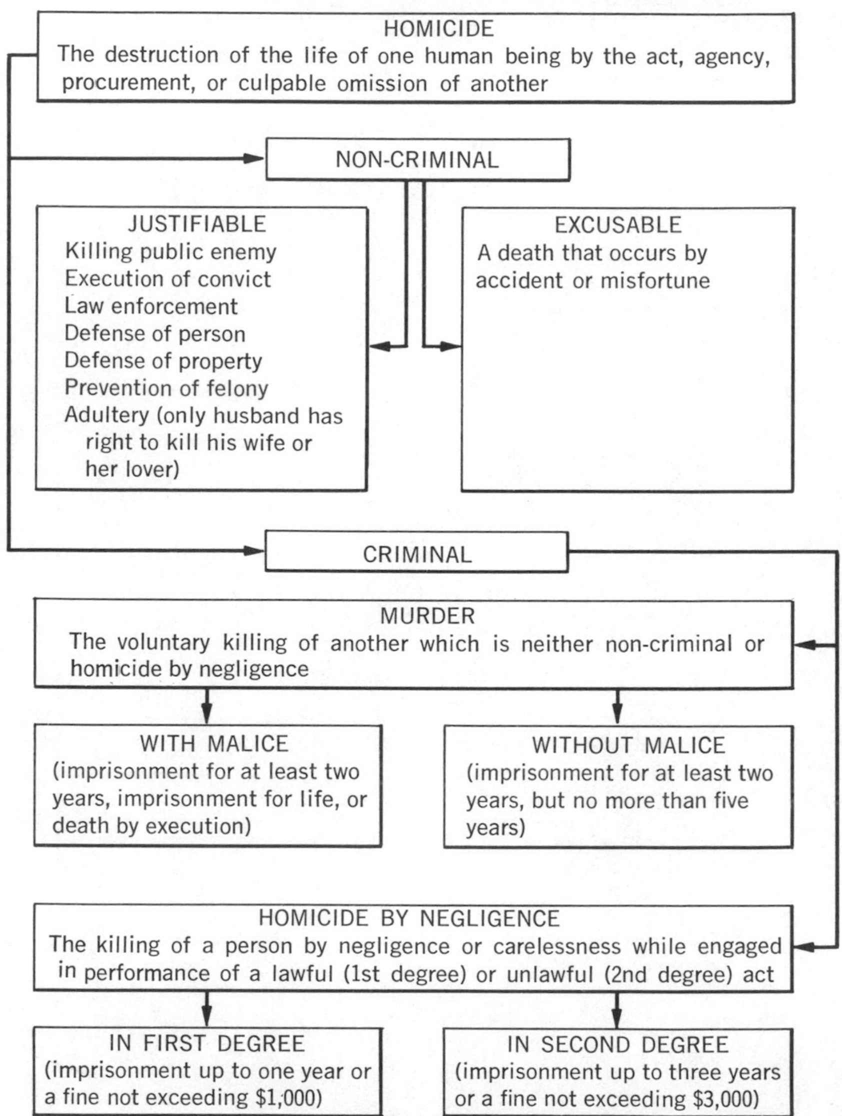

Source: Vernon's Annotated Penal Code of the State of Texas, 1961

CHART III

A SCHEMATIC VIEW OF TEXAS HOMICIDE STATUTES APPLICABLE TO ALL ACTS COMMITTED AFTER 1974

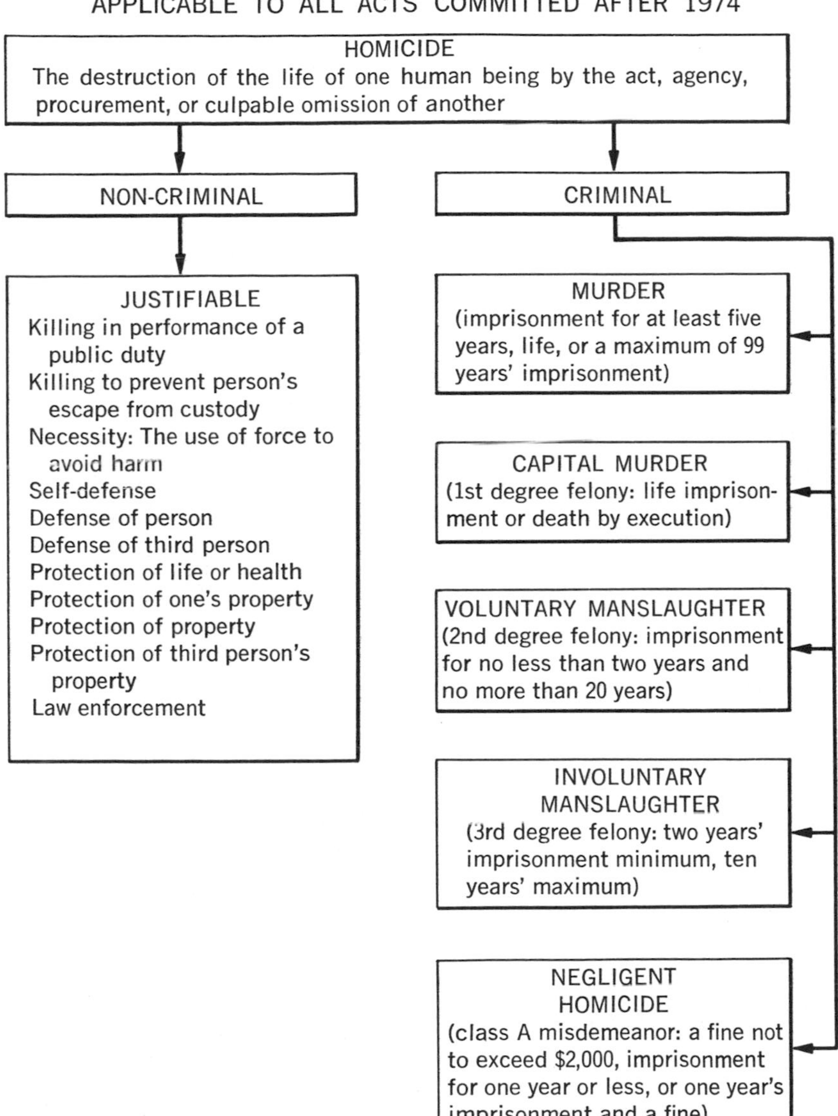

Source: Vernon's Texas Codes Annotated: Penal Code, 1974

APPENDIX E
Data on Homicide

TABLE I

TEN PRINCIPAL CAUSES OF DEATH IN THE STATE OF TEXAS, 1967

Cause of death	number of deaths	death rate per 100,000 population	percent of total
Heart disease	29,741	273.9	35
Cancer	14,103	129.9	16
Apoplexy	9,957	91.7	12
Accidents	6,513	60.0	8
Diseases of early infancy	2,879	26.5	3
Pneumonia	2,727	25.1	3
General arteriosclerosis	1,560	14.4	2
Diabetes mellitus	1,511	14.0	2
Homicide	1,152	10.6	1
Cirrhosis of the liver	1,068	9.8	1
All other causes	14,983	138.0	17
Total	86,194	793.9	100

Source: Texas Almanac—1970–1971:589

Note: All percentages have been rounded to the nearest whole number.

TABLE II

GEOGRAPHICAL DISTRIBUTION OF HOMICIDE RATES PER 100,000 POPULATION IN THE FIFTY STATES, 1969

State	population	number of homicides	homicide rate
Alabama	3,531,000	485	13.7
South Carolina	2,692,000	336	12.5
Georgia	4,641,000	551	11.9
Florida	6,354,000	720	11.3
Texas	11,187,000	1,264	11.3
North Carolina	5,205,000	556	10.7
Alaska	282,000	30	10.6
Missouri	4,651,000	485	10.4
Kentucky	3,232,000	336	10.4
Wyoming	320,000	33	10.3
Arkansas	1,995,000	197	9.9
Tennessee	3,985,000	382	9.6
Louisiana	3,745,000	356	9.5
Maryland	3,765,000	350	9.3
Nevada	457,000	41	9.0

TABLE II (Continued)

State	population	number of homicides	homicide rate
Illinois	11,047,000	950	8.6
Michigan	8,766,000	729	8.3
Mississippi	2,360,000	192	8.1
New York	18,321,000	1,320	7.2
Delaware	540,000	39	7.2
California	19,443,000	1,386	7.1
Ohio	10,740,000	685	6.4
New Mexico	994,000	61	6.1
Arizona	1,693,000	102	6.0
Virginia	4,669,000	276	5.9
Oklahoma	2,568,000	148	5.8
West Virginia	1,819,000	102	5.6
Colorado	2,100,000	112	5.3
New Jersey	7,148,000	369	5.2
Indiana	5,118,000	252	4.9
Pennsylvania	11,803,000	482	4.1
Oregon	2,032,000	81	4.0
Montana	694,000	25	3.6
Washington	3,402,000	124	3.6
Kansas	2,321,000	81	3.5
Massachusetts	5,467,000	191	3.5
Hawaii	794,000	27	3.4
Rhode Island	911,000	28	3.1
Connecticut	3,000,000	86	2.9
Utah	1,045,000	26	2.5
New Hampshire	717,000	18	2.5
Nebraska	1,449,000	36	2.5
Vermont	439,000	11	2.5
Wisconsin	4,233,000	87	2.1
South Dakota	659,000	13	2.0
Idaho	718,000	14	1.9
Minnesota	3,700,000	69	1.9
Maine	978,000	16	1.6
Iowa	2,781,000	39	1.4
North Dakota	615,000	1	.2
Total	201,921,000	14,587	7.2

Source: Uniform Crime Reports—1969:58–62

Note: There is a slight, but statistically insignificant, variation between the number of murder and nonnegligent manslaughter reported for individual states and the total figure of 14,587.

TABLE III

SERIOUS OFFENSES AGAINST THE PERSON KNOWN TO THE HOUSTON POLICE, 1969

Classification of offenses	number of actual offenses	Number of Offenses in 1969 Cleared by Arrest: total offenses cleared	by arrest of persons under 18 (included in total offenses)
Criminal Homicide:			
Murder and nonnegligent manslaughter	281	236	12
Forcible Rape Total:	405	209	23
Rape by force	320	171	17
Assault to rape—attempts	85	38	6
Robbery:	5,395	1,682	146
Armed—any weapon	4,940	1,548	111
Strong-arm—no weapon	455	134	35
Assault Total:	8,994	6,012	512
Gun	1,151	677	34
Knife or cutting instrument	1,086	565	50
Other dangerous weapon	388	228	25
Hands, fists, feet, etc. aggravated	128	77	9
Other assaults—not aggravated	6,241	4,465	394
Total	29,869	16,042	1,374

Source: Annual Report, Police Department, City of Houston, Texas, 1969

Note: The number of actual offenses reported by the Police Department between 1970 and 1975 show a slight rise in the homicide rate: 1969 (281), 1970 (289), 1971 (303), 1972 (294), 1973 (263), 1974 (330), and 1975 (342).

TABLE IV

REPORTED HOMICIDE AND AGGRAVATED ASSAULT RATES PER 100,000 INHABITANTS IN THE UNITED STATES, 1960–1969

Year	homicide rate	aggravated assault rate	ratio of homicide to aggravated assault
1960	5.0	84.7	1 : 17
1961	4.7	84.4	1 : 18
1962	4.5	87.3	1 : 19
1963	4.5	91.0	1 : 20
1964	4.8	104.5	1 : 22
1965	5.1	109.5	1 : 21
1966	5.6	118.4	1 : 21
1967	6.1	128.0	1 : 21
1968	6.8	141.3	1 : 21
1969	7.2	151.8	1 : 21
Ten-year average	5.43	110.09	1 : 20

Source: Uniform Crime Reports—1969:57

TABLE V

RACIAL AND MARITAL CHARACTERISTICS OF SAMPLE POPULATION

	Average persons per tract	percent
Race:		
White	475	5
Black	8,426	94
Mexican-American	68	1
Total	8,969	100
Marital Status:		
Male, 14 years and over		
Single	900	32
Married	1,539	54
Separated	(237)	
Widowed	193	7
Divorced	192	7
Total	2,824	100
Female, 14 years and over		
Single	864	25
Married	1,657	49
Separated	(351)	
Widowed	565	16
Divorced	331	10
Total	3,417	100

TABLE VI

DISTRIBUTION OF HOMICIDES IN RELATIONSHIP TO RACIAL COMPOSITION OF CENSUS TRACTS

	Tracts in which Homicides Took Place		Tracts in which Victims Resided		Tracts in which Offenders Resided	
	number of tracts	percent	number of tracts	percent	number of tracts	percent
Census tracts with less than 400 Black population	29	37	31	40	21	30
Census tracts with 400 or more Black population	49	63	47	60	48	70
Total	78	100	78	100	69	100

TABLE VII

EMPLOYMENT CHARACTERISTICS OF SAMPLE POPULATION

Employment status	tract average	percent
Male, 16 years old and over	2,628	
Labor force:	1,877	
Percent of total		70
Civilian labor force:	1,877	
Employed	1,790	95
Unemployed	87	5

TABLE VIII

EDUCATIONAL ACHIEVEMENT LEVELS OF SAMPLE POPULATION

		Tract average	percent
Persons, 25 years old and over		4,354	
School years completed		160	4
Elementary: 1 to 4 years		527	12
5 to 7 years		908	21
8 years		442	10
High school: 1 to 3 years		1,224	28
4 years		720	16
College: 1 to 3 years		242	6
4 years or more		131	3
Median school years completed (%)	9		
Percent high school graduates (%)	24		

TABLE IX

COMPARISON OF BLACK TENANCY STATUS WITH GENERAL POPULATION

	General population	Black population
Tenancy Status:		
Owner occupied (%)	17	12
Renter occupied (%)	83	88
Lacking Some or All Plumbing Facilities:		
All housing units (%)	7	10
Contract Rent:		
Median	$57.25	$57.50

TABLE X

DISPOSITION OF HOMICIDE CASES IN TERMS OF THE STATUS CATEGORY OF KILLERS

Killer's status category	case number	disposition
Husband	125	suicide
	167	suicide
	70	no bill*
	92	not guilty
	67	charge pending
	168	3-month jail sentence
	102	7-year jail sentence
	190	10-year jail sentence
	233	90-year jail sentence
Wife	2	no bill
	15	no bill
	38	no bill
	49	no bill
	64	no bill
	93	no bill
	140	no bill
	159	no bill
	198	no bill
	82	no charge filed
	69	dismissed
	76	reset for trial
	86	3 years' probation
	117	outcome undetermined
	9	outcome undetermined
Father	193	10-year jail sentence
Mother	164	5-year jail sentence
Son	99	life sentence
	63	99-year jail sentence
Brother	206	no bill
	42	no charge filed
	170	nolle prosequi
	225	2-year jail sentence
	131	outcome undetermined
Uncle	129	no bill
	226	no bill
	105	nolle prosequi
Tertiary relatives	17	5 years' probation
	35	12-year jail sentence
Boyfriend	73	suicide
	43	no bill
	50	3-month jail sentence

TABLE X (Continued)

Killer's status category	case number	disposition
	75	20-month jail sentence
Girl friend	74	suicide
	179	no bill
	227	no bill
	234	no bill
	11	probation
Cohabitant	132	no bill
Close friend	94	no bill
	145	no bill
	171	no bill
	220	dismissed
	44	3-month jail sentence
	77	3-year jail sentence
	183	5-year jail sentence
	19	10-year jail sentence
Casual acquaintance	23	no bill
	48	no bill
	65	no bill
	96	no bill
	101	no bill
	114	no bill
	187	no bill
	210	no bill
	57	nolle prosequi
	20	3 years' probation
	148	5 years' probation
	97	1-year jail sentence
	52	2-year jail sentence
	62	3-year jail sentence
	209	4-year jail sentence
	89	5-year jail sentence
	110	5-year jail sentence
	36 (2)**	12-year jail sentence
	36 (2)**	75-year jail sentence
	32	outcome undetermined
	37	outcome undetermined
	68	outcome undetermined
	211	outcome undetermined
Friend, closeness undetermined	230	no bill
	212	nolle prosequi
	154	5 years' probation
	203	2-year jail sentence
	84	5-year jail sentence
	121	5-year jail sentence

TABLE X (Continued)

Killer's status category	case number	disposition
	87	10-year jail sentence
	144	40-year jail sentence
Gambling associate	95	nolle prosequi
	178	not guilty
	239	not guilty
	109	5 years' probation
	138	2-month jail sentence
	85	3-year jail sentence
	91	life sentence
Neighbor	56	no bill
	122	nolle prosequi
	143	nolle prosequi
	142	1-year jail sentence
	47	3-year jail sentence
Colleague	13	suicide
	185	no bill
	152	3 years' probation
Roommate	135 (2)**	8-year jail sentence
	135	10-year jail sentence
Employer	161	no bill
	83	life sentence
Employee	195 (2)**	not guilty
Customer	22	nolle prosequi
	34	5-years' probation
	169	5-year jail sentence
	238	10-year jail sentence
	127	25-year jail sentence
	61	40-year jail sentence
Proprietor	16	no bill
	147	no bill
	165	no bill
	228	no bill
	54	3 years' probation
	29	2-month jail sentence
	60	3-year jail sentence
	130	5-year jail sentence
	166	charge pending
Husband		
Separated or divorced	224	suicide
	26	dismissed
	66	dismissed
	98	4-year jail sentence
	180	4-year jail sentence
	18	5-year jail sentence

TABLE X (Continued)

Killer's status category	case number	disposition
Wife		
Separated or divorced	24	3 years' probation
Ex-boyfriend	103	10 years' probation
	115	10-year jail sentence
Ex-girl friend	157	no bill
	217	2 years' probation
Paramour	106	no bill
	40	nolle prosequi
	123	nolle prosequi
	176	nolle prosequi
	137	5 years' probation
	194	5-year jail sentence
	223	5-year jail sentence
	172	outcome undetermined
	177	charge pending
Common-law husband	200	no bill
	71	reset for trial
	25	5-year jail sentence
	182	19-year jail sentence
Comon-law wife	46	no bill
	53	no bill
	55	no bill
	120	no bill
	213	no bill
	134	not guilty
	195	not guilty
	33	5 years' probation
	186	outcome undetermined
Stepfather, Father-in-law	139	not guilty
	205	outcome undetermined
Stepmother, Mother-in-law	196	7 years' probation
Stepson, Son-in-law	181	no bill
	146	not guilty
	80	outcome undetermined
Stepdaughter, Daughter-in-law	112	outcome undetermined
Brother-in-law	126	no bill
	215	no bill
Sister-in-law	1	referred directly to grand jury
Stranger	222 (2)†	50-year jail sentence
	27	no bill
	51	no bill
	128	no bill
	175	no bill

TABLE X (Continued)

Killer's status category	case number	disposition
	192	no bill
	207	no bill
	235	no bill
	3	nolle prosequi
	10	nolle prosequi
	30	dismissed
	118 (2)†	dismissed
	231	not guilty
	174	not guilty
	14	3 years' probation
	107	5 years' probation
	133	7-month jail sentence
	10 (3)†	3-year jail sentence
	113	4-year jail sentence
	229	5-year jail sentence
	31	7-year jail sentence
	90	10-year jail sentence
	7	15-year jail sentence
	8	15-year jail sentence
	8 (2)†	15-year jail sentence
	39 (2)†	30-year jail sentence
	118	30-year jail sentence
	45 (2)†	40-year jail sentence
	8 (3)†	50-year jail sentence
	222 (2)**	50-year jail sentence
	10 (2)**	65-year jail sentence
	45	90-year jail sentence
	218	99-year jail sentence
	150	life sentence
	39	death penalty
	59	death penalty
	81	death penalty
	136	death penalty
	237	death penalty
	12	charge pending
	156	charge pending
	219	charge pending
	78	outcome undetermined
	163	outcome undetermined
Relationship unknown	111	suicide
	188	suicide
	28	no bill
	41	no bill
	58	no bill

TABLE X (Continued)

Killer's status category	case number	disposition
	88	no bill
	116	no bill
	119	no bill
	151	no bill
	153	no bill
	189	no bill
	199	no bill
	204	no bill
	236	no bill
	201	nolle prosequi
	201 (2)**	nolle prosequi
	210 (2)**	nolle prosequi
	210 (2)**	nolle prosequi
	221	nolle prosequi
	5	dismissed
	4	not guilty
	232	not guilty
	184	3 years' probation
	160	5 years' probation
	162	5 years' probation
	197	5 years' probation
	158	10 years' probation
	124	6-month jail sentence
	79	5-year jail sentence
	173	5-year jail sentence
	202	7-year jail sentence
	149	10-year jail sentence
	155	15-year jail sentence
	208	15-year jail sentence
	237 (2)**	30-year jail sentence
	214	charge pending
	141	outcome undetermined

* A grand jury issues a "no bill" if it finds the evidence against an accused person insufficient for indictment.
** Two defendants.
† Two or three defendants.

TABLE XI

STATUS POSITION OF KILLERS

Status position	number	percent
Husband	9	4.30
Wife	15	7.17
Father	1	.48
Mother	1	.48
Son	2	.96
Brother	5	2.39
Uncle	3	1.44
Relatives farther removed	2	.96
Boyfriend	4	1.91
Girl friend	5	2.39
Cohabitant, sexual partner	1	.48
Close friend	8	3.83
Casual acquaintance	23	10.90
Friend, closeness undetermined	8	3.83
Gamble-mate	7	3.35
Neighbor	5	2.39
Colleague, coworker	3	1.44
Roommate	2	.96
Employer	2	.96
Employee	1	.48
Customer	6	2.87
Proprietor	9	4.30
Separated or divorced husband	6	2.87
Separated or divorced wife	1	.48
Ex-boyfriend	2	.96
Ex-girl friend	2	.96
Paramour	9	4.30
Common-law husband	4	1.91
Common-law wife	9	4.30
Stepfather, Father-in-law	2	.96
Stepmother, Mother-in-law	1	.48
Stepson, Son-in-law	3	1.44
Stepdaughter, Daughter-in-law	1	.48
Brother-in-law	2	.96
Sister-in-law	1	.48
Stranger	42	20.09
Accomplice	2	.96
Total	209	100.00

TABLE XII

STATUS POSITION OF HOMICIDE VICTIMS

Status position	number	percent
Husband	15	7.50
Wife	9	4.50
Father	2	1.00
Son	2	1.00
Brother	5	2.50
Sister	1	.50
Nephew	3	1.50
Relatives farther removed	2	1.00
Boyfriend	5	2.50
Girl friend	4	2.00
Cohabitant, sexual partner	1	.50
Close friend	8	4.00
Casual acquaintance	22	11.00
Friend, closeness undetermined	8	4.00
Gamble-mate	7	3.50
Neighbor	5	2.50
Colleague, coworker	3	1.50
Roommate	1	.50
Employee	2	1.00
Customer	9	4.50
Proprietor	6	3.00
Separated or divorced husband	1	.50
Separated or divorced wife	5	2.50
Ex-boyfriend	2	1.00
Ex-girl friend	2	1.00
Paramour	11	5.50
Common-law husband	10	5.00
Common-law wife	4	2.00
Stepfather, Father-in-law	4	2.00
Stepson, Son-in-law	3	1.50
Brother-in-law	2	1.00
Stranger	35	17.50
Accomplice	1	.50
Total	200	100.00

TABLE XIII

THREE MAJOR KILLER AND VICTIM RELATIONSHIPS EXPRESSED IN REFERENCE TO FINAL CASE DISPOSITION

	Relatives		Friends/Associates		Strangers	
Case disposition	frequency	percent	frequency	percent	frequency	percent
Offender deceased	3	3.90	3	4.41		
No bill	24		20		10	
No charge filed	2 } 31	40.26	} 25	36.77	} 13	23.64
Nolle prosequi	5		5		3	
Dismissed	3	3.90	2	2.94	1	1.82
Not guilty	5	6.49	3	4.41	2	3.64
Probation	8	10.39	6	8.82	4	7.27
Death penalty					5	9.09
Outcome undetermined	8	10.39	2	2.94	2	3.64
Charge pending	2	2.30			4	7.27
Life sentence	1	1.29	2	2.94	1	1.82
Sentenced	16	20.78	25	36.77	23	41.82
Total	77	100.00	68	100.00	55	100.00
Average sentence (years)	13* 8** 20		10		28	

* Case No. 63 excluded.
** Cases Nos. 63 and 233 excluded.

TABLE XIV

STATISTICAL VALUES FOR PRISON TERMS IN YEARS AMONG THE THREE PRINCIPAL OFFENDER CATEGORIES

	Relatives ($n = 13$)	friends/ associates ($n = 22$)	strangers ($n = 21$)
Mean	7.62	10.09	27.90
Standard deviation	4.52	16.01	28.75
Maximum	19.00	75.00	99.00
Minimum	2.00	1.00	3.00
Range	17.00	74.00	96.00

TABLE XV

PERCENT HOMICIDE CASES ACCORDING TO DISTANCES BETWEEN ASSAILANT, VICTIM, AND PLACE OF OCCURRENCE

Distance (miles)	assailant/victim	assailant/occurrence	victim/occurrence
0.0–0.4	46.7	57.0	61.0
0.5–0.9	10.8	10.0	14.3
1.0–1.4	5.8	5.0	8.2
1.5–1.9	6.9	2.2	3.9
2.0–2.4	4.1	2.8	2.8
2.5–2.9	1.1	1.5	1.1
3.0–3.4	3.0	2.8	2.6
3.5–3.9	2.8	1.7	1.5
4.0–4.4	1.1	1.3	1.3
4.5–4.9	1.1	0.4	0.6
5.0–5.4	0.2	0.2	0.6
5.5–5.9	1.5	0.6	0.2
6.0–6.4	0.9	0.6	0.4
6.5–6.9	0.4	0.2	0.4
7.0 and over	13.6	13.7	1.1
Total	100.0	100.0	100.0

Source: Bullock, Urban homicide in theory and fact (1955, p. 571)

TABLE XVI

FREQUENCY AND PERCENT OF HOMICIDE CASES ACCORDING TO RESIDENTIAL DISTANCE BETWEEN VICTIMS, KILLERS, AND LOCATION OF HOMICIDE*

	Frequency			Percent		
Distance (miles)	victim/ killer	victim/ location	killer/ location	victim/ killer	victim/ location	killer/ location
0.0–0.4	81	122	109	47	59	60
0.5–0.9	18	20	23	11	10	13
1.0–1.4	13	9	12	8	4	7
1.5–1.9	9	8	3	5	4	2
2.0–2.4	4	3	5	2	1	3
2.5–2.9	3	8	2	2	4	1
3.0–3.4	5	4	3	3	2	2
3.5–3.9	4	3	3	2	2	2
4.0–4.4	7	6	6	4	3	3
4.5–4.9	4	0	1	2	0	0
5.0–5.4	4	6	1	2	3	0
5.5–5.9	5	5	5	3	2	3
6.0–6.4	2	2	1	1	1	0
6.5–6.9	3	0	2	2	0	1
7.0 and over	11	10	6	6	5	3
Total	173	206	182	100	100	100

* Only homicides within the Houston city limits and those cases for which the home address of the principals are known have been tabulated.

TABLE XVII

DISTRIBUTION OF KILLERS AND VICTIMS BY RACE AND SEX

	Killers		Victims	
	number	percent	number	percent
Males:				
White	46	23	51	26
Black	134	69	134	67
Mexican-American	15	8	13	7
Other	—	—	1	—
	195	100	199	100
Females:				
White	10	20	10	28
Black	38	74	20	55
Mexican-American	3	6	6	17
Other	—	—	—	—
	51	100	36	100

TABLE XVIII

JUSTIFIABLE HOMICIDES REPORTED, 1969

Case No.	killer	victim	circumstances	weapon
240	WM 60	MEX 39	burglary	rifle
241	BM 47	BM 16	burglary	handgun
242	MEX 16	MEX 30	defense of other person	rifle
243	WM 57	BM 33	burglary	handgun
244	police officer	WM 21	robbery	rifle
245	police officers (2)	BM 17	robbery	shotgun
246	police officer	BM 18	burglary	shotgun
247	WM 49	WM 35	burglary	handgun
248	BF 70	BM*	self-defense	handgun
249	police officer	WM 28	unknown	handgun
250	police officer	BM 28	self-defense	handgun
251	WM 44	BM 24	burglary	shotgun
252	WM 52	BM 18	robbery	handgun
253	police officer	BM 20	self-defense	shotgun
254	police officer	BM 21	burglary	shotgun
255	WM 54	BM 14	burglary	shotgun
256	police officer	BM 29	robbery	handgun
257	police officer	BM 29	robbery	handgun
258	WM 54	BM 25	burglary	shotgun
259	WM 57	MEX 27	robbery	handgun
260	WM 60	BM 17	robbery	shotgun
261	WM 33	MEX 21	burglary	handgun
262	WM 45	BM 25	robbery	handgun
263	WM 33	BM 14	burglary	rifle
264	police officer	BM 23	robbery	handgun
265	WM 60	BF 24	robbery	shotgun
266	BM 56	BM 22	robbery	handgun
267	BM 56	BM 28	burglary	handgun
268	WM 53	BM 17	robbery	handgun

* Age unknown.

TABLE XIX

MOTIVE OR FACT LEADING TO COMMISSION OF HOMICIDE

Motive or fact	number	percent
Quarrel	50	22
Provoked	28	12
Self-defense	26	11
Domestic quarrel	25	11
Quarrel over sex	22	10
Robbery involved	16	7
Quarrel over money	14	6
Malicious intention	13	6
Accident	8	3
Quarrel over money in gambling	8	3
Domestic quarrel between in-laws	5	2
Intoxication	4	2
Suicide	4	2
Accidental homicide of a third party in a quarrel or fight	4	2
Fight	2	1
Rubout, conspiracy	1	—
Negligent homicide	1	—
Unknown	1	—
Total	232	100

TABLE XX

OBSERVED AND EXPECTED HOMICIDE FREQUENCY DISTRIBUTION BY DAY OF THE WEEK

	Monday	Tuesday	Wednesday	Thursday	Friday	Saturday	Sunday	Total
Observed	27	21	21	18	29	70	46	232
Expected	33	33	33	33	33	33	33	231
Total	60	54	54	51	62	103	79	463

$Chi^2 = 63.73$

TABLE XXI

HOMICIDE SCENES BY TYPE AND FREQUENCY OF LOCATION

Type of location	frequency	percent
Home:		
In general	5	
Living room	24	
Bedroom	23	
Kitchen, dining room	10	
Hallway	4	
Yard	7	
Driveway	7	
Porch, outside house	14	
	94	40
Bar	46	20
Street	26	11
In front of or in the vicinity of a bar	18	8
Store	12	5
Unspecified	12	5
Parking lot	11	5
Inside a car	6	3
Motel	2	1
Vacant lot	2	1
Place of work	2	1
Public place	1	—
Total	232	100

TABLE XXII

DISTRIBUTION OF HOMICIDE WEAPONS BY TYPE AND FREQUENCY

Weapon	number	percent
Firearms	199	86
Knife	25	11
Tool	4	2
Arms, hands	3	1
Cloth (rag)	1	—
Total	232	100

TABLE XXIII

DISTRIBUTION OF HOMICIDE FIREARMS BY TYPE AND FREQUENCY

Firearms	number	percent
Pistol:		
Caliber unknown	16	
.22	80	
.25	12	
.32	23	
9 mm	1	
.38	39	
.45	5	
	176	88
Rifle:		
Caliber unknown	3	
.22	7	
	10	5
Shotgun:		
Caliber unknown	3	
12	5	
16	3	
20	1	
.410	1	
	13	7
Total	199	100

Notes

Chapter 1

1. The book-length studies of homicide represented by Bromberg's *The Mold of Murder* (1961), Macdonald's *The Murderer and His Victim* (1961), Palmer's *The Psychology of Murder* (1960), and Wertham's *The Show of Violence* (1949) and *A Sign for Cain* (1966) illustrate how psychologists and psychiatrists have broached the question of normalcy in relationship to personal violence and criminal culpability. Wegrocki's article on "A Critique of Cultural and Statistical Concepts of Abnormality" (1939) critically examines the problem of how to conceptualize abnormality as a universalistic and cross-cultural form of human behavior.

2. See, for example, Brearley's study, *Homicide in the United States* (1932), for an early and general overview of homicide incidents in the nation. A five-volume book by Warren and Bilas entitled *Warren on Homicide* (1938) provides a comprehensive review of different state criminal statutes and leading case decisions on homicide. Comparative statistical data on violent crimes have, since 1930, been collected and published by the Federal Bureau of Investigation. The Uniform Crime Reports, which only include information on crimes known to or reported by different state police agencies, provide a general overview of the relative volume of homicide in the different states. Although there may be fewer numerical discrepancies between the frequency of actual and reported homicide than may be the case for other serious crimes, such as rape, the criticisms embodied in the following journal articles serve to caution us that the crime indices of the Uniform Crime Reports cannot be accepted at face value: Biderman, "Surveys of Population Samples for Estimating Crime Incidence" (1967); Biderman and Reiss, "On Exploring the 'Dark Figure' of Crime" (1967); Beattie, "Problems of Criminal Statistics in the United States" (1955); Cressey, "The State of Criminal Statistics" (1957); Kitsuse and Cicourel, "A Note on the Use of Official Statistics" (1963); Sellin, "The Basis of a Crime Index" (1931); and Wolfgang, "Uniform Crime Reports: A Critical Appraisal" (1963).

3. See, for example, Montagu, *Man and Aggression* (1973).

4. Mulvihill and Tumin, *Crimes of Violence* (1969).

5. Couzens, "Reflections on the Study of Violence" (1971).

6. See Kuhn's *The Structure of Scientific Revolutions* (1970) for a detailed discussion of the notion of "paradigm."

7. See, for example, Brown, *Explanation in Social Science* (1963), and von Wright, *Explanation and Understanding* (1971).

8. Margaret Mead has provided a brief but insightful analysis of some of the differences between American and English cultural differences in her article, "The Application of Anthropological Techniques to Cross-National Communication" (1947).

9. Kirkham et al. furnish a detailed view of political assassination in their work, *Assassination and Political Violence* (1970).

10. Toch, *Violent Men* (1969, p. 225).

11. See, for example, Sellin's article, "The Significance of Records of Crime" (1951), and Van Vechten's study, "Differential Criminal Case Mortality in Selected Jurisdictions" (1942).

12. Nash, "Death as a Way of Life: The Increasing Resort to Homicide in a Maya Indian Community" (1967, p. 456).

13. Eisenhower, *Progress Report of the National Commission on the Causes and Prevention of Violence to President Lyndon B. Johnson* (1969, p. 1).

14. See Eisenhower, *To Establish Justice, to Insure Domestic Tranquility . . .* (1969), and Katzenbach, *The Challenge of Crime in a Free Society . . .* (1967).

15. Clark, *Crime in America* (1971, p. 29).

16. See, for example, Cressey, "Epidemiology and Individual Conduct" (1960), and Glueck, "Theory and Fact in Criminology" (1956). Both articles consider the pros and cons of the late Professor Sutherland's theory of differential association.

17. Sapir, "The Unconscious Patterning of Behavior in Society," in Mandelbaum, *Selected Writings . . .* (1963, pp. 546, 548).

18. Professor Taft's article, "Influence of the General Culture on Crime" (1966), emphatically supports the need, indeed the necessity, for changing the emphasis in criminological studies from a concern with the correlational

analysis of specific criminogenic variables to a much broader and cultural framework of analysis and explanation.

19. Langness, "Violence in the New Guinea Highlands" (1972, pp. 171–185).

20. Chagnon, *Yanomamö: The Fierce People* (1968).

Chapter 2

1. See, for example, Wechsler and Michael, "A Rationale of the Law of Homicide" (1937), Collings, "Offenses of Violence Against the Person" (1962), and Boudouris, "A Classification of Homicides" (1974).

2. Although the Danish jurist and sociologist Verner Goldschmidt draws from his experience with Scandinavian criminal law, his characterization of the norms that guide the behavior of police officers as sanctioning agents applies to the judicial procedures described in this study. Goldschmidt's article, "Primary Sanction Behavior" (1966), illustrates how "The agent is expected not to regard everything he perceives in his job as relevant facts. . . . Secondly, the agent is expected only to disapprove of certain modes of behavior, the selection of which is based on values in the social system concerned . . ." (ibid., p. 178). See, also, Skolnick's study, *Justice Without Trial* (1966), for a descriptive account of police behavior and investigative activities. Deputy Chief Caldwell's book, *Basic Law Enforcement* (1972), is valuable because the author uses many examples drawn from his long career with the Houston Police Department.

3. See, for example, any of the following works for a more detailed and illustrated account of the procedures followed in an autopsy: Hendrix, *Investigation of Violent and Sudden Death* (1972); Karsner, "Autopsy (Necropsy)" (1948); and Weber et al., *Autopsy Pathology Procedure and Protocol* (1973).

4. See, for example, Collins, *Homicide Squad* (1944), and Snyder, *Homicide Investigation* (1944), for different descriptions of a homicide investigation.

5. Until quite recently it was a common sight to witness a steady stream of persons visiting the Homicide Division for the specific purpose of filing formal complaints against a spouse. Since the majority of such complaints are dropped after a few days of cooling off, or reconciliation, the police have

adopted new procedural guidelines that have helped to discriminate between serious and frivolous complaints. A person, therefore, who appears personally at the Homicide Division to file a complaint against a spouse—which inevitably in the majority of cases is a woman wishing to file charges against her legal or common-law husband—is asked to read the following instructions before formally filing the complaint:

To: All wives wanting to file assault charges on a husband

Before discussing the filing of a charge on your husband, you must consider the following:

1. If charges are filed, you cannot come back later and recommend that charges be dismissed.
2. If charges are filed, your husband will be placed in jail and will have to post a $400.00 bond in order to be released. In all probability this money will come from his paycheck and your family budget.
3. On coming to court, at a minimum, your husband will have to pay a fine and court cost, which will also probably come from your family budget.
4. If your husband is employed, chances are good that he will lose his job.
5. If your husband has never been arrested, he will now have a police record.
6. The filing of charges will not make him stop "hitting" you. There is nothing the District Attorney or police can do to guarantee a husband and wife to live in peace.
7. We will not consider the filing of a charge unless you have now left your husband and have filed for a divorce.
8. If you have not filed for divorce and this is your intention, we recommend that you do so. Your attorney can ask the court for a restraining order to keep your husband away from you.
9. If you wish, the Assistant District Attorney will give you a note which will indicate you have requested that charges be filed which you may show to your husband should you desire to continue living with him.
10. The District Attorney's Office does not issue "Peace Bonds."

If, after considering all of the above, you still wish to discuss the filing of charges, give this back to the receptionist and she will give you a form to prepare prior to talking to the Assistant District Attorney.

(Houston Police Department, n.d.)

6. The gruesome sex-torture murders, which involved no less than 27 young victims, received wide publicity in the national press. The two youths, Brooks and Henley, who had procured victims for the 33-year-old Dean Corll, were

indicted, tried, and found guilty of murder. Brooks was sentenced to life imprisonment, whereas Henley was sentenced to serve five concurrent 99-year prison sentences.

Chapter 3

1. See, for example, Bender, "A Refinement of the Concept of Household" (1967), and Goody, *Domestic Groups* (1972), for a more detailed discussion of the concepts of "household" and "domestic group."

2. As this study progressed, it became increasingly obvious that there is a paucity of empirical and specifically ethnographic studies of American social organization. As members of the culture we quite naturally assume, like most people in the world, that our everyday knowledge of our own society and culture is both accurate and valid. My articles, on "Privacy" (1971) and "Racial and Ethnic Classifications" (1973), illustrate how so-called "folk concepts" should not be confused with either empirical knowledge or the conceptual vocabulary employed in scientific discourse. Recent anthropological field studies of family and kinship patterns in different Black communities—for example, Aschenbrenner's *Lifelines* (1975), Billingsley's *Black Families in White America* (1968), Hannerz's *Soulside* (1969), and Stack's *All Our Kin* (1974)—vividly illustrate the many discrepancies between commonly held notions about, say, "life among the poor" and the many different life-styles found among different segments of minority communities. The many social and racial issues associated with the problems of poverty, and the explosive political and economical factors of inequality in a democratic society, are as capable of generating divisiveness among citizens as between members of the scientific community. Montagu's brief article, "Sociogenic Brain Damage" (1972), in which he called attention to the possibilities of "sociogenic brain damage" among persons subjected to an impoverished early childhood environment (as would be the case for many if not most of the lowest economic classes in the United States), has provoked a controversial and polemical essay by Valentine and Valentine, "Brain Damage and the Intellectual Defense of Inequality" (1975).

Edward Banfield's *The Unheavenly City* (1970) and Arthur Jensen's "How Much Can We Boost I.Q. and Scholastic Achievement?" (1969) address the issues very bluntly and, in turn, their efforts have generated personal criticism from colleagues and, in Jensen's case, precipitated the birth of an additional booklength treatment of the subject in his *Educability and Group Differences* (1973). See, also Denniston's review of Professor Jensen's book in *Science* (1975). These books and articles, and many others like them, attest to the simple truth that scientists are only beginning to formulate working hypotheses about the very complex cultural and biological determinants of human behavior. It may finally be added that although my data do not include any information on the relative social intelligence of either killers or victims, it does seem permissible to suggest that agonistic and fighting behavior may be more highly valued by some members of American culture and less highly valued by others. This is not to say that all persons who happen to live in a social milieu that fosters and even values fighting behavior must necessarily manifest such behavior.

The important study by Schatzman and Strauss, "Social Class and Modes of Communication" (1955), of different individual perceptions of the events surrounding a natural disaster in a small community, indicates that thought and communication patterns correlate with membership in different social classes. A principle finding of that study, and one that can be applied to the explanation of homicidal behavior, is that "lower class persons" frequently fail to see any need to adjust their personal views of a situation with those of others. The cases in this and the two following chapters illustrate how killers and victims often engage in hostile verbal exchanges that acerbate egocentric feelings of self-righteousness. Such persons seem unable to engage in a dialectical exchange and, more seriously, to disengage issues from personalities. Arguments, therefore, are resolved by recourse to physical rather than intellectual mechanisms of conflict resolution.

3. See, for example, Rotenberg et al., "Legal Services for the Poor–Houston" (1969), for a description and analysis of poverty in Houston by a group of lawyers charged with the evaluation of the effectiveness of services provided by the Houston Legal Foundation.

4. It may be noted that Wolfgang's study, *Patterns in Criminal Homicide* (1958), in Philadelphia is based exclusively on information from "police records, coroners' reports, court or judicial records, and records of prison commitments" (ibid., pp. 10–11). In this study I have relied upon similar sources. Unlike Wolfgang, however, I have included as much descriptive case material as possible. The cases have been selected to illustrate different kinds of killer-victim relationships and, most significantly, the social contexts in which the final homicide drama takes place.

5. Although police clerks in the Homicide Division make an effort to update cases that have been cleared by recording the final disposition of the individual cases, it is not uncommon to find a case that lacks this information. The case disposition data in this study were laboriously culled from handwritten entries in city and county records.

6. The subject of filicide should also be viewed in relationship to child abuse in particular and intra-family violence in general. See, for example, Fontana's *The Maltreated Child* (1964), Helfer and Kempe's *The Battered Child* (1969), Myers' "The Child Slayer" (1967), and Young's *Wednesday's Children* (1964). For a recent study of physical aggression between husbands and wives see Gelles's *The Violent Home* (1972).

Chapter 4

1. See, for example, Schneider's *American Kinship* (1968).

2. The very complex biological and cultural bases for "bonding behavior" have been extensively treated in Tiger's book, *Men in Groups* (1969) and by Tiger and Fox, *The Imperial Animal* (1971). Eibl-Eibensfeldt's most recent study, *Ethology: The Biology of Behavior* (1975), provides an excellent summary of the biological bases of human behavior.

3. Bullock's "Urban Homicide in Theory and Fact" (1955, p. 575).

4. The literature on the subject of the interrelations among law, custom, and morality is indeed very extensive and controversial. Studies by Hoebel, *The Law of Primitive Man* (1954), Bohannan, "The Differing Realms of the Law" (1965), and Pospisil, *Kapauku Papuans and Their Law* (1958) and *The Ethnology of Law* (1972), provide a good overview of how different anthropologists have addressed themselves to the problems of law and custom in non-Western societies. The debate between H. L. A. Hart in *The Concept of Law* (1961) and Lon L. Fuller in *The Morality of Law* (1969) illustrates the theoretical and conceptual issues among analytical jurists, and Leiser's *Custom, Law, and Morality* (1969) provides a brief perspective on the problems from the vantage point of a philosopher.

Chapter 5

1. Black, *Black's Law Dictionary* (1951, p. 1590).

2. Wolfgang, *Patterns in Criminal Homicide* (1958, p. 205).

3. Zimbardo's provocative essay, "The Human Choice: Individuation, Reason and Order vs. Deindividuation, Impulse and Chaos" (1973), under-

scores the point made in this paragraph. He says: "When a person wants to engage in behavior solely for self-gratification and doesn't want to take into consideration the mutual needs of the other interacting person, he can best achieve that end by dehumanizing the other . . ." (p. 229).

4. The early contributions by Ruesh and Bateson (1951) to human communication and interaction theory, together with E. T. Hall's (1959, 1964, and 1966) applications of both linguistic and ethological concepts and methods to the analysis of cultural phenomena, emphasize how even seemingly trivial forms of human interaction in reality are the product of exceedingly complex cultural rules. Frake's essay, "How to Ask for A Drink in Subanum" (1964), and Murphy's study, "Social Distance and the Veil" (1964), represent some of the best examples of how specific forms of human interactions are, in fact, generated by complex cultural rules. Sherri Cavan's book, *Liquor License* (1966), represents one of a growing number of ethnomethodological studies that focus attention on what is called taken-for-granted or common-sense features of social organization.

5. Goffman, in his book, *Interaction Ritual* (1967), suggests that "different individuals and groups have somewhat different personal base-lines from which to measure risk and opportunity" (p. 157). This helps to explain why some individuuals may kill others in response to the slightest threat or provocation, whether actual or perceived, and why, for example, a holdup man will kill a storekeeper to obtain an "insignificant" amount of cash. Although Banfield's *The Unheavenly City* (1970) is charged with profound insights and generalizations, it is clear that we lack substantial ethnographic data on people growing up in a milieu where the values and value orientations may, in fact, precipitate what to others may appear like utterly senseless behavior.

6. Although it is not known how many persons in the Houston community either carry a concealed weapon or have access to a firearm, the possession of firearms by private citizens is so common as to be viewed as entirely normal and acceptable. In Houston, as in the nation as a whole, the majority of violent crimes are committed with the use of firearms.

7. It would be interesting to know, other things being equal, whether the formal legal sanctions applied to resolve this particular case would have been different if the killing had occurred in a more exclusive drinking establishment and if the victim had been a respected Houston businessman, a lawyer, or maybe an off-duty police officer.

8. The possible relationship between the value of stolen goods and the length of the sentence for a robber-thief is, of course, only suggestive. It is

not unlikely, however, that future research may uncover statistically insignificant correlations between the economic status of a victim and the degree and relative severity of punishment for a killer.

9. Merton in his book, *Social Theory and Social Structure* (1957), and Dubin in his article, "Deviant Behavior and Social Structure" (1959), discuss different modes of social adaptation (innovation, ritualism, retreatism, rebellion, and conformity) that are directly relevant to our understanding of how strangers cope with life in the urban environment.

10. See, for example, Wilson's *Sociobiology* (1975) for a recent discussion of altruistic behavior from both biological and sociological perspectives. Foster's *Tzintzuntzan* (1967) vividly illustrates how, in a small Mexican peasant community, "dyadic contracts" are used to define mutual obligations and structure interpersonal relationships.

11. Packard, *A Nation of Strangers* (1972).

Chapter 6

1. Prosser, *Handbook of the Law of Torts* (1964, p. 7).

2. Ibid., p. 7.

3. See, for example, the following studies of victim compensation programs: Brooks' "Compensating Victims of Crime" (1973), Cameron's "Compensation for Victims of Crime" (1963), Edelhertz and Geis' *Public Compensation to Victims of Crime* (1974), Geis' "State Compensation to Victims of Crime" (1967), Lamborn's "Toward a Victim Orientation in Criminal Theory" (1968), Rothstein's "State Compensation for Criminally Inflicted Injuries" (1965), and Sandler's "Compensation for Victims of Crime" (1966).

4. See, for example, *Vernon's Texas Codes Annotated: Penal Code* (1974), Vol. 1, pp. ix–x, 82–90.

5. Bubany, "The Texas Penal Code of 1974" (1974, p. 306). See, also, O'Donnel "Problems with the Texas Penal Code" (1974).

6. It is difficult to take issue with the views of criminal law expressed by Norbert Wiener in his book, *The Human Use of Human Beings* (1954). Professor Wiener, who is a mathematician and not a legal scholar, sums up

his views by stating that "the criminal law speaks now in one language, and now in another. Until we in the community have made up our minds that what we really want is expiation, or removal, or reform, or the discouragement of potential criminals, we shall get none of these, but only a confusion in which crime breeds more crime. Any code which is made, one-fourth on the eighteenth-century British prejudice in favor of hanging, one-fourth on the removal of the criminal from society, one-fourth on halfhearted policy of reform and one-fourth on the policy of hanging up a dead crow to scare away the rest, is going to get us precisely nowhere" (p. 110).

A slightly different view of the law and the legal profession is presented in Llewellyn's delightful book with the appropriate title *The Bramble Bush* (1951). Professor Mellinkoff's book, *The Language of the Law,* probes the historical background of legal terms and expressions.

7. See, for example, Marshall's *Law and Psychology in Conflict* (1966) and Menninger's *The Crime of Punishment* (1966).

8. Hoebel, *The Law of Primitive Man* (1954) (Chapter 5).

9. Stephen, *A History of the Criminal Law of England* (1883, p. 21).

10. See, Holmes' *The Common Law* (1881, esp. Lecture II).

11. Michael and Wechsler, "A Rationale of the Law of Homicide" (1937, p. 731).

12. *Vernon's Texas Codes Annotated: Penal Code* (1974, Vol. 1, p. xxi). See, also, Baab and Furgeson, "Texas Sentencing Practices" (1967), for a discussion of how analogous criminal offenses result in variable sentences and punishments for offenders.

13. *Vernon's Annotated Penal Code* (1961, p. 633).

14. See, for example, F. Time, "Murder by Any Name Ain't the Same" (1971), McGregor, "Homicide Charge in Texas" (1953), Stumberg, "Criminal Homicide in Texas" (1938), and Raymond, "What Constitutes Murder in Texas" (1939).

15. *Vernon's Annotated Penal Code* (1961, p. 639).

16. Ibid., p. 640.

17. Ibid., p. 640.

18. Ibid., p. 643.

19. Ibid., p. 764.

20. Ibid., p. 770.

21. Ibid., p. 807.

22. Bard's and Zacker's article, "Assaultiveness and Alcohol Use in Family Disputes" (1974), recently emphasized the danger of attributing complex life situations to the appearance of a single independent variable. This brief but excellent article concludes their 22-month study of 1,388 family disputes by stating: "Alcohol and aggression have long been paired. . . . Both the victims and those who commit homicides and assaults have long been known to show blood concentrations of alcohol. But alcohol is an extraordinarily common social lubricant in this country–so common that many, if not most, social occasions are marked by its use. It would not be unreasonable to expect then that homicide and assaults (which mostly occur between intimates and in a social context) would show evidence of alcohol use. The error may be merely in associating the two causally. Indeed, given the extent of drinking in our society, if there were a simple causal relationship we would be a far more bloody society than we are" (p. 292).

23. *Vernon's Annotated Penal Code* (1961, p. 203).

24. Ibid., p. 177.

25. Ibid., p. 191.

26. The discussion of legal statutes implicitly assumes that formal and public laws are known to the people protected by such laws. Williams and Hall in their study, "Knowledge of the Law in Texas" (1972), found, however, that many areas of the law remain unknown to most people and that knowledge of the law is not equal for all groups in the population. It would, of course, be of enormous interest to find out the degree of familiarity with the homicide statutes exhibited by offenders.

27. *Vernon's Annotated Penal Code* (1961, p. 272).

28. *Vernon's Annotated Constitution of the State of Texas* (1955, p. 491).

29. Ibid.

30. *Vernon's Annotated Penal Code* (1961, p. 280).

31. Ravkind, "Justifiable Homicide in Texas" (1959, p. 524). See, also, the 1974 Code, Chapter 9.

32. Chapter 9 of the 1974 Penal Code has omitted adultery as a category of justifiable homicide.

33. Stumberg, "Defense of Person and Property under Texas Criminal Law" (1942, p. 21).

34. *Vernon's Annotated Penal Code* (1961, p. 469).

35. Ibid., p. 547.

36. Ibid., p. 549.

37. Hohfeld, "Some Fundamental Legal Conceptions as Applied in Judicial Reasoning" (1913 and 1917).

38. See, for example, Davidson's *Chicano Prisoners* (1974) and Sykes' *The Society of Captives* (1958).

39. Davenport, "Twenty Years of Homicide in Texas" (1947, p. 638).

Chapter 7

1. See, for example, R. Brown, *Explanation in Social Science* (1963), or T. S. Kuhn, *The Structure of Scientific Revolutions* (1970).

2. Wolfgang, *Patterns in Criminal Homicide* (1958, p. 83).

3. For a more detailed view of these arguments see, for example, Seitz, "Firearms, Homicides, and Gun Control Effectiveness" (1972), and Zimring, "Is Gun Control Likely to Reduce Violent Killings?" (1968).

4. Berkowitz and LePage, "Weapons as Aggression-Eliciting Stimuli" (1967).

5. See, for example, Gibbons, *Society, Crime, and Criminal Careers* (1968).

6. Kluckhohn and Kelly, "The Concept of Culture" (1945). See, also, Kroeber and Kluckhohn, *Culture* (1952); Kaplan and Manners, *Culture*

Theory (1972); White, "The Concept of Culture" (1959); and Weiss, "A Scientific Concept of Culture" (1973).

7. Radcliffe-Brown, "Social Sanction" (1934, p. 531).

8. See, for example, Cohen, *Deviance and Control* (1966).

9. See, for example, the following general studies in the field of legal anthropology: Hoebel, *The Law of Primitive Man* (1954); Nader, *The Anthropological Study of Law* (1965); Bohannan, "The Differing Realms of the Law" (1965); Friedman, "Legal Culture and Social Development"; and Pospisil, *The Ethnology of Law* (1972).

10. Goldschmidt, "Primary Sanction Behavior" (1966, p. 179).

11. Compare, for example, Packer's book, *The Limits of the Criminal Sanction* (1968).

12. Epstein, "Sanctions" (1968, p. 1).

13. Goldschmidt (ibid., p. 177) defines "sanction-threshold" as *"the total amount of conditions for releasing an organized negative sanction in a given social situation.* The sanction-threshold is not fixed but is assumed to vary like the tolerance limits from situation to situation." He further notes that "The concept of sanction-threshold is especially important when defining social norms and social sanctions as separate phenomena. The basic assumption . . . is that norm deviations do not always release sanctions and, on the other hand, the sanctions can be released without any norm violation."

14. Schneider, "Political Organization, Supernatural Sanctions, and the Punishment for Incest on Yap" (1957, p. 800).

References

[Anon.]. *Texas Code of Criminal Procedure*. St. Paul, Minn.: West Publishing Co., 1971.

[Anon.]. *Vernon's Annotated Penal Code of the State of Texas*. Vol. 2A. St. Paul, Minn.: West Publishing Co., 1961.

[Anon.]. *Vernon's Texas Codes Annotated: Penal Code* (Sections 1.01 to 18). St. Paul, Minn.: West Publishing Co., 1974.

[Anon.]. *Vernon's Annotated Constitution of the State of Texas*. Vol. 1. Kansas City, Mo.: Vernon Law Book Co., 1955.

[Anon.]. *Big Town, Big Money: The Business of Houston*. Houston: Cordovan Press, 1973.

Ardrey, Robert. *The Territorial Imperative: A Personal Inquiry into the Animal Origins of Property and Nations*. New York: Dell Publishing Co., Inc., 1966.

Ardrey, Robert. *The Social Contract: A Personal Inquiry into the Evolutionary Sources of Order and Disorder*. New York: Dell Publishing Co., Inc., 1970.

Aschenbrenner, Joyce. *Lifelines: Black Families in Chicago*. New York: Holt, Rinehart and Winston, Inc., 1975.

Aubert, Vilhelm. Some Social Functions of Legislation. *Acta Sociologica* 10:99–110, 1966.

Baab, George William, and Furgeson, William Royal, Jr. Texas Sentencing Practices: A Statistical Study. *Texas Law Review* 45:471–503, 1967.

Bainbridge, John. *The Super-Americans*. New York: Holt, Rinehart and Winston, Inc., 1961.

Banfield, Edward. *The Unheavenly City*. Boston: Little, Brown, 1970.

Bard, Morton, and Zacker, Joseph. Assaultiveness and Alcohol Use in Family Disputes. *Criminology* 12:281–92, 1974.

Beattie, Ronald H. Problems of Criminal Statistics in the United States. *The Journal of Criminal Law, Criminology, and Police Science* 46:178–86, 1955.

Bender, Donald R. A Refinement of the Concept of Household: Families, Co-Residence, and Domestic Functions. *American Anthropologist* 69:493–504, 1967.

Bensing, Robert C., and Schroeder, Oliver J. *Homicide in an Urban Community*. Springfield, Ill.: Charles C. Thomas Publisher, 1960.

Berkowitz, Leonard, and LePage, Anthony. Weapons as Aggression-Eliciting Stimuli. *Journal of Personality and Social Psychology* 7:202–7, 1967.

Biderman, Albert D. Surveys of Population Samples for Estimating Crime Incidence. *Annals of the American Academy of Political and Social Science* 374:16–33, 1967.

Biderman, Albert D., and Reiss, Albert J., Jr. On Exploring the "Dark Figure" of Crime. *Annals of the American Academy of Political and Social Science* 374:1–15, 1967.

Billingsley, Andrew. *Black Families in White America*. Englewood, N.J.: Prentice-Hall, Inc., 1968.

Black, Henry C. *Black's Law Dictionary*. 4th ed. St. Paul, Minn.: West Publishing Co., 1951.

Bohannan, Paul, ed. *African Homicide and Suicide*. Princeton: Princeton University Press, 1960.

Bohannan, Paul. The Differing Realms of the Law. *American Anthropologist* 67:33–42, 1965.

Boudouris, James. A Classification of Homicides. *Criminology* 11:525–40, 1974.

Brearley, Harrington C. *Homicide in the United States*. Chapel Hill, N.C.: The University of North Carolina Press, 1932.

Bromberg, Walter. *The Mold of Murder: A Psychiatric Study of Homicide*. WestPort, Conn.: Greenwood Press, 1961.

Brooks, James. Compensating Victims of Crime: The Recommendations of Program Administrators. *Law and Society Review* 7:445–71, 1973.

Brown, Robert. *Explanation in Social Science*. Chicago: Aldine Publishing Co., 1963.

Bubany, Charles P. The Texas Penal Code of 1974. *Southwestern Law Journal* 28:292–339, 1974.

Bullock, Henry A. Urban Homicide in Theory and Fact. *Journal of Criminal Law, Criminology, and Police Science* 45:565–75, 1955.

Caldwell, Harry. The Relationship of Houston Homicide to Racial Segregation and Total Crime. Master's thesis, University of Houston, 1963.

Caldwell, Harry. *Basic Law Enforcement*. California: Goodyear Publishing Co., 1972.

Cameron, Bruce J. Compensation for Victims of Crime: The New Zealand Experiment. *Journal of Public Law* 12:367–75, 1963.

Carp, Robert A. The Harris County Grand Jury–A Case Study. *Houston Law Review* 12:90–120, 1974.

Cavan, Sherri. *Liquor License: An Ethnography of Bar Behavior*. Chicago: Aldine Publishing Co., 1966.

Chagnon, Napoleon. *Yanomamö: The Fierce People*. New York: Holt, Rinehart and Winston, Inc., 1968.

City of Houston Police Department. *Annual Report*. 1969.

Clark, Ramsey. *Crime in America: Observations on its Nature, Causes, Prevention and Control*. New York: Simon and Schuster, Inc., 1971.

Cohen, Albert K. *Deviance and Control*. Englewood Cliffs, N.J.: Prentice-Hall, Inc., 1966.

Collings, Rex A., Jr. Offenses of Violence against the Person. *The Annals of the American Academy of Political and Social Science* 339:42–56, 1962.

Collins, Frederick L. *Homicide Squad*. New York: G. P. Putnam's Sons, 1944.

Couzens, Michael. Reflections on the Study of Violence. *Law and Society Review* 5:583–604, 1971.

Cressey, Donald R. The State of Criminal Statistics. *National Probation and Parole Association Journal* 3:230–41, 1957.

Cressey, Donald R. Epidemiology and Individual Conduct: A Case from Criminology. *The Pacific Sociological Review* 3:47–54, 1960.

The Dallas Morning News. Texas Almanac and State Industrial Guide. Dallas: A. H. Belo Corp., 1970–1971.

Davenport, John. Twenty Years of Homicide in Texas. [Comment] *Texas Law Review* 25:634–40, 1947.

Davidson, R. Theodore. *Chicano Prisoners: The Key to San Quentin*. New York: Holt, Rinehart and Winston, Inc., 1974.

Denniston, Carter. Accounting for Differences in Mean I.Q. (Book review) *Science* 187:161–62, 1975.

Dubin, Robert. Deviant Behavior and Social Structure: Continuities and Social Theory. *American Sociological Review* 24:147–64, 1959.

Edelhertz, Herbert, and Geis, Gilbert. *Public Compensation to Victims of Crime.* New York: Praeger Publishers, Inc., 1974.

Eibl-Eibensfeldt, Irenäus. *Ethology: The Biology of Behavior.* 2nd ed. New York: Holt, Rinehart and Winston, Inc., 1975.

[Eisenhower, Milton S.] *Progress Report of the National Commission on the Causes and Prevention of Violence to President Lyndon B. Johnson.* Washington, D.C.: U.S. Government Printing Office, 1969.

[Eisenhower, Milton S.] *To Establish Justice, to Insure Domestic Tranquility: Final Report of the National Commission on the Causes and Prevention of Violence.* Washington, D.C.: U.S. Government Printing Office, 1969.

Epstein, Arnold L. Sanctions. In *International Encyclopedia of the Social Sciences,* Vol. 14, edited by David L. Sills. New York: The Macmillan Company and the Free Press, 1968.

Fitzgerald, Patrick J. *Criminal Law and Punishment.* London: Oxford University Press, 1962.

Fontana, Vincent J. *The Maltreated Child.* Springfield, Ill.: Charles C. Thomas Publisher, 1964.

Foster, George M. *Tzintzuntzan: Mexican Peasants in a Changing World.* Boston: Little, Brown, 1967.

Frake, Charles O. How to Ask for a Drink in Subanun. *American Anthropologist* 66:127–32, 1964.

Friedman, Lawrence M. Legal Culture and Social Development. In Friedman, Lawrence M. and Stewart Macaulay [comp.]. *Law and the Behavioral Sciences.* New York: The Bobbs-Merrill Co., Inc., 1969.

Fuller, Lon L. *The Morality of Law.* Rev. ed. New Haven, Conn.: Yale University Press, 1969.

Geis, Gilbert. State Compensation to Victims of Violent Crime. In The President's Commission on Law Enforcement and Administration of Justice. *Task Force Report: Crime and Its Impact–An Assessment.* Washington, D.C.: U.S. Government Printing Office, 1967, pp. 157–77.

Gelles, Richard. *The Violent Home: A Study of Physical Aggression between Husbands and Wives.* Beverly Hills: Sage Publications, Inc., 1972.

Gibbons, Don C. *Society, Crime and Criminal Careers.* Englewood Cliffs, N.J.: Prentice-Hall, Inc., 1968.

Glueck, Sheldon. Theory and Fact in Criminology. *British Journal of Deliquency* 7:92–98, 1956.

Goffman, Erving. *Interaction Ritual: Essays on Face-to-Face Behavior.* Garden City, N.Y.: Doubleday and Co., Inc., 1967.

Goldschmidt, Verner. Primary Sanction Behaviour. *Acta Sociologica* 10:173–90, 1966.

Goody, Jack. *Domestic Groups.* Addison-Wesley Modular Publications, No. 28, pp. 1–32, 1972.

Hall, Edward T. *The Silent Language.* Garden City, N.Y.: Doubleday and Co., Inc., 1959.

Hall, Edward T. Adumbration in Intercultural Communication. *American Anthropologist* 66:154–63, 1964.

Hall, Edward T. *The Hidden Dimension.* Garden City, N.Y.: Doubleday and Co., Inc., 1966.

Hannerz, Ulf. *Soulside: Inquiries into Ghetto Culture and Community.* New York: Columbia University Press, 1969.

Hart, Herbert L. A. *The Concept of Law.* London: Oxford University Press, 1961.

Helfer, Ray E., and Kempe, C. Henry, eds. *The Battered Child.* Chicago: The University of Chicago Press, 1968.

Hendrix, Robert C. *Investigation of Violent and Sudden Death: A Manual for Medical Examiners*. Springfield, Ill.: Charles C. Thomas Publisher, 1972.

Hoebel, E. Adamson. *The Law of Primitive Man*. Cambridge: Harvard University Press, 1954.

Hohfeld, Wesley N. Some Fundamental Legal Conceptions as Applied in Judicial Reasoning. *Yale Law Journal* 23:16–59, 1913.

Hohfeld, Wesley N. Fundamental Legal Conceptions as Applied in Judicial Reasoning. *Yale Law Journal* 26:710–70, 1917.

Holmes, Oliver W., Jr. *The Common Law*. Boston: Little, Brown, 1881 [Mark DeWolfe Howe, ed. Cambridge: Harvard University Press, 1963].

Jensen, Arthur R. How Much Can We Boost I.Q. and Scholastic Achievement? *Harvard Educational Review* 39:1–123, 1969.

Jensen, Arthur R. *Educability and Group Differences*. New York: Harper & Row, Inc., 1973.

Justice, Blair. *Violence in the City*. Fort Worth, Tex.: Texas Christian University Press, 1969.

Kaplan, David, and Manners, Robert A. *Culture Theory*. Englewood Cliffs, N.J.: Prentice-Hall, Inc., 1972.

Karsner, Howard T. "Autopsy (Necropsy)." In *The Cyclopedia of Medicine, Surgery and Specialties,* Vol. 1, edited by G. M. Piersol. Philadelphia, Pa.: F. A. Davis Co., 1948, pp. 858–72.

[Katzenbach, Nicholas deB.]. *The Challenge of Crime in a Free Society: A Report by the President's Commission on Law Enforcement and Administration of Justice*. Washington, D.C.: U.S. Government Printing Office, 1967.

Kirkham, James F., Levy, Sheldon G, and Crotty, William J. *Assassination and Political Violence: A Report to the National Commission on the Causes and Prevention of Violence*. New York: Bantam Books, 1970.

Kitsuse, John I., and Cicourel, Aaron V. A Note on the Use of Official Statistics. *Social Problems* 11:131–39, 1963.

Kluckhohn, Clyde, and Kelly, William H. The Concept of Culture. In *The Science of Man in the World Crisis,* edited by Ralph Linton. New York: Columbia University Press, 1945, pp. 78–106.

Kluckhohn, Florence R., and Strodtbeck, Fred L. *Variations in Value Orientations*. New York: Row, Peterson and Co., 1961.

Kroeber, Alfred L., and Kluckhohn, Clyde. *Culture: A Critical Review of Concepts and Definitions*. Papers of the Peabody Museum of American Archaeology and Ethnology, Vol. 47, No. 1. Cambridge: The Peabody Museum, 1952.

Kuhn, Thomas S. *The Structure of Scientific Revolutions*. 2nd ed., enlarged ["Second Edition, Enlarged" from title page: the book was "enlarged" for the second edition to permit the author to expand his use of the concept paradigm]. Chicago: The University of Chicago Press, 1970.

Lamborn, Leroy L. Toward a Victim Orientation in Criminal Theory. *Rutgers Law Review* 22:733–68, 1968.

Langness, Lewis L. Violence in the New Guinea Highlands. In *Collective Violence,* edited by James F. Short, Jr., and Marvin E. Wolfgang. Chicago: Aldine Atherton, 1972, pp. 171–85.

Leiser, Burton M. *Custom, Law, and Morality: Conflict and Continuity in Social Behavior*. New York: Doubleday and Co., Inc., 1969.

Llewellyn, Karl N. *The Bramble Bush: On Our Law and Its Study*. New York: Oceana Publications, 1951.

Lofland, Lyn H. *A World of Strangers: Order and Action in Urban Public Space*. New York: Basic Books, Inc., 1973.

Lorenz, Konrad. *On Aggression*. New York: Harcourt, Brace, and World, Inc., 1966.

Lundsgaarde, Henry P. Privacy: An Anthropological Perspective on the Right to be Let Alone. *Houston Law Review* 8:858–75, 1971.

Lundsgaarde, Henry P. Racial and Ethnic Classifications: An Appraisal of the Role of Anthropology in the Lawmaking Process. *Houston Law Review* 10:641–54, 1973.

Macdonald, John M. *The Murderer and His Victim*. Springfield, Ill.: Charles C. Thomas Publisher, 1961.

Malinowski, Bronislaw. *Crime and Custom in Savage Society*. London: Routledge and Kegan Paul, Ltd., 1926.

Marshall, James. *Law and Psychology in Conflict*. New York: The Bobbs-Merrill Co., 1966.

McGregor, Charles B. Homicide Charge in Texas. *Baylor Law Review* 6:40–58, 1953.

Mead, Margaret. The Application of Anthropological Techniques to Cross-National Communication. *Transactions of the New York Academy of Sciences* 9:133–52, 1947.

Mellinkoff, David. *The Language of the Law*. Boston: Little, Brown, 1963.

Menninger, Karl. *The Crime of Punishment*. New York: The Viking Press, Inc., 1966.

Merton, Robert K. *Social Theory and Social Structure*. Rev. and enlarged edition. New York: The Free Press of Glencoe, 1957.

Montagu, Ashley. Sociogenic Brain Damage. *American Anthropologist* 74:1045–61, 1972.

Montagu, Ashley, ed. *Man and Aggression*. 2nd ed. New York: Oxford University Press, 1973.

Mulvihill, Donald J., and Tumin, Melvin M. *Crimes of Violence*, Vols. 12 and 13. [A Staff Report Submitted to the National Commission on the Causes and Prevention of Violence.] Washington, D.C.: U.S. Government Printing Office, 1969.

Murphy, Robert F. Social Distance and the Veil. *American Anthropologist*, 66: 1257–74, 1964.

Myers, Steven A. The Child Slayer: A 25-Year Survey of Homicides Involving Preadolescent Victims. *Archives of General Psychiatry* 17:211–13, 1967.

Nader, Laura. The Anthropological Study of Law. *American Anthropologist* [Special Publication] 67:3–32, 1965.

Nash, June. Death as a Way of Life: The Increasing Resort to Homicide in a Maya Indian Community. *American Anthropologist* 69:455–70, 1967.

O'Donnell, James. Problems with the Texas Penal Code. *Houston Law Review* 11:1229–49, 1974.

Packer, Herbert L. *The Limits of the Criminal Sanction*. Stanford, Calif.: Stanford University Press, 1968.

Packard, Vance. *A Nation of Strangers*. New York: David McKay Co., Inc., 1972.

Palmer, Stuart. *The Psychology of Murder*. New York: Thomas Crowell Co., 1960.

Pokorny, Alex. A Comparison of Homicides in Two Cities. *Journal of Criminal Law, Criminology, and Police Science* 56:479–87, 1965.

Pospisil, Leopold. *Kapauku Papuans and Their Law*. Yale University Publications in Anthropology, No. 54. New Haven, Conn.: Yale University Press, 1958.

Pospisil, Leopold. *The Ethnology of Law*. Addison-Wesley Modular Publications, No. 12:1–40, 1972.

Prosser, William L. *Handbook of the Law of Torts.* 3rd ed. St. Paul, Minn.: West Publishing Co., 1964.

Radcliffe-Brown, Alfred R. Social Sanction. *Encyclopaedia of the Social Sciences* 13:531–34. New York: Macmillan Co., 1934.

Ravkind, William M. Justifiable Homicide in Texas [Comment]. *Southwestern Law Journal* 13:508–24, 1959.

Raymond, Jesse Andrews. What Constitutes Murder in Texas [Comment]. *Texas Law Review* 8:391–98, 1930.

Rotenberg, Daniel L., ed. Legal Services for the Poor–Houston. *Houston Law Review* 6:941–1228, 1969.

Rothstein, Paul F. State Compensation for Criminally Inflicted Injuries. *Texas Law Review* 44:38–54, 1965.

Ruesch, Jurgen, and Bateson, Gregory. *Communication: The Social Matrix of Psychiatry.* New York: W. W. Norton and Co., Inc., 1951.

Sandler, Robert A. Compensation for Victims of Crime–Some Practical Considerations. *Buffalo Law Review* 15:645–55, 1966.

Sapir, Edward. The Unconscious Patterning of Behavior in Society. In *Selected Writings of Edward Sapir in Language, Culture and Personality,* edited by David G. Mandelbaum. Berkeley: University of California Press, 1963, pp. 544–59.

Schatzman, Leonard, and Strauss, Anselm. Social Class and Modes of Communication. *The American Journal of Sociology* 60:329–38, 1955.

Schneider, David M. Political Organization, Supernatural Sanctions, and the Punishment for Incest on Yap. *American Anthropologist* 59:791–800, 1957.

Schneider, David M. *American Kinship: A Cultural Account.* Englewood Cliffs, N.J.: Prentice-Hall, Inc., 1968.

Seitz, Steven T. Firearms, Homicides, and Gun Control Effectiveness. *Law and Society Review* 6:395–613, 1972.

Sellin, Thorsten. The Basis of a Crime Index. *Journal of Criminal Law and Criminology* 22:335–56, 1931.

Sellin, Thorsten. The Significance of Records of Crime. *The Law Quarterly Review* 67:489–504, 1951.

Shirley, Glenn. *Law West of Forth Smith.* Lincoln, Neb., University of Nebraska Press, 1968.

Skolnick, Jerome H. *Justice Without Trial: Law Enforcement in Democratic Society.* New York: John Wiley and Sons, Inc., 1966.

Snyder, LeMoyne. *Homicide Investigation: Practical Information for Coroners, Police Officers, and Other Investigators.* Springfield, Ill.: Charles C. Thomas Publisher, 1944.

Stack, Carol B. *All Our Kin: Strategies for Survival in a Black Community.* New York: Harper & Row, Inc., 1974.

Stephen, Sir James F. *A History of the Criminal Law of England,* Vol. III. London: MacMillan Co., 1883.

Stumberg, George W. Criminal Homicide in Texas. *Texas Law Review* 16:305–34, 1938.

Stumberg, George W. Defense of Person and Property under Texas Criminal Law. *Texas Law Review* 21:17–35, 1942.

Sykes, Gresham M. *The Society of Captives: A Study of a Maximum Security Prison.* Princeton: Princeton University Press, 1958.

Taft, Donald R. Influence of the General Culture on Crime. *Federal Probation* 30:16–23, 1966.

Tiger, Lionel. *Men in Groups.* New York: Random House, 1969.

Tiger, Lionel, and Robin, Fox. *The Imperial Animal*. New York: Holt, Rinehart and Winston, Inc., 1971.

Time, Fred. Murder by Any Name Ain't the Same. *Texas Bar Journal* 34:1065–74, 1971.

Toch, Hans. *Violent Men: An Inquiry into the Psychology of Violence*. Chicago: Aldine Publishing Co., 1969.

U.S. Department of Justice, Federal Bureau of Investigation. *Crime in the United States, Uniform Crime Reports—1969*. Washington, D.C.: U.S. Government Printing Office, 1969.

Valentine, Charles A., and Valentine, Bettylou. Brain Damage and the Intellectual Defense of Inequality. *Current Anthropology* 16:117–50, 1975.

Van Vechten, Courtlandt C. Differential Criminal Case Mortality in Selected Jurisdictions. *American Sociological Review* 7:833–39, 1942.

Von Wright, Georg H. *Explanation and Understanding*. Ithaca, N.Y.: Cornell University Press, 1971.

Warren, Oscar L., and Bilas, Basil M. *Warren on Homicide,* vols. 1–5. Permanent ed. Buffalo, N.Y.: Dennis and Co., 1938.

Weber, Dudley L.; Fazzini, Eugene P., and Reagen, Thomas J. *Autopsy Pathology Procedure and Protocol*. Springfield, Ill.: Charles C. Thomas Publisher, 1973.

Wechsler, Herbert, and Michael, Jerome. A Rationale of the Law of Homicide (I and II). *Columbia Law Review* 37:701–61, 37:1261–1325, 1937.

Wegrocki, Henry J. A Critique of Cultural and Statistical Concepts of Abnormality. *Journal of Abnormal and Social Psychology* 34:166:178, 1939.

Weiss, Gerald. A Scientific Concept of Culture. *American Anthropologist* 75: 1376–1413, 1973.

Wertham, Fredric. *The Show of Violence*. New York: Doubleday and Co., Inc., 1949.

Wertham, Fredric. *A Sign for Cain*. New York: Macmillan Co., 1966.

White, Leslie. The Concept of Culture. *American Anthropologist* 61:227–51, 1959.

Wiener, Norbert. *The Human Use of Human Beings: Cybernetics and Society*. Rev. ed. Garden City, N.Y.: Doubleday and Co., Inc., 1954.

Williams, Martha, and Hall, Jay. Knowledge of the Law in Texas: Socioeconomic and Ethnic Differences. *Law and Society Review* 7:99–118, 1972.

Wilson, Edward O. *Sociobiology: The New Synthesis*. Cambridge, Mass.: Harvard University Press, 1975.

Wolfgang, Marvin E. *Patterns in Criminal Homicide*. Philadelphia, Pa.: University of Pennsylvania, 1958.

Wolfgang, Marvin E. Uniform Crime Reports: A Critical Appraisal. *University of Pennsylvania Law Review* 111:708–38, 1963.

Wolfgang, Marvin E., and Ferracuti, Franco. *The Subculture of Violence: Towards an Integrated Theory in Criminology*. London: Tavistock Publications, 1967.

Young, Leontine. *Wednesday's Children: A Study of Child Neglect and Abuse*. New York: McGraw-Hill Book Co., 1964.

Zimbardo, Philip G. The Human Choice: Individuation, Reason and Order vs. Deindividuation, Impulse and Chaos. In *Urbanman: The Psychology of Urban Survival,* edited by T. Helmer and N. A. Eddington. New York: The Free Press, 1973, pp. 196–238.

Zimring, Franklin, E. Is Gun Control Likely to Reduce Violent Killings? *The University of Chicago Law Review* 35:721–37, 1968.

INDEX